7/60

ENJOY,

ENJOY!

Also by Harry Golden

ONLY IN AMERICA

FOR 2¢ PLAIN

HARRY GOLDEN

Enjoy,
Enjoy!

FOREWORD BY *Harry Golden, Jr.*

 CLEVELAND AND NEW YORK

THE WORLD PUBLISHING COMPANY

PUBLISHED BY The World Publishing Company
2231 West 110th Street, Cleveland 2, Ohio

PUBLISHED SIMULTANEOUSLY IN CANADA BY
Nelson, Foster & Scott Ltd.

Library of Congress Catalog Card Number: 60-6691

FIRST EDITION

Several of these essays have appeared in a syndicated column,
distributed by The McClure Newspaper Syndicate.

To the Sandburgs,

Carl,

Paula,

Margaret,

and Janet

Contents

CONTENTS

CONTENTS

CONTENTS

CONTENTS

CONTENTS

CONTENTS

CONTENTS

Foreword

BEHIND his desk in Charlotte, North Carolina, the improbable Harry Golden gnaws black cigars and explores new ideas.

I asked him once, after the successes of *Only in America* and *For 2¢ Plain*, why he still traipsed around the country making speeches.

He looked up at his target board, on a wall in his office, where he flips darts in moments of unhurried reflection, and said, "I don't need the money. I didn't need the money, in fact, when I *needed* it. I make speeches because of the Evil Eye. The alternative would be to sit home and bask. But the Evil Eye sees me huffing and puffing through the airport, seventy pounds overweight, and the Evil Eye thinks, 'Why bother with him? There are a lot of happy people to bother with.'"

My father, Harry Golden, has put one over on the Evil Eye, because this North Carolina author—editor and publisher of *The Carolina Israelite* and character witness for America—is really the happiest man I know.

I screened and edited my father's thousands of newspaper stories, magazine articles, speeches, new material, and even fragments of conversation, and I put these things into the form of his books.

A newspaperman myself, a feature writer for *The Detroit Free Press*, I can only marvel at the kind of announcement my father made in the *Israelite* in 1953: "The next issue will be in September . . . I will omit August because of the terrible heat wave."

I was down in Charlotte not long ago and I happened to catch him in the moment of his preparation for one of his national television appearances.

He put down the telephone at his desk and looked at his bare, scuffed floor. Then he bellowed a command to his staff: "Mr. Edward R. Murrow's men are coming here!" he cried. "Send the bedspread to the laundry!"

An overnight guest there must rise at seven, when the daily turmoil begins. He will find that what he thought was a bed is quickly converted into a couch in the visitors' reception area. What he thought was a night stand becomes a desk at which an advertising salesman placidly seats himself for another day's work.

Upstairs, in what apparently once served as a hallway, circulation assistants cast letters into peach baskets and cardboard cartons.

The cartons, it turns out, are trash receptacles. The peach baskets are repositories of important correspondence.

The strains of a Rachmaninoff concerto issue from a phonograph perched precariously on a shallow mantel.

And there is a ceaseless flow of callers—some of them among the most distinguished people of our time.

Once he was being interviewed on the contemporary South by a representative of the ultra-leftist *National Guardian*, and a second reporter walked into his house. It was a member of the Washington staff of *The Wall Street Journal*.

His first thought was: "If I could only get these two to interview each other—what a story!"

And he observed, "Moving from one office to another, between *The Wall Street Journal* and the *National Guardian*, I felt like Groucho Marx supervising a bar mitzvah."

Harry Golden, self-described fat little guy, short of breath, lives and writes in the clatter of this rambling frame structure that was a middle-class home in the Victorian Era.

His only concession to convention is that for speeches he wears a necktie.

I suppose I was called upon as a preposterous pinch hitter for Carl Sandburg (who introduced the last two books) to give some insight into the real, backstage Harry Golden.

But there is no backstage Harry Golden. When you read *Enjoy, Enjoy!* you will know this man. He writes his heart out, which, of course, is the secret.

HARRY GOLDEN, JR.

Introduction

SINCE the publication of *Only in America* and *For 2¢ Plain*, I have received as many as one thousand letters a week, and these letters provide a clue to the hunger and the longing, and the need for identity that one feels in this America of the mid-twentieth century. These letters wistfully recall a time and a place that is lost; a happiness that has vanished. Almost all of these letters are from people comfortably settled in the middle class. Yet these writers confess to loneliness. Do not underestimate this problem of loneliness, this unhappiness in a rootless society.

Sometimes this loneliness is relieved by the stories I write about the Lower East Side of New York, the milieu of the one and a half million immigrants from 1890 to 1914.

And it's more than nostalgia that inspires the many confessions of longing. Sentiment alone wouldn't provide an empathic identification for many thousands of people who never saw New York. What does emerge is that the strongest memory of life is *the family*.

The happiest memory of family life on the Lower East Side is that the father was not only an ever-present household head, but had to be respected. The father was always the figure of authority. This does not mean that Pop was a tyrant. No, it meant simply that no one sat down at the dinner table until he came home from work; and that we didn't speak until he spoke first, or until he asked us a question.

Jews call this "derekh eretz." The phrase is literally translated as "the custom of the land," but in actual usage it means respect for elders and particularly for parents.

Religion also played an important part in the unification of the family. Quite frankly, I did not realize how important a part religion played in our lives until quite recently.

There was always a religious service every time we sat down at the table. What strengthened the family relationship was that the religious service could not begin until every member of the family was present.

Looking back over forty years I realize what our religion did for us on the Lower East Side—we were sure that what disgraced one disgraced us all.

It is true that there were gangsters, but no glamour attached to them. No one ever mentioned their names in the home. When other parents spoke to the mother of a gangster, they would never tell this sorrowing woman about a son that had just been graduated from City College or a daughter that was teaching kindergarten. A gangster was an intrusion, not only upon the family but upon one million other people.

The Fascists, Nazis, and Communists understood the dangers of familial loyalty. To gain perfect loyalty for the state, they all knew that the family tie must be eliminated. The first thing they did was establish their "youth" organizations, with their widespread activities *outside* the home.

And history is not totally without its lessons. Its most important lesson is how a civilization survives. The civilization which perpetuates itself is the civilization which lives for tomorrow.

Has the Amercan civilization lost this? Sometimes I think so. Cook in a mechanical kitchen, listen to a rigged television quiz show, point with pride to the new white-wall tires—these are all costly distractions. We need distractions because inwardly we fear that the present is empty.

The stern Pilgrims who landed on the New England coast found it nothing but rock ledge yet made from it a garden—for tomorrow. The Englishmen and the Scots who came into North Carolina with an ax and a rifle also lived for tomorrow. The courthouses they built are filled with the land deeds they signed with an X— "his mark." But the children of these people were among the first professors in the land-grant universities built for still another tomorrow.

And the Jews who came from the ghettos of Europe and settled on the East Side entered the American middle class so readily because the mothers and fathers lived solely for tomorrow.

My mother didn't learn English. It was enough for her to stay home and cook and sew. But she wanted her children to learn English. And to see that they were educated she worked as a dress-maker in the tenement late at night. The words she mastered in English, "Enjoy! Enjoy!" meant—Tomorrow.

HARRY GOLDEN

June 1960
Charlotte, N. C.

PART 1

We're Completely Homogenized

The rocking chair

In the days when my mother had to empty the drip pan under the icebox she still had time to sit in the rocking chair for an hour or two every day. The rocking chair was among the most valuable of all our inventions. It provided both relaxation and the opportunity to think out our problems and have a good look at the world.

The rocking chair not only provided relaxation, comfort, and intellectual stimulation, but if something began to boil on the stove or if the doorbell rang, you could step out of it on its very next forward go-round, with the ease of stepping off a low and convenient platform. And unless you have read the Bible, Shakespeare, Longfellow, or Sandburg in a rocking chair, you've missed one of the truly great joys of living.

Sitting in a modern contour chair is like falling into a coalbin, and you cannot get out of it without assistance. If you read the memoirs of the Count de Sade you will find that he was the one who really invented this contraption. And I suspect that the modern poetry fellows have had a lot to do with it. They would never trust you with their stuff in a rocking chair. They want you to stay on edge all the time—they want everything to be a "challenge" to you, and, my friends, I think the time has come for a few less challenges. The crying need of the moment is a good comfortable rocking chair going back and forth, back and forth, and restoring the importance and the dignity of the *individual*.

A nice old lady

I had to spend a few days in the South Carolina city of Florence, and since my advertising manager went there frequently,

I asked him to suggest a place for me to stay. He told me he always checked in at a tourist place called For-Rest Tourist Home at 279 West Cheves Street. It was operated, he said, by a Mrs. Mattie Taylor, who was "a nice old lady."

So I made my trip and I learned that this "nice old lady" was about eighty years old and that she not only actively managed her tourist business, but she drove into North Carolina near Wilson once a week to supervise two tobacco farms which she inherited years past from her father and her husband. But that was only the beginning. She attended the Woman's College at Greensboro, long before it became part of the Consolidated University of North Carolina, and upon her graduation took a secretarial position with Congressman MacLean. She later became the first female court stenographer in North Carolina. Her classmates, trained in the arts of taffy pulling and club meetings, raised their eyebrows when this Southern belle went to work "for wages." At their twenty-fifth reunion, however, all had been forgiven; and at their fiftieth reunion, the remaining members of the class stood up and cheered her.

Mrs. Taylor's home was next door to the home of the late U. S. Senator Cotton Ed Smith, and she had a hundred stories to tell about that. The Smith home is empty now and the neighborhood today is one of the business centers of that thriving, typically Southern city of 35,000. "Typically Southern" is correct too, because it was in Mrs. Taylor's home that Edna Ferber lived for a few weeks, gathering "color" and "Southern accent" for her novel, *Show Boat*, but that's another story.

Mrs. Taylor was the first lady in Florence to convert her home to the tourist trade. They called it then, "opening your door to guests." One day, after her husband died, she took careful inventory of her assets, which included two growing boys, and she came downstairs and opened her door to the public.

Her friends were shocked: "Mattie is opening her home to guests, some may even come from the North, and to think she's the daughter of Colonel Moore, who lost an arm at Fort Sumter!" But that's another story. My visit was several years back and she's gone now, Mrs. Mattie Taylor, this nice old lady.

I was just trying to point out the difference between an advertising manager and a reporter.

Company's coming

I WOULD recommend that we straighten out a few things before we contemplate any interplanetary transportation system. Suppose a man from Mars should suddenly appear on Earth? I think it would be terribly embarrassing if he learned that a second-rate singer in a night club makes four thousand dollars a week, and a high-school teacher makes three thousand eight hundred and ninety dollars a year. This and many other things should be straightened out first if we intend to maintain our dignity when planet folks start visiting us.

We are colorless

SINCE we use the term "colored" for the Negro race, I suggest that the Negro use the term "colorless" for the white race. "A group of colored and colorless got together for a meeting."

The march to the sea

IN EVERY city I visit, I make it my business to study the sociological terrain. I usually ask, "Where are the Gentiles making their stand?"

Take Boston as an example—Boston with its tremendous Irish Catholic influence and sizable Jewish and Italian communities. The Jews began to move into the better residential areas, while the Irish were fanning out in another direction. The Protestants began to run into the suburbs, with the Irish, the Jews, and the

Italians at their heels, and the pursuers themselves being chased
by the Negroes. But from all indications it appears that the Protestants have decided to make a firm stand at Concord and at Lexington. The Jews are now at the approaches to Old Concord Bridge;
at Newton, Wayland, Lincoln, Sudbury; they hold Brookline and
parts of Wellesley, and from the other side both the Irish and the
Jews are attacking by way of Natick, with the Italians preparing
to mount a major offensive of their own. The Protestants, behind
their fortification at Concord and Lexington, have revived the old
signal system to alert the inhabitants—"One if by land, and two if
by sea."

I have never been greatly disturbed about the fact that some
resort hotels do not cater to "Jewish clientele." Let those hotel
managers worry. Every time they get a telegram requesting a reser-
vation, the poor fellows take an ulcer pill and say, "I wonder if he
is one."

I expressed these views once to a committee of people seriously
concerned about the late Vice-President Alben Barkley's honeymoon. This good man had married the charming widow, Mrs.
Hadley, and they were honeymooning at a place called The Clois-
ters at Sea Island, Georgia. The "committee" was worried: Did
the Vice-President know that this hotel refuses to accept Jewish
guests? And all sorts of proposals were made. One man said that
we should get in touch with the Vice-President. Another, that
maybe we should merely notify his office. Finally it was my turn,
and I suggested that we leave the Vice-President and his bride
alone, let them enjoy their honeymoon in peace. I expanded my
argument to a recital of this entire campaign which I called: "The
March to the Sea."

When I was a little boy on the Lower East Side of New York
we all used to go to Coney Island. In Coney Island there was a
"segregated" section called Sea Gate. No Jews could go to Sea
Gate. I remember watching some of the folks go through "the
gate"; and it didn't concern me then, and it doesn't concern me
now. A few Jews, however, began to infiltrate. Pretty soon the Jews
were going to Sea Gate. When we got to Sea Gate, however, the
other folks left, and they took up positions along the Jersey coast.

And it was right there in the State of New Jersey that we fought the decisive battle in the March to the Sea, a sort of sociological Battle of Saratoga.

This decisive battle was fought at Lakewood, New Jersey. Now Lakewood was a very fancy resort nestling in the pines. In those days it was frequented by the Morgans, the Rockefellers, and the Vanderbilts. The Jewish salient backed by the Sea Gate forces split the defenders crucially. The main body of Gentiles retreated south in wild disorder. A smaller body "escaped" to the north, gaining refuge in the White Mountains and the Berkshires. We Jews decided then and there to follow the main body retreating down the Atlantic coast and to permit the smaller force to escape, figuring that we could initiate mopping-up operations later.

The next major encounter was at Asbury Park, which had been a Methodist retreat named after one of that church's early bishops. The retreating Gentiles, however, were able to exploit the advantages of the coastal terrain. While Jewish forces fanned out in a double-pronged advance, the Gentiles were able to build strong defenses in several inlets and enclaves in the area. The hope of the defending forces was that the Jews would not penetrate these strongly defended pockets of resistance. And they were correct in their judgment, although the Jewish advance pushed forward along the coast without any serious interruption. Strategy dictated that Jews by-pass these redoubts so as not to slow the advance, and let the rear echelons engage in another mopping-up campaign. At Virginia Beach, the Gentiles held out a long time until only the leading hotel was left, but its position was precarious; it soon reached the stage where the only remaining "exit" was to the sea. Luckily this outpost forced a narrow passageway by land and fled. At this moment the Gentile retreat turned into a major disorganized rout, and they were not able to regroup until they reached Florida. It took two years to reinforce both sides. And when all is said and done, strategically and tactically, the Miami siege made brilliant military history. The regrouped Gentiles faced their forces northward. They had strong supporting columns from Palm Beach and hundreds of enclaves and fortresses to buffer the attack. They also had received considerable help from the St. Petersburg–Tampa

area as well as from the Orlando sector. The Jews, however, re-
sorted to a flanking movement and then a beautiful pincers attack.
The beleaguered Gentiles fell back into the city. The armies finally
met face to face at Fifteenth Street in hand-to-hand fighting.
Grudgingly the Gentiles gave up half a block at a time, and while
they did not evacuate all the hotels and rooming houses, they left
them isolated in enemy territory. The block-by-block struggle in
Miami reached its climax at the end of the 1940's. The defenses
of the Gentiles were breached, then broken forever. Most of the
survivors fell behind hastily prepared breastworks at Palm Beach,
determined to make a last-ditch stand. But many of them fled to
the St. Petersburg–Tampa area and to other resorts far, far away
on the Gulf of Mexico.

I explained to the committee that each of the great fortresses
had surrendered without too much of a struggle—Long Branch,
Deal, Asbury Park, Atlantic City, Virginia Beach, Myrtle Beach,
and finally Miami, and I would not start a new campaign for Sea
Island, Georgia, which is nothing more than an inoperable beach-
head, a Formosa with only a history and a fast-receding future.

So now you have an insight into the historical fact that this great
and good man, the late Vice-President Alben Barkley, was not
disturbed on his honeymoon.

The question is, why were the Gentiles running away and why
were the Jews pursuing them? What is this war all about? *Bigotry*
would be an oversimplification. You must remember that the running Gentiles and the chasing Jews are both newcomers to the
American middle class. The Gentiles were actually running away
from their own people, from the fellows who drive trucks, dig coal,
work in the mills, and pump gas. The guilt of the "exclusive" Gentile is intolerable, and to ask him to accept an outsider, like a Jew,
is just too much. The Jews have been winning these battles because they, too, are running away from their own. They forced the
fortifications of the Gentiles on Fifteenth Street in Miami because
behind them, coming along fast, were the lower-echelon Jews with
the salami and the baby carriages.

It was inevitable that these two groups of exclusive middle-
classniks would wage war up and down the Atlantic seaboard. In

recent years there appears to have been a more determined Gentile stand in the St. Petersburg–Tampa area. Resistance has been great, and only a few Jews have been able to make it, although they fully appreciate the status significance. Today when you ask a few of the fancy folks, "How was Miami?" they answer with deep indignation: "What do you mean Miami? We go to the West Coast." But I think that the "West Coast" has now been conceded to the Gentile forces. I suspect it might even be wise now to enter into negotiations for the exchange of populations; the Gentiles who are hidden in the inlets and up the river branches around Miami to be exchanged for the Jews who are percolating in the St. Petersburg–Tampa sector.

It would be advisable to choose a negotiation site midway between Florida's West Coast and the Jewish stronghold in the Catskill Mountains.

I was a guest in a Catskill hotel called The Pines, and I have never seen anything like it. This fabulous hostelry has swimming pools for children and adults, steam rooms, card rooms, playrooms, ballrooms, and a thousand-seat theater. The food they serve you has not been placed on any table since Petronius threw his big party during the Second Roman Empire. On top of all of that, there's a two-hour show with professional Broadway performers of top rank.

Why would anyone want to go to Sea Island when they can have Fallsburg with lox, bagels, challah, sweet-and-sour meat balls, onion rolls, and a fine master of ceremonies who uses the name of Hopalong Kishkidick? If someone gave me a written guarantee that the Jews would be secure forever in the Catskill Mountains, I would gladly sign away all my rights to Sea Island, and throw in Grosse Pointe, Pinehurst, White Sulphur Springs, and clear across to the Camelback Inn as a bonus.

We're completely homogenized

This is the age of the Deodorized American.

When we took a bath once a week (in the summer, that is), there were no deodorants. But now when our bathtub culture has reached such tremendous proportions, we buy millions of dollars' worth of deodorants.

This is what we would call "Moishe Kapoyer" (a fictional character of the ghetto, a sort of lovable idiot, who did everything backward or upside down).

The advertising boys had a product to sell and so they invented the disease which the product was advertised to cure. This is not to say that "body odor" does not exist. Of course it does, but it has little to do with deodorants. It has everything to do with diet and economic status, which includes occupation and living quarters, and it also involves the lack of reasonable sanitary precautions.

Actually the American bathtub culture is a comparatively recent development, no more than about a half-century old. In fact the tradition of the New England Puritans and the Southern Calvinists was entirely against any undue concern for the physical body. No one mentioned taking a bath or anything of that sort. The Hebraic culture never discussed bathing except in terms of a religious ritual. Now it has become the style for people to open a conversation (before the TV is turned on) with the statement: "I take two showers a day."

Anything to achieve status.

There's nothing to do

It is hard to fathom the next turn American civilization will take. Where will we go? What will become of us? This is a question that frames itself unavoidably as one walks past the great stores of Fifth Avenue. Where once suits and shirts and an

occasional scarf were sold, now ski togs, plastic helmets for motorboat enthusiasts, and skin-diving equipment are displayed. In
specialty shops where once a fellow could buy a one-dollar Brownie
to take a picture of his kids he can now buy a gold golf ball or
pick from a thousand different styles of decanters.

And a result is that if you take a flight and confide in your
fellow passenger that you are deplaning at Dayton, he will say,
"There's nothing to do there." And children who have received
toys the like of which have never been seen before will say Christmas morning, "There's nothing to do."

In every American city there's a roadside night club called Grove
Terrace or Terrace Grove, which is supposed to represent something to do, except that too soon it becomes obvious what it is—a
partial disguise for the emptiness of suburban and urban life.

There is nothing to do, except imitate and become like the
Athenians, the Carthaginians, and the Romans. Each of them
ended their civilization during an era of "nothing to do."

Swimming in the suburbs

IN THE rich suburbs the folks have begun building private
swimming pools. These aren't any backyard affairs, lined with
plastic. These are T-shaped, forty-by-sixty-foot jobs with two
diving boards. But the folks aren't always getting what they're
paying for.

One night, after a couple of highballs, one suburbanite says to
his neighbor, "Wouldn't it be nice if we could get some of our
friends together and build a private swimming pool? Cost us
about three thousand dollars and we wouldn't need more than
twelve families. And the kids wouldn't have to travel all the way
to that municipal pool."

Done, quick as a wink. What's better as a status symbol than a
private swimming pool? The articles of incorporation are drawn
up and there are just twelve families. A few families who believed
they were part of the inner set are aggrieved because they weren't

asked. There's a little tension over the highballs for a couple of weeks, but this tension is relieved because the pool doesn't cost three thousand dollars. No siree, what with the inflated realty values and whatnot, the swimming pool comes to about six thousand nine hundred dollars. So those aggrieved families are hustled into the corporation pretty fast; in fact, they're even pressured to get in some of their friends who belong to another inner circle. The pool has grown now from twelve families to twenty-four, but it's still pretty exclusive in that everyone has the same attitudes.

The foundation's been dug and the pipes are laid. The workmen are about to pour the cement when a commissioner from the Zoning Board shows up and addresses himself to the first highball drinker.

It seems a swimming pool is an "attractive nuisance" and if any kid other than the child of a member falls in and drowns, the corporation will be held liable. So the Zoning Board of the town has decreed some time before that all swimming pools be surrounded by a ten-foot-high wire-mesh fence. That fence is going to cost about nine hundred dollars plus another three hundred dollars for labor and, what with costs on the pool running a bit high to get it finished in time for the summer, the number of the corporation grows to thirty families. Of course, thirty families of the right background and manners are not easy to find, and the highball folks now go out searching for all sorts of odds and ends, and now that Syrian architect who has seven kids (and an extra four hundred dollars) is dragged into the circle, too.

The fence is posted, the pool is readied, and the first day of summer dawns. But now who should come plodding up the road but an assistant to the health commissioner. It seems there's a State law that demands a certified lifeguard preside over every swimming pool. These certified lifeguards don't cost any thirty dollars a week either. But the corporation locates a Harvard sophomore, home for the summer, at the bargain price of fifty-five dollars. But that's another four families. Plus the fact that the pool must be drained every three days in accordance with local health laws, which means another three families.

But the kids splash and play and romp in their exclusive swimming pool and the wives watch and play canasta and the only fly in the ointment is that the municipal pool is so uncrowded now it's positively pleasant to go there. But of course the municipal pool isn't exclusive. It doesn't cost anything. Ah, it's not all honey to be a middle-classnik in mid-twentieth-century America.

"My son-in-law, the doctor"

A JEWISH father or mother never said," My son-in-law Joe," or "My son-in-law Harry," it was always, "My son-in-law the doctor," or "My son-in-law the lawyer," or "My son-in-law the dentist." In recent months I have even heard, "My son-in-law the lawyer, who also is a professor at N.Y.U. at night."

When the father or the mother said, "My son-in-law who is very good to my daughter," you knew that this was bad—very bad —the son-in-law was a factory worker, a cloaks operator, a peddler, a mechanic, or a taxi driver.

This was also the protocol concerning marriageable daughters. When the parents (or the marriage broker) of a marriageable girl said, "She is very smart," or "She's a wonderful cook and also sews beautifully," you had to prepare yourself for a shock when you finally met the gal. A pretty girl needed no other "virtues," and this is part of the culture of all mankind.

There have been some new developments in this quest for status. As I tour the country and meet committeewomen, they tell me about "my six-foot-two son who is at Yale," or "my son, who is six feet." Apparently, six feet is the cutoff point. Nothing shorter confers status. No one has ever described to me a five-foot-ten-and-a-half-inch son-in-law.

Southern cooking

MANY Southern writers have made the point that Southern cooking is not what it used to be. I should say it is not! Out of the forty most popular eating places in Charlotte, twenty-two are southern Greek, three are Nationalist Chinese, two are kosher delicatessens, two others are "kosher style" places operated by northern Greeks, one is French, and one is "Italian style." The rest include the three or four hotel dining rooms, a Howard Johnson's, a large cafeteria, and a large dining room. The latter two are local enterprises and may rightfully be called "Southern."

The point I make is that more than the Southern *viewpoint* is changing. There are a few "why don'tcha go back where you came from" boys left, but their stupid little world is disappearing before their eyes. And so when a patriot rises in righteous indignation to defend the honor of our Southern restaurants, he doesn't know what the hell he's talking about.

Southern viewpoint

IN GEORGIA the governor vowed to "champion the Southern viewpoint at all times." In North Carolina a bright young office visitor inquired: "Do you subscribe to the Southern viewpoint?"

What is this Southern viewpoint? Who speaks for the South?

James Byrnes expresses a Southern viewpoint. So do Lillian Smith, John Temple Graves, William Faulkner. And Benjamin Mays, the Grahams, Frank and Billy. So do Jonathan Daniels, Harry Byrd, Tom Linder, Lister Hill, Kelly Alexander, Paul Green, Kermit Hunter, Junius Scales, and Virginius Dabney. Herman Talmadge, Ellis Arnall, John Sparkman, William Fulbright, Hodding Carter, and Erskine Caldwell. Each expresses his Southern viewpoint. So do I.

If the above-mentioned Southern "spokesmen" are found to agree on one important or unimportant issue, I will nose-roll peanuts from Atlanta to the sea.

The tears of mobility

ON NEW YORK'S East Side, when a family moved from Eldridge to Rivington Street, it was an occasion of grievous sorrow to the children. The parents steeled themselves against the children's tears. The children cried at leaving the familiar street, their friends, and the safety of the nearby candy store where they were known and accepted.

Nowadays parents don't move within a ten-block area. They move over the length and breadth of the continent. And they move often. The statistics say a family moves once every five and a half years. I wonder if we understand the sorrow of the children when we make these moves. Though you try to tell a child that in a new place he will find new interests, new friends, and new happiness, he doesn't believe you and you know it. It will not be the same. It will not be the same because no family is ever the same after it has been uprooted. The children know the house they live in will be a temporary home, their friends transitory acquaintances, and the father's profession only a passing job.

The Chosen People

SEVERAL civic clubs in Texas and South Carolina have eliminated the singing of "The Star-Spangled Banner" at their meetings and have substituted "Dixie." Ah, how wonderful it is to be a Southerner—one of the true Chosen People. Can you imagine some labor union up North eliminating "The Star-Spangled Banner" and substituting the song about old Joe Hill? Senator McClellan would call for an emergency meeting.

At most of our meetings and conventions we Jews sing the "Hatikvah," that beautiful poem of Zion; but we are extremely cautious. First we sing "My Country, 'Tis of Thee," then "Hatikvah," and finally "The Star-Spangled Banner." Thus we protect ourselves at both ends. At a Seaboard Zionist Conference some years ago someone goofed and we did not follow "Hatikvah" with "The Star-Spangled Banner" (it shouldn't happen), and some of the folks who attended that conference are still shaking.

That the Southern white Protestant is conscious of his complete political and social pre-eminence and immunity is evidenced by the fact that he is a "bellyacher," which is the occupational disease of Chosen People.

Everybody's after him. The North is after him. Since 1935, through his Congressional seniority, he has been running the North (not a single piece of legislation could get through without his knowledge and consent), but nevertheless he says the North is after him. Everybody's after him. The "foreigners" are after him. As one of the native-born, he represents ninety-nine-point-four per cent of the population in his section, but he sits up night and day worrying about that naught-naught-point-six of a per cent who are after him. Now he has a new worry. The NAACP is after him. Big deal! A year ago a large industrial company decided to add two Negro filing clerks to its office staff of two hundred and eighteen clerks. But the Negroes had to be super. So the committee dug up two doctors of philosophy for these filing-clerk jobs. And the industrial concern told the committee, fine, but no publicity about this for at least three years. Let's see how it works out first.

Big deal!

He fragmentizes himself into many societies and organizations for "protection," when all the time he carries with him the only carte-blanche membership in this world, that of a Southern white Protestant, the open sesame to every nook and corner of our civilization. He has written thousands of last wills and testaments in which the number one bequest was "the copper still on the back porch," but he remains the undisputed symbol of piety, acknowledged by all the world as the true custodian of the Hebrew God and all the works of Jeremiah and Isaiah. He remains the Undisputed Custodian of Love of Country and American Patriotism. He is the only man in our society who can even tell jokes about God and it is not blasphemy. Tomorrow morning, if a Southern white Protestant in the Senate were to say, "Let's go over there to Mao Tse-tung and do some trading," a hush would fall over the legislative halls of the land, and you could bet your bottom dollar that America would be embarking on a new phase of foreign policy.

When you no longer feel the need to prove your patriotism, that, my friends, is the alpha and the omega of political freedom.

They do not even hang out the flag on the Fourth of July in the South, and when you see one you can be sure it is the home of some fellow who has just come down from the North. Why, on the Fourth of July my mother hung out two flags, one in the front window facing Eldridge Street and the other in the back facing what we called the yard. Some yard!

This is what makes the South so interesting. I listen to the reporters and feature writers from the North who visit me, and they tell me all sorts of tales; how bad it is down here, and I give them a drink and a dart. I have a dart board and everyone must shoot at least one dart; and we talk about the South and I usually detect that faraway look in the fellow's eye.

But with all the whining, the Southern white Protestant carries with him the seeds of freedom, and the price he exacts may not be too high at that. And because he remains the One True Individualist left in this world, I love him with all my heart, bellyaching and all.

Singing with the Salvation Army

ON A SATURDAY night one time I was making my way through Charlotte's main thoroughfare to the big newsstand to buy my out-of-town newspapers. On the corner was a Salvation Army band. There were five of them: two men with trumpets, two women with a drum and cymbals, and a leader who conducted the concert. They were playing "What a Friend We Have in Jesus."

I know almost all of the gospel hymns and this is a particular
favorite. So I stood at the edge of the crowd and began to hum
along with the band:

> What a friend we have in Jesus
> All our sins and griefs to bear.
> What a privilege to carry
> All our woes to God in prayer.

I had no sooner started than the conductor was in front of me,
waving his baton to lead me onward. He was trying to edge me
into the solo spot in front of the band.

I had two alternatives. I could run away, but I am no coward;
or I could sing along with him, which I did. First thing you know
I was right there in deep center field among the folks with the
trumpets and the drum and the cymbals, and they all seemed to
perk up and take on a new exhilaration. We were in "Blessed Assurance" as the great hymn rolled from our efforts. I had to sing
several verses before I found the opportunity to make a graceful
exit.

Nor was this the end of it. On a Saturday night in Charlotte,
as elsewhere, you would think all the fancy folks would be off
disporting themselves in the lounges of the country clubs. No,
not on this Saturday night. More people saw me singing with the
Salvation Army (or so they said) than read my paper. The rumor
went about that I had joined, repented, that now I was a Salva-
tionist, and it spread from Richmond, Virginia, to Augusta,
Georgia. I had reached "Blessed Assurance."

Bible teaching in the South

RECENTLY in a senior class of a high school in Charlotte,
the teacher took up the essays of Ralph Waldo Emerson and called
upon one of the students to read a short biographical sketch of
the American philosopher. After the reading, one of the boys rose
and demanded that the essays be withdrawn: "It says that Emer-

son was a Unitarian. He was not a Christian and we shouldn't read anything by a man who was not saved." The teacher laughed it off and proceeded with the lesson. The next morning eleven pupils took their places beside the teacher's desk. They were dead serious. They had asked their Bible teacher about it and she had confirmed their fears. Mr. Emerson was not saved; in fact, he was burning in hell at this very moment.

This is not an isolated case. The teaching of religion outside the home and organized church has created many new and serious problems. It has reached the stage where some of the clergymen who had hitherto supported the program are now beginning to question its consequences, not for the "minorities," but for themselves.

I'd like to explain how it works in the South. The several local Protestant churches make up a fund out of which they pay the Bible teacher in the public schools. A committee of laymen representing the churches supervises this fund and the selection of the teachers. Usually these instructors are Sunday School teachers in their respective churches, but they must also meet the qualifications of the public school system.

The Baptists openly oppose the system, at least at the level of their clergy. Their protests are usually answered effectively by the supervising committee: "Your church is against our program, but the majority of the children 'electing' Bible study are Baptists." This is true, of course, since the Baptists are by far the largest Protestant denomination in the South.

But even this idea of "electing" the subject is open to question. Upon admission each student is given a card for the signature of either of his parents: "Do you want your child to take Bible study as one of his elective subjects?" The card must be returned with either "Yes" or "No."

However, what is *not* elective, even in the high schools, is the daily devotional in every homeroom class, in the form of a prayer prepared by the Bible teacher (King James Version). Every Monday morning the "outside" Bible instructor provides each homeroom teacher with a set of five devotionals for the week, passages from the Gospels.

The influence of the Bible teacher goes far beyond the room of her own elective class.

In the elementary schools there are no separate rooms for Bible study, and both the daily devotional and the religious lesson are conducted by the regular teacher. The committee claims that this too is elective, since the child has the privilege of walking out. But this unhappy decision had been resolved long ago. The vast majority of the parents involved feel that their child would be less conspicuous (and less bewildered) if he remained seated than if he walked out of a room of forty or forty-five of his classmates "because he does not want to hear about God."

The Bible teacher paid by these "outside" funds is formally under the supervision of the public school authorities, but this is only a technicality. The committees of church laymen include business and political leaders, the most important citizens of the community. This gives the Bible teacher a special status which she cannot avoid even if she tries. The result is a pressure on the school authorities and the teachers which represents the truly great tragedy, particularly because these people lack the freedom to condemn it.

The Bible teacher may be both sincere and high-minded, but it is inescapable—she brings *fear* with her the moment she enters the school building. Thus the most innocuous note from the Bible teacher, asking for a student to come to her class, will set the entire building into feverish action. On occasions such as picnics or special meetings, the first thing the regular teachers will say to each other on the phone is, "Be careful, *she* will be there."

The school authorities and teachers have another serious problem. The elective religious study usually has the largest enrollment. This is understandable. The study involves reading from the Gospels and hymn singing. There is considerable emotion built up among one hundred young people singing "The Old Rugged Cross" at nine o'clock in the morning. The regular teachers have found that it takes an extra period for the children to be unwound sufficiently to proceed with grammar or geography.

In fact it is this emotionalism which, in some cases, has reached fantastic proportions. Groups of these young high-school students have recently decided to conduct their own religious services in a supercharged atmosphere, without trained supervision or religious wisdom. The result has been that a few of the less orthodox Protestant clergymen have received abusive phone calls from young people demanding: "When are you going to begin to really preach the Gospel, the Blood, and the Atonement?"

A Baptist clergyman who is also active in the work of mental hygiene told me, "I know better than anyone else of the tragedy of this religious instruction in the public schools. I have been called in as counselor to get some of these children down from their high emotional pitch, but I am sorry to say that some of them will require far more serious treatment than I can give them."

To baseball, long life

AT EVERY level of our culture we reflect the habits and mores of the society that surrounds us. I watch this carefully when I go about the country making speeches.

In Milwaukee the Jews were all hot and bothered about the World Series and the Braves. While I was in Milwaukee, Hank Aaron had broken up a ball game with a home run and the folks were flushed with victory. One elderly lady said to me in Yiddish: "A leban uff zein schwartzen keppele" (A long life to his little black head).

The same thing happened the year before in Kansas City. Kansas City had just acquired a major-league baseball team—the Athletics —and like the rest of the city, the Jewish middle class was beside itself with joy. I was sitting on the dais with the dignitaries when I noticed that a note was handed by an usher to a man in the last row. From hand to hand the note went, through forty rows of people, until it reached the chairman on the dais, who accepted it and solemnly read its contents. In fifteen minutes another note made its way from the usher over the forty rows up to the chairman. Again he read the note solemnly. After finishing it, he walked purposefully to the lectern and announced loudly: "End of the sixth inning: Kansas City Athletics 4, Washington Senators o." I said to myself, What did they need me to make a speech for? They could sit here and pass these notes all night.

Of course, I can understand why baseball is our national sport. It offers an exhibition of national virtues, like stamina, skill, and courage. It is a team effort that nevertheless allows a display of personality and virtuosity. Sometimes I think we try to deny this and it is always dismaying when the radio announcers keep describing all of the players as "fine gentlemen" and "all-around fellows." I remember when Ty Cobb vaulted into the stands and poked a heckler. And when Ted Williams spat at the crowd I was glad to think the sport hadn't changed. Since then I've learned that there are pitchers invariably described as brilliant and intelligent who spend the afternoon in the dugout reading *Superman Comics* and outfielders described as alert who can't stop thinking or talking about their avocado ranches.

But what really makes baseball the great American pastime is the fact that it is the only sport which lends itself completely to our passion for statistical assessment.

I mean the averages: the batting averages, the won-lost pitching records, the earned-run averages, and the fielding averages, as well as the standings of the teams, represented not only fractionally but in percentages, too. It is true that the averages do not always reflect every part of the game. There are shortstops who can stop the ball only with their elbows and their fielding averages are very high because they never get near enough to the ball to make an error, but to follow the game completely, you've got to go out and watch that short-stop once in a while.

The expense account

It is impossible to buy the best meats in a butcher shop any more. Even the giant supermarkets don't have them. And the

vegetable delicacies like endive or truffles have similarly disappeared. Where have they gone?

To the restaurants. There you can eat the best of everything.
Don't make the mistake, however, of thinking the customer pays
for them. No siree, don't let appearances deceive you. The United
States Government pays, because all these foods and fine dishes
are just so many more items on the expense account.

The expense account, which comes right off the top of the
income tax, has led to the formation of countless credit card
systems. These credit card systems provide two things: convenience
in declaring income-tax exemptions and prestige. The man with
the credit card is the man with status. If you offer to pay cash for
your tab in a swell restaurant, the cashier and the waiters rub you
off their sleeves like so many flyspecks.

I have seen men with credit cards that unfold and drop from
their wallets like those old-time scenic postal cards where you got
twelve for the price of one.

Sorrow in the valley

THE country trembled when John L. Lewis sent the simple
telegram, "Come up out of the mines." It trembled when he wired
the A.F. of L. man, William Green, "We disaffiliate." Gone, gone
are those days when a telegram from a John L. Lewis could make
the nation sit up or make Congress ask the President for direction.

For some time before he announced his retirement last December, John L. Lewis was in decline, not because of any reaction on
the part of the miners, nor because labor-management problems
were solved, nor because he'd lost any vigor as one of the great
labor leaders of our time. John L. Lewis was in decline because
coal was no longer king.

From a high production yield of seventy million tons, anthracite
coal has slipped to about eighteen million tons. And this is not
the bottom. On a recent trip to Hazleton, Pennsylvania, I found
the folks are all using oil burners, a phenomenon that could not

have been imagined in this famous anthracite region twenty-five years ago. So we close the book on the era of John L. Lewis and the United Mine Workers.

But the story is not that simple.

In the heart of Pennsylvania, in Scranton, Wilkes-Barre, and Hazleton, there are thousands of men unemployed, miners who have been unemployed for years. And there is little other industry to absorb them. These miners glumly suspect they will never go back into the mines. Almost all mining now is "stripping"—taking the coal from the surface.

The women talk and say, "It's a funny thing, Min. When the floods hit the valley, everyone pitched in to help us. Unemployment is worse than the floods and yet it just drags on for years and years."

David Dubinsky and the International Ladies' Garment Workers' Union have tried to help. There are dozens of garment factories and sewing shops in the coal regions. But this only mutes the tragedy. Miners and their sons stand aside while their wives, mothers, and sisters earn the living. For the miner who has spent twenty years in the pits the chances for employment are scarce. If the unemployed miner has silicosis (miners' asthma), and most miners have it in varying degrees, no other industry will touch him. All that he has left is the hope that if he keeps up his union dues—one dollar a month if he is unemployed—he will collect pension benefits at sixty. Even here he is disillusioned since recently these benefits were cut in half, from one hundred dollars a month to fifty dollars.

The new garment industry tried to bring the men in. But the miners were embarrassed sitting in front of a sewing machine and their gnarled hands were clumsy and their fingers could not manage the fine work of an unfamiliar trade.

A man who once was master of the house, who earned good money, now sits on the porch and listens for the lunch whistle, and he goes into the house and comes out with his wife's lunch and takes it to her at the factory. He will drive her to work in the morning and call for her at night, and he tries to hide his face from his fellow miners who are doing the same thing.

And the responsibility for this heartbreak and poignant degradation of a strong workingman's spirit can be laid at the door of the short-sighted coal operators of the 1920's who opposed the coming of other industry that would drain off from their own pool of workingmen. Let us look toward the anthracite region of Pennsylvania. Big, strong Americans, Americans who gave much to our country, are being degraded and humiliated.

East Carolina's "cousins"

THERE'S something very fascinating about the towns and cities in eastern North Carolina. They have retained much of their original character, refusing to break their long-cherished continuity with the past. As you cross the Rip-Roaring, Ruby-Red Roanoke and enter the town of Windsor, it is like going back into the civilization of Charles II. The term "cousin" is used with considerable justification. Most of these old Anglo-Saxon communities of eastern Carolina can trace their earliest beginnings to a single Englishman who had been given a large land grant from the king. The folks kept themselves "intact," and thus can easily trace their whole family tree back to this one man. In a sense this was like Jewish ghetto life in Europe between the third and seventeenth centuries, and is not unusual. As a matter of fact I believe that at least two out of every five Englishmen living today have had a common ancestor, the good King Edward III. By the same token at least half of the people of western Europe are direct descendants of Charlemagne. If each of us were somehow able to extend our family tree along parallel lines, there would have to have been no fewer than four billion people on this planet one thousand years ago. But as a matter of fact there was not one tenth of that number, and thus somewhere along the line most of us "crossed." The world is full of cousins. In a more or less isolated community such as Windsor, this becomes particularly clear.

Windsor was settled in 1750 by eight Englishmen, John Gray

and several others; two were "esquires" and the other six were
"gentlemen." Gray bought some land from Cullen Pollock, son
of Thomas Pollock, who got the land from the Lords Proprietors.
Everybody in Windsor is either a direct descendant of John Gray
or of Cullen Pollock. What made Bertie County even more
"cousin" territory than usual was the fact that it was landlocked
for most of its existence—the only way you could get out was by
boat, and thus there was nobody else to choose from except their
own, and they married and intermarried all over the place.

These people once printed their own money, and they cherish
their eccentrics. They have a town drunk, a village atheist, a
female whom they refer to only as "that woman," a town "queer,"
and a sprinkling of folks without visible means of support who
sit on a bench outside the poolroom. They also have their stock
Negro characters, the "Vegetable Man," and the "Preacher," with
his pushcart built like a locomotive, a character who would rival
Porgy.

But the main characteristic of this leisured rural society is that
old Anglo-Saxon devotion to individualism. What has held them
back, of course, is the same thing that has held back dozens of
such wonderful communities throughout the South. It is the fetish
about the Negro. Once that fear is thrown off, these people will
go forward with a tremendous bang. They are the salt of the earth.
When you scratch away this unwarranted surface fear, you'll find
the people who gave Western civilization most of its treasures of
law, freedom, and dignity.

Armour and Manischewitz

SEVEN or eight years ago Elliott Roosevelt did a commentary on the radio with a few sponsors, one of which was the
Manischewitz Company. At that time I published one of Elliott's
commercials:

"I don't have to tell you about Armour's Star Brand Ham,
sweet as honey, just heat it, it tastes so good, and here we have

Manischewitz's matzoh balls and kreplach soup—a delight which no family should miss. For extra pleasure throw in three of four slices of Armour's best grade of bacon. And let us not forget that Manischewitz is now offering strictly kosher gefilte fish in jars. Manischewitz used to offer matzohs for the Passover season but now they are available during the entire year. Between the two of them—Armour and Manischewitz—any family's dining needs should be taken care of."

But when it came to the pronunciation of Manischewitz—oy vey iz mir. What that boy did to the commercial! He pronounced it in every conceivable way. Many-shoe-itz . . . Mon-o-shay-witz . . . Minny-shay-yits . . . the listener could never tell whether Elliott was advertising wine, a Japanese department store, or some obscure African tribe. I do not know how the Manischewitz sales made out, but the stores did a large trade in pronouncing dictionaries and the *Jewish Daily Forward* switchboard was lit up like a Menorah by elderly women in the Bronx asking if Elliott was really the son of Eleanor Roosevelt or just an enemy Arab trying to drive down the price of Manischewitz stock.

The white-clock cab

HUMAN nature is funny, especially where money is concerned. I have seen men in my time who have written checks for five thousand dollars for some charity, but who would lock you out of your apartment and foreclose on the pillows and mattress if you did not pay them a twenty-five-dollar debt on time.

A fellow will throw a ten-dollar bill across the bar and buy drinks all around a few hours after he has turned his wife down for an extra five dollars. And these are good people I am talking about. Men devoted to their families.

It is the desire to be well-liked. Only a few have reached the status where they do not need to be well-liked. The rest of us hunger for the accolade and hope it comes when we are not present: "He's a good fellow."

This drive takes on many forms. If the fellow is rich and it is no longer a problem for him to pick up the check, he will seek it in other ways—becoming president of the lodge or introducing the guest speaker at the big banquet. I knew a fellow in New Jersey who had a railroad pass on the commuters' train. When the conductor came around to the smoking car to pick up the commutation stubs, this fellow whipped out his wallet and showed his pass. He did that every day, coming and going. This pass cost him three or four times as much as the regular book of tickets, but it was a very big deal for him when he showed that wallet.

Years ago I knew a famous Wall Street gambler by the name of Bill Ebel. Mr. Ebel was one of the most dynamic gamblers on the exchanges. It was not unusual for him to sell five thousand shares of stock in one day, taking a position on the short side of the market. Those were the days when he and his more famous partner, Jesse Livermore, were the leading bears in Wall Street. Mr. Ebel could lose twenty-five thousand dollars without batting an eyelash. One night he was standing on the corner of Broadway and Exchange Place in a terrible downpour; he was being drenched to the skin but he allowed four or five taxicabs to pass.

In those days there were two kinds of taxicabs. One with a red clock charged a higher rate, and one with a white clock had the lower rate, and as each empty red-clock taxi pulled up to him he waved it away and said, "Gyp taxi, gyp taxi"—and he waited and waited till he got a white-clock cab. Mr. Ebel lived at the Hotel Astor and the difference between a "gyp taxi" and a "cheap taxi" was forty-five cents.

Will success spoil...?

THE deep concern about whether success will spoil this or that man is reserved only for writers, composers, artists, teachers, and clergymen.

No such worry concerns anyone in the commerical society. I have seen fellows come to Charlotte, borrow money to pay the rent for their families, and after a few years build a house for seventy-five thousand dollars. These are houses equipped with swimming pool and broad veranda. This phenomenon, I am sure, has been repeated a hundred times in every city and suburb throughout the country.

No one worries about these men. No one keeps expressing concern about whether or not success will spoil them. Unlike the writers, composers, artists, teachers, and clergymen, if a commercial man makes money, it is considered his just reward. It is coming to him.

The businessmen who hit it lucky with some deodorant (the advertisement of which costs infinitely more than the product) buy two Cadillacs and this is considered normal and routine. But these Cadillac owners watch the clergyman, the song writer, and the novelist like a hawk. They will proclaim they have detected a change if he buys a stripped-down Chevrolet.

A New York myth

THE power structure of our country remains the same. It is a white Protestant society. And it remains a white Protestant society despite the attention focused on the emergence of several ethnic groups.

Recently in an anti-Semitic journal I read, ". . . That Noo Yawk should be blown off the face of the earth." To which I say, "You poor benighted ignoramus, if anything should happen to New York (God forbid), there would be more grieving families in the South than there were after Gettysburg."

This is a good time to explode a myth. When I was a kid on the Lower East Side of New York, I repeated an old jingle about New York: *"The Italians built it, the Irish run it, and the Jews own it."* Years later it began to dawn on me that this was a hoax. So while the bigots shook their fists at "that old debil Noo Yawk," the shrewd Protestants just went about the business of directing the whole show.

In Detroit, New York, Chicago, and Boston, with their large

Jewish, Irish, Polish, Italian, and Negro communities, the white Protestant power structure has been tolerant through the years in letting a James Michael Curley or a Tammany boss Charles Murphy run the cities, and they smile tolerantly when they see a Negro, a Jew, an Irishman, an Italian, or a Pole elected to public office. These are the shavings, so to speak. The things that really matter in our society—the insurance company, the bank, the railroad, the airline, the daily newspaper, the national magazine, the oil, steel, glass, building materials, and automobile industries (and the government)—all remain in the complete and undisputed control of the white Protestants.

Two or three times a year they take enough time out to throw a little confetti out the window when one of the "minority groups" is passing by with a big drum.

Textile workers and the South

THE Textile Workers Union of America is spending a million dollars a year in its operations in the South—a million dollars a year and in six years they have not produced a thousand new members. On the contrary, the Textile Workers Union has lost about half its dues-paying membership since 1950.

When Eisenhower became President, there were 1,300,000 textile workers in the country. Today there are 890,000. Of this number 600,000 are in the South and of these 600,000 textile workers, the union has perhaps 70,000 dues-paying members.

The loss of membership can be traced to several factors. Mergers and dissolutions have taken their toll. When I was selling advertising in Gastonia, North Carolina, in 1940, I had one hundred and thirty-two proprietors to call on. Today the advertising men tell me that there are fewer than seventy individuals with the authority to place an advertisement.

The union has lost election after election, which brings us to the main factor—the use of the Taft-Hartley Act which makes organization almost impossible wherever there is resistance on the part of the employer.

The first thing to ask is why the union continues to spend a million dollars a year under such near-hopeless conditions.

The answer is simple. To withdraw from the South would mean the destruction of the entire union. The Northern textile workers would drop out or organize a unit of their own. The Northern workers insist upon a militant organizing force in the South to try to bring into line the runaway plants from the North. If the Textile Workers Union withdrew, the movement of the industry into the South would accelerate at a tremendous pace, and the Northern textile worker knows he would eventually be eliminated entirely.

I think the best way to discuss this entire situation is in terms of the current strike in Henderson, North Carolina. This dispute involves the Harriet and Henderson Cotton Mills and eleven hundred members of the Textile Workers Union of America, AFL-CIO. The strike began on November 17, 1958, as a result of the company's refusal to renew its standard contract which had been in effect since 1944.

The union made no new demands in negotiations. Management however insisted on a long list of changes, the heart of which was the demand that the standard arbitration clause in the agreement be eliminated and a no-strike clause be added. Obviously to have agreed to such demands would have watered down the contract to a point where the employees would have had no voice at all in their working conditions.

So far it has been one of the most costly, violence-ridden strikes in many years. Not only are eleven hundred people out of work, but the twenty thousand people living in and around Henderson have been split into factions by bitterness and hate. The strikers have received no cash benefits from the union since they walked off; but the union has established a commissary where the strikers draw free groceries and household supplies. Light and water bills and emergency hospital bills are also paid by the union.

The union feels that the issues at Henderson are far more im-

portant than those found in just a local labor dispute. And they
are right. The entire structure of textile trade unionism in the
South may be at stake. Governor Luther H. Hodges stepped in
and achieved a settlement. It gave the union an opportunity to
save face and the workers were ordered back to work. The mills
however would only take back about two hundred of the strikers.
Mr. John D. Cooper, Jr., the mill owner, regarded as a staunch
individualist, insisted that the scabs he had hired (half of them
from the State of Virginia) held seniority. The workers of course
returned to the picket lines and the bitterness increased and so
did the violence. National Guard units went to Henderson to
keep the mill open and to protect the scabs. The streets of Henderson are deserted after 10:00 except for the patrol cruisers and
through traffic on the highway. Any pedestrian or motorist found
on the streets after 10:00 is stopped and asked to identify himself. On the side streets there are anonymous members of a
vigilante committee who keep watch in their homes. They report
their suspicions to a special communications center, identifying
themselves by code names. The State Bureau of Investigation has
set up a special office in Henderson and the State Police patrol
has been increased from four men to nearly two hundred.

There are some interesting aspects to this strike. First of all,
Mr. Cooper was once a great "friend" of the union. The Textile
Workers Union used to take pride in their locals in Henderson.

What happened to change this atmosphere?

About three months earlier there had been an announcement
by Charles A. Cannon (Cannon Mills), who has resisted union
organization for many years, that he would grant an increase in
wages to a minimum of $1.25 an hour—in the main, the equal of
the union wages. This was followed by a general increase in most
of the nonunion plants. The general policy of the textile owners
in recent years has been to "keep five cents an hour ahead of the
union."

This increase in wages by the nonunion plants was followed by
a wholesale challenge of union contracts throughout the South.
The public has been fed an image which pictures the unions

"running" America. Yet here is a major union of a major American industry fighting for its very existence.

But let us get back to Mr. Cooper's side of it—his anger at the arbitration clauses. He has a case there. This arbitration clause has not been handled with wisdom by the union. During the long periods of "peace" the union seems to feel that it must show some activity. I know of a case in which they called the employer to arbitration over a matter of thirteen dollars. It cost both sides about five hundred dollars to settle the matter.

All right, if the mill owners pay union wages and offer other benefits, including pension plans, why should there be such resistance to organization? The reason is that unionization in the textile mills of the South is not wholly a matter of economics. It is also political. Right there in Henderson most of the county officials were elected with the support of those two strong textile locals which are now on strike. Political education and activity *always* follow the organization of a plant.

A good example is my own city, Charlotte. In an area known as Hoskins (union textile plants), the liberal Senator Frank Graham received a majority of nearly six to one, while the rest of the city went nearly three to one for his highly conservative opponent, the late Senator Willis Smith!

South Carolina, the most conservative state in the Old South, is a better example. The precinct boxes which include the (organized) workers of the Celanese plant and the Rock Hill Finishing plant give a majority to the liberal candidate for State and national offices, and in the capital city of Columbia, the precinct boxes which include the (organized) Pacific, Mt. Vernon-Woodbury Mills give an impressive majority to the liberal candidates against the trend in the rest of South Carolina. In all of these instances you have essentially the same people, the same traditions, the same religion, but a different vote.

Thus the prospect of an increased liberal electorate involved in trade unionism is really the most important factor in the resistance to organization which we have seen accelerated in recent years.

The Senator McClellan-Robert Kennedy hearings have added to the woes of the textile union. Because the South does not have the organized labor structure of the North (with its thousands of different craft, transportation, and industrial locals), the Southern millworker usually identifies unions as a single unit ("Unions are crooked" or "Unions are all right"). The proof of Dave Beck's thievery and Jimmy Hoffa's arrogance did greater damage to the organizers of the textile union in the South than it did to the teamster hierarchy of the North.

Even some liberals have praised the Taft-Hartley Act and have said that all it needed was "a little modification." When it comes to the interpretation of the rules and regulations concerning the Taft-Hartley Act by the National Labor Relations Board, it is an entirely different story.

For example, today it is impossible to win a decision against an employer for "discriminatory firing." The Taft-Hartley Act only enjoins an employee of the firm from propagandizing against trade unionism. So the wife of the superintendent visits the homes of each of the workers suspected of favoring the union. The superintendent's wife is not an employee of the mill. One huge mill in North Carolina had a clergyman hold prayer meetings during "vote week" and he prayed against the union.

In addition, the big headache for the Textile Workers Union is time. In four recent elections in North Carolina and Alabama, the union had won the election by a narrow margin. The employer challenged enough of the pro-union voters to gain a hearing before the National Labor Relations Board. The "challenges" are now the rule. The employer knows more or less who will vote for the union and he challenges the margin of the majority. These challenges are made on several grounds; the employer says that there was undue pressure exerted on the voter or the employer claims that a few days before the election he had assigned the employee to a supervisory task, thus making him ineligible to vote. In deciding these hearings the National Labor Relations Board takes from six months to two years, and during this time the employer is able to fire most of the union organizers.

One management charged that a circular claimed that an organized mill in another city paid $1.40 an hour and management claimed that this was fallacious; the mill paid $1.38 an hour, not $1.40. Result: another six months' delay, and more opportunity to switch pro-union voters.

The Textile Workers Union of America has not come to grips with the situation as it exists in the year 1960.

In the old days the superintendent of the mill came from the ranks. He had been a "doffer" or a "spinner." To some extent he was in sympathy with his fellow workers who were seeking to organize. But today the superintendent of the mill is a college graduate, often trained in public relations. In addition, the mills now employ public relations men and highly trained sociologists who know how to talk to workers. The unions have not kept pace with this development in the textile industry. Most of their organizers still belong to the old class-war school of trade unionism. And this is a dead issue!

Twenty years ago there were millworkers making sheets but who themselves did not have two sheets for their bed. That condition is entirely changed. Not only does the mill hand's wife have several sets of sheets, she also goes to the beauty parlor, and she has a washing machine on the porch and a television set and she owns her own home.

It is true that the mill family owes money for everything but this is no radical change from their previous condition. It is much better to be in debt and have all these things than to be in debt and have nothing.

No union organizer impresses a millworker today by promising him five cents an hour more pay. This is nonsense. The mills are paying union wages. It is true that they are paying union wages in order to avoid the union, and it is true that the unorganized millworker reaps benefits secured for him through the pioneering travail of the trade unionists. But you cannot use this as an argument. It simply does not convince.

And here again the Negro intrudes himself, as he intrudes himself at every level of the Southern culture. From the day the Southerner is born until he dies, the Negro intrudes himself.

The union is called "segregationist" by the Northern textile workers and "integrationist" by the Southern textile workers. The Northern textile workers call the union "segregationist" because it has not thrown out of the union the locals in the South which refuse to permit Negroes to sit at meetings.

But it goes deeper than this. The charge is not only made against the union by its own members but by the employers, too. A recent circular distributed by employers showed a picture of Mr. James Carey of the Phillip Murray Foundation handing a check to Roy Wilkins of the NAACP. This of course was Foundation money and had nothing to do with Textile Workers' money. But the circular had a big heading on it: "Your dues are going to the NAACP." And this is a most potent argument against trade unionism in the South.

My own observation is that the Textile Workers Union of America will make no real headway in the South until this integration matter is settled in accordance with law. And then when an employer asks: "Do you want a nigger to work beside you?" the millworker will say: "Why, they're going to school with my kids." The schoolhouse is the heart of the entire matter. The entire pattern of segregation will crumble the moment the schools are integrated. Nothing else will do it.

The future of trade unionism and the Textile Workers Union in the South hinges on the challenge made to their existence in Henderson and the other challenges which are sure to come. The union to survive must keep pace with the tremendous strides the employers have made in the field of public relations. It must stress the fringe benefits accruing to a man who belongs to a labor union, and most important of all—*job security*. This no employer public relations can as yet give him. The unions do not have the personnel who know how to emphasize and exploit these matters convincingly enough to impress the worker. The personnel still live in the days when the worker put in eleven hours a day at thirty-five cents an hour. Those days are gone. The unionists, with all their resources and with all their history, did not adapt their philosophy to the moment, and this is essentially their real problem, although hovering over them and their members is the Negro, and as long as the Negro remains a "weapon" the unions will make very little progress. You can try to minimize the racial matter all you want, but there can be no substantial trade-union structure in the South until the Southerner is ready to accept the reality that racial segregation is not only illegal and immoral but is also depriving the New South of a vast wealth and a great prosperity.

The loneliest woman

THERE is no lonelier woman in our country than a white nursemaid, governess, cook, or other household employee; and that is why there are no American-born white domestics. In the South this noble profession is identified with the Negro, and in the North they are "foreigners," and so you have the two "qualifications" for the very bottom of the totem pole. The girl who sells ribbons in the five-and-ten-cent store would not go to the movies with a white nursemaid or domestic—whose only chance for some "belonging" is when she actually is made part of the family she serves and fortunately this happens with fair regularity. One lady working for a family here told me of a few of her experiences. She had come from England and she was chagrined to learn that she had no American colleagues, but her sense of humor carried her through for a while.

With her first month's pay check she went to the bank to open an account. All through the negotiations the bank clerk kept saying: "Yes, Mrs. Clark," "Certainly, Mrs. Clark," "Of course, Mrs. Clark." A few minutes later when she had filled out her form and indicated her occupation the rest of the conversation was, "Of course, Louise," "Certainly, Louise," "Any time at all, Louise."

Jobs at the curb

IN EVERY large city of the South there is a street corner where you will find a group of Negroes waiting to be "picked up" for a day's work, perhaps even a regular job. In Charlotte the Negroes line up against a wall of an old railroad freight station, and they can be seen lounging, laughing, and wrestling with one another until they see a car slowing down as it approaches the corner. This may be an "employer"; the fellow sitting on the curb stands up and the others clowning or lounging along the wall also seem to stand up straight as if for inspection. You can stand and watch this scene for an hour and nothing happens, yet the fellow I picked up assured me that they do get work. I wanted to know why they do not go to the employment office, but they told me that unskilled jobs are getting scarce.

As a boy I remember such a market on the East Side of New York. It was at the corner of Ludlow and Hester Streets, near P.S. 62, and was known as the Khazar Market (Pig Market). The immigrants stood around in droves waiting for employers to pick them up. Often the men would hold their tools aloft, not only to attract attention but to indicate their skills. I saw fellows holding up hammers and others holding the carpenter's saw, unsheathed as if it were a sword. Others I recall carried windowpanes under their arms with a glass cutter prominently displayed.

The Negro curb market in the South operates under the same system as the East Side employment corner of long ago. The contract is made on the spot and when an agreement is reached the employer takes the worker to the job, but he is not required to bring him back.

The New South

NAPOLEON BONAPARTE had received from the Pope the crown of Charlemagne after he had smashed the armies of Europe at the Battle of Austerlitz. He dealt the greatest blow to the Austrian Hapsburgs, the very custodians of the Holy Roman Empire. But on the day he married the Hapsburg princess, Marie Louise, he turned to his brother and said, "Ah, Joseph, if our father were to see us now."

Smashing the armies of the Hapsburgs was one thing, marrying a Hapsburg princess another.

"Who was she before her marriage?" This was at the very foundation of the Southern culture, a way of life which is no more.

The mark of social distinction in the Old South was based on land, lineage, learning, and leadership. Actually the Southerner was the last American to maintain status-without-money.

Some of the Southern writers have understood this very well, and their stories about *Tobacco Road* and *Baby Doll* were less a reflection of the life in the South than the intent to satisfy a hunger in the North. These writers knew that a story of incest in Mississippi would help ease the jealousy the Northerners had for this amazing old culture.

Some of the streetwalkers I met on Broadway years ago, with their keen insight into life, also understood this, and these women from the Bronx, Brooklyn, and New Jersey would simulate a Southern accent to add to their desirability.

I suspect that this is part of the answer to the question which has puzzled our historians for a generation: why the unending interest in Civil War books? Sir Winston Churchill has said that it was "the last war between gentlemen." The late novelist, Jimmy Street, Mississippi born, wrote that this same war was "a slaughter between two undisciplined mobs." The Northerners share with the Southerners the need to accept the Churchillian version.

The South is exciting—emergent. The South is wonderful. I see evidences of this everywhere I look, in everything I read, and in everything I hear.

I think that some of the Southern writers have gone overboard in their "debunking" of the "moonlight and magnolias" of the South. When they point to the fact that only a very small percentage of Southerners had plantations and owned slaves, they miss the point. The moonlight, the magnolias, and the dueling pistol did not have to be universal to possess validity, because it was all a state of mind anyway, and this often prevails against armies as well as statistics.

And we must relate the carping at the South and often the sense of outrage that Northerners have expressed to this attitude of admiration, desire to emulate, and jealousy. It was based primarily on this rare gift the Southerner possessed—status-without-money. But he has lost it now and this is part of his great struggle against the recent laws to end racial segregation. Because the end of racial segregation dramatizes for him, or makes public, that which he knows is gone. This great culture which was based on family, tradition, and history was never really a myth. It had its parallel among the early Jewish immigrants to America. I saw many elderly Jews sitting in damp stores picking rags. It was no myth to them that they were of the chosen people. Thus when we speak of the old "Southern aristocracy" we are joking and at the same time we are not joking.

Land was the basis of it. It started with the people who got here first and had the most energy to get land away from the Indians and the least compunction about using the slaves to till the land. Then came learning. The county courthouses are filled with deeds of land grants from George II and George III, all signed with an X—his mark; but we find that twenty-five years later the sons of these men were the teachers at the university. Finally came leadership. This followed in the tradition of the Whigs of the mother country—England. The responsibility of the landowner was to serve, to be the magistrate, the sheriff, or the county commissioner. The sheriff and the county commissioner may have fallen in recent years in standard, but at one time they were the mark of responsibility. Money played little part in the social distinctions. It was a world such as Van Wyck Brooks described in another context, a world of being and becoming instead of doing. This status-without-money also brought in its wake a humanism of a sort. If you claimed kinship to the Chief Justice of the Supreme Court this also included, on equal terms, kinship with the second cousin who was fired from the bread route every two months because his accounts were short, and when he was brought into court the whole clan sat in the front row. "We've got to do something for Jim." When you have this sense of family, you are not allowed to pick and choose, you must claim them all.

When the immigrants came to America in the 1890's and in the first decade of the twentieth century, many of them took to ped-

dling or working in the needle trades in the factories or dealing in
scrap metal and old clothes. But the immigrants who had yikhus
(status) in Europe, and who tried so desperately to maintain status
in America, did not go into the factories and they did not take to
peddling or hustling of any kind. Lacking the capital and the talent
to achieve an upper echelon place for themselves in the economic
structure, they did nothing. Because dirty hands were the sign of
the peasant, the evidence of lower status. The lower echelon immigrant who "dirtied" his hands and peddled and collected scrap
metal went up and up and sent his sons on to Cornell and the University of Pennsylvania. The "status" fellows became lost souls.

And this is exactly what happened in the South. Instead of the
peasant, the Southerner had the Negro, and the Negro intruded
himself at every level of the Southerner's life. Because of the enforced lower status of the Negro, first through slavery and then
through racial segregation, the life of the white man was conditioned by this Negro from the day he was born to the day he died.
Many of these men throughout the South are today between fifty
and sixty-five years old. They lacked the capital and the talent to
achieve an upper echelon trade or occupation, and so they did not
dare dig tunnels, or work in the factories, or do anything which
the Negro was doing, because this would have identified them with
the lower status of the black man.

Now what has happened to the Southerner is that a few million
"immigrants" have arrived in this wake of urbanization. And these
immigrants are of two classes; Anglo-Saxons from the farms, the
mountains, and the rural sections of the South; and the Northern
managers of the national concerns. Now the former chore-boy from
the farm and the mountains did not have this old Southern status
and so he did not mind digging the tunnels and working the
gasoline pumps, and he quickly became the fuel-oil distributor,
the contractor, the lumber dealer, the owner of a fleet of trucks,
and a member of the school board. Now this fellow entering the
new urban middle class knew that he did not possess the ingredients
which made up the old Southerner of status-without-money. He
knew that he was not a Southern "aristocrat." And it was necessary
for him to avoid the question: "Who was she before she was

married?" And so what did he do? He made a wild dash for the country club, just as his new fellow middle-classniks did in Westchester County of New York. And he established "exclusive" city and luncheon clubs.

The Northern managers of the national concerns who began to come down South twenty-five years ago also lacked the ingredients, but they were even more desirous of becoming Southern aristocrats than the farm boys. When the employer up North notified this fellow that he was being transferred South, he went out and bought himself a book on "How To Make Mint Juleps," and then his wife briefed him on the South of *Gone With the Wind*. The second day after he moved down here he wrote a "letter to the editor" about the Supreme Court decisions against racial segregation. The newspaper put his letter on top of the "Open Forum" with the headline, "Northern Man Has His Say on Mixing":

"Dear Editor: We have just moved to this wonderful city from White Plains, N. Y., and the mixing of us whites and Negroes will never work. We know . . ."

This immediately made the Northern manager a Southern aristocrat. And he, too, made a wild dash for the country club and the "exclusive" city and luncheon clubs.

The farm boy and the mountaineer who were now the contractor and fuel-oil distributor welcomed these Northern managers with open arms, because by sheer weight of numbers they could actually eliminate the "old" Southerner and avoid the question: "Who was she before her marriage?"

And as the South has advanced from an agrarian to an industrial economy, and grown more wealthy in the process, there has been this new stratification of social classes in the urban centers. Gone forever is the democracy of equal poverty.

In a religious community it is not surprising that this stratification expresses itself in the churches. Episcopalians tended to look down on the Presbyterians, who in turn showed little enthusiasm for the Methodists. And if a man announced he had become a Baptist (through marriage) both Presbyterians and Methodists had a standing joke: "Boy, you can't become a Baptist, you have to be born one." And, of course, they all look down on the more primitive sects: The Church of God, Holiness, Free Will Baptist, etc. These were the sects of the millworkers, the sharecroppers, the propertyless.

The process did not end there. Within the various creeds, divisions based on wealth and growing social prestige began to take place. In an earlier day when a man suddenly acquired wealth, he would pass into the Episcopal Church itself. But with the expansion of the Southern economy, too many of them were entering the middle class, and so Presbyterians, Methodists, and Baptists, instead of joining the Episcopalians, proceeded to make their individual churches as "Episcopalian" as possible.

The working people were left to their own devices. Shut out for the most part from the established churches, they passed by the thousands into the tents of the itinerant evangelists and eventually began to form new sects. But now they, too, are following the pattern of the great church denominations. As these people acquire electric washing machines, television, and their own homes, they seek a more intellectual approach to their religion, and the sect which started in a tent now has a beautiful church edifice and the preachers wear claw-hammer coats and flowers in their lapels and have taken their places in Rotary, Kiwanis, Civitan, and Lions Clubs. It was within this same quarter of a century that the South lost its Bible Belt coloration and today the laymen have taken over—the trustees, the elders, the fellows in the economic power structure of the city. The Protestant clergyman no longer stands on the doorstep of his church shooing in the last child before mounting the pulpit. Today he stands at the door as the folks leave and he shakes hands with them, and he is wearing robes and vestments exactly as they do at St. Bartholomew's on Park Avenue and at the Church of the Heavenly Rest on Fifth Avenue. (The Jews, of course, are "more so" in reflecting the habits and the mores of the society in which they live. The rabbi has lost his classical function, and on public occasions the rabbi rarely has an opportunity of expression beyond what the laymen call "the Invocation and the Benediction.")

There is one thing more we must bear in mind in a discussion of the South—the South is *people*. The South is people who are trying to get along the same as the rest of the country—pay the bills, send the children to school, prove their individual worth, and achieve self-esteem. And above all else the yearning for status, the driving force which is equal to the need for food, shelter, and clothing; it is life itself. Except that the Southerner has this added problem. He knows that he once possessed this greatest of all gifts, status-without-money; and he's trying to hang on to a dream of the old agrarian life and he is dreaming of it in an industrial age.

The house once stood upon the hill and in the twilight the smoke came out of the chimney, and everybody knew his place in society—but today the Diesel truck goes up that road at twilight and the Diesel truck doesn't care who drives it, who his wife was before her marriage, or what color he is. The agrarian civilization is gone and with it all the ingredients which made up the Southern Way of Life. It's a different world today. It is an urban way of life, and when you are on the freeway outside of Charlotte, Atlanta, Memphis, or Birmingham, it is the same as being on the freeway outside of Toledo, Boston, Spokane, or Detroit.

Rent control and babies

RECENT controls in New York City are not working out as well as some of us had hoped. They have introduced a new factor into the life of the city. Because of this factor, slum areas are more hopelessly bad than ever. In the old days when the collector came for the rent, you said, "Not on your life, no rent until you fix that ceiling." But today rent controls have conspired to produce a sort of unwritten agreement between landlord and tenants: in return for the guarantee of a stable rent the tenant makes no maintenance demands upon the landlord.

The disturbing result is that now new slums are beginning to appear. It is impossible to keep up with the new slums of New York. Have you seen Washington Heights lately? Forty years ago I delivered packages in that area and it was a pleasure simply to walk along its streets. In those days, Mr. Maurice Costello, the early silent-movie hero and the father of the famous Dolores Costello, owned a movie house on Fort Washington Avenue. Many folks wore dinner jackets when they paid their admission. The beauty of the streets of Washington Heights has lived in my memory all these years. But today it is as though people set out to deface the property by neglect and carelessness and deliberate vandalism. These once beautiful streets are worse than anything we saw down on Allen Street in 1910.

The slums are expanding. And although I was a militant fighter for rent controls I am not sure now that they are an unalloyed good. It is true that they have helped thousands of low-income families, but they have also granted an immunity to the landlord. This is a bad exchange, and probably not worth it.

I was in the office of a real-estate agent recently talking to him about his great battle of day-to-day living. He told me about one landlord who will rent only to young married couples. Young married couples, this landlord insists, are his specialty. His apartments are filled with newlyweds. Why is this Cupid so interested in the young marrieds? Because of rent controls. Under the rent-control law, the landlord is permitted a 15 per cent increase for every new tenant, provided the previous tenant has occupied the apartment for two years. Young married couples move in and they have a baby, and they get along in the three-room apartment until the baby starts to crawl and a second baby is about to come and then they're off to one of the suburbs. The whole process takes two years. The next newlyweds will pay 15 per cent more for those three rooms. This landlord prays for babies night and day.

Prohibition at sunset

THE Charlotte liquor stores (under State control) should really open at 8:30 in the morning instead of 9 o'clock. Usually I see a few men waiting around in the morning and thus wasting nearly a half-hour of valuable time. Most men have their breakfast between 8 and 8:30, which means that they must wait around that half-hour for the liquor stores to open, or go to their offices and then make a second trip, which is a great inconvenience. Now if the stores opened at 8:30, things could follow in proper sequence. This was one of the reasons many of the folks were against the repeal of the local prohibition laws. The bootlegger brought the stuff to you a few minutes after you placed your order. One fellow I knew carried his deliveries in a fine cowhide brief case. He was well dressed and looked like a lawyer. When you were alone with him he opened the brief case and there was the stuff.

In South Carolina the liquor stores are privately owned and the law provides for the sale of liquor from "sunrise to sunset." In the window of every liquor store is a sign which tells you the exact moment of the sunset on that day. Every time I see one of these signs, "SUNSET TODAY AT 7:12 P.M.," I realize how much the South Carolinians owe to the culture of the East. It's like the sunset notice calling the worshipers to "Maariv" (evening prayer) . . . It would be nice if the Governor hired a few fellows who could blow the "shofar" (ram's horn), and stationed them on centrally located rooftops. As the sun began to sink below the western horizon, they could sound the warning to the faithful . . . time is running out.

Sales manager's tempo

SALES manager, general sales manager, vice-president in charge of sales—whatever his title, this is the fellow who whirls America away from itself and makes it fall into his lap. THIS IS IT, MEN—NOW IS THE TIME—YOU ARE THE SPARK, FELLOWS—DON'T FUMBLE THE BALL FOR A. K.'S BIRTHDAY CELEBRATION!!

This is the man who lives in the world of the metaphor, and who dares not relax for a single moment.

He always refers to the boss by the initials to bring the men in the field closer to the situation, but he lives in deadly fear of any one of the salesmen communicating "direct."

"Don't bother A. K. with such details—clear through me. I'll take it up with A. K." This is the man in our society who has tremendous influence. His art is to *stimulate*, his true belief is that "they will buy anything in a little red box." And with these two basic qualifications he is on his way, by letter, bulletin, telegram, and telephone. Now he can pick up the phone and talk to the men in all fifty States at the same time: "Listen, fellows, I'm out of breath. This is *it*, men. Not five minutes ago A. K. himself came out of the factory with our long-promised model T-45. I wish you all were here to have witnessed the scene. As A. K. put the garment on my desk, I saw tears in his eyes. Now is the time, men. The samples are going off air-mail-special. I'm all filled up, men, and can't say any more right now, but a special bulletin on T-45 will be in the mail together with your sample. God bless you, men. This is It; and, by the way, good work, Jim Backus, up there in Oregon, are you listening? Congratulations on again winning first place in the "100 per cent club."

The advertising men only make the ammunition. The sales manager is the man who fires the gun. He is the true "huckster," and his bulletins will be a source of special interest to the philosophers from the planet Mars some day.

"Hello, fellows: I still can't get over the look in A. K.'s eyes when he officially brought out model T-45 into the open. It is all history now, and we can be part of that history by getting the buyers to take the stuff away from us. I am not unmindful of the competition. I understand that the Missy-Shmissy Frock is also coming out with a pattern similar to T-45, but where is the comparison price-wise, or quality-wise, or even delivery-wise? Were they able to do anything with our whole line of Shmendrick Classics last year? Now is the time, fellows. The good salesman is like Shakespeare said: 'Neither snow, nor rain, nor wind, etc.'

"Now, fellows, about the new $44,000 Club. I argued with A. K. all night about that $44,000 quota, and finally we decided on that figure because it was such an easy-to-beat quota. And that is why we decided to make this Easy-To-Beat-Quota Week. And remember that each month the prize changes. Last month's prize, which Jim Backus won, was a pair of horse figurine book ends. Next month the prize is an Indian blanket. Well, so long, fellows. A. K. joins me in wishing you Godspeed and we are all very, very happy that T-45 is now in your hands."

And so it goes, a new rabbit out of the hat every morning, and with eleven of those fifty salesmen always gunning for his job, the sales manager is really the pivot around which our commercial society revolves, the society of which F. Scott Fitzgerald once wrote: "There are only the pursued, the pursuers, the busy, and the tired."

The one-legged treasurer

FOR many years the candidates with the best chance to win public office in the South were the men who had lost an arm or a leg in the Civil War.

The young public-spirited lawyers who wanted a start in politics were up against it.

But around 1910 a lot of young fellows figured the war had been glorified long enough. I know of a particular campaign that took place over in Anson County, North Carolina. The three candidates for sheriff sat on the platform, each speaking in his turn to the constituents below. The first speaker was an old fellow who had been an incumbent on and off since 1876. He told the crowd how he had lost his arm at Shiloh. His opponent, who also had filled the office on and off, described how he had lost his leg at Chancellorsville. Finally the young lawyer took the rostrum. He said, "I did not have the opportunity of fighting in the war. I am just a young lawyer, and I have both arms and both legs, but I want to assure you citizens that I have the biggest rupture in Anson County."

Nevertheless the lost-limb tradition continued in Southern politics far beyond the time that the loss was associated with "wounds of battle." Finally it made no difference how you lost the leg or the arm, you had the best chance of winning public office—especially county treasurer. It was a matter of principle or prudence that a one-legged man or a one-armed man would make the most satisfactory treasurer. Perhaps the voters felt that a one-legged man could not run very fast or get very far, and the one-armed man could dip only one hand into the till, which of course reduced the risk by one half. At any rate dozens of counties in the South had one-legged or one-armed treasurers.

Los Angeles, Los Angeles

THE City of Los Angeles lies in the flat part of a huge saucer. The Indians, who prowled and hunted in this saucer long before the arrival of the white men, called it, "the place of the everlasting smoke." Long after they had broken up their hunting camps, the smoke from their fires would hang over the saucer. Today Los Angeles is enveloped by a smog from the factories which makes the eyes sting and produces a rasping cough. Eventually, however, they will dissipate this smog—as soon as the Los Angelenos muster the courage to stand up to the oil and rubber industries which produce it. Right now these industries pay over a hundred million dollars in taxes, but the day is fast coming when the citizens of the city will no longer tolerate this blemish, a hundred million or not.

Because Los Angeles will one day have twenty-five million people. It is inevitable. Even now it is the phenomenon of mid-twentieth-century America. It has been described as two hundred suburbs in search of a city, but this is only because Los Angeles is the new frontier. The reason writers have not made literature out of this fantastic city is that they associate the frontier with the wide-open spaces, Tonto, and the six-shooter. They have not yet realized that there is an urban frontier, too. Los Angeles in 1960 is the perfect symbol of the urbanization of our civilization.

In Los Angeles there are thousands of fraternal organizations and societies based on place of origin. There is the Minneapolis Canasta Club, the Iowa Society, the Friends of the Mid-West, the Lower East Side Association, the Oregon Friendly Social Club.

In this, the newcomers to California are following the pattern of

America's immigrants from Europe, who organized themselves into fraternal societies of people from the same town or area.

One of the real reasons for so many societies was the fact that a fraternity could have only one president, one secretary, and one treasurer, and there was always the need for another organization. History hasn't changed much since those days. Many of our organizations today are broken down into five or six separate groups —Mr. and Mrs. clubs, adult study groups, auxiliaries, and of course "youth." And each organization has a staff of officers, banquets, and social functions.

I can just see the old gents of the "Zegeefska Chevra" stroking their beards in wonder at the "Tuesday Ladies of Flatbush" playing canasta in a vestry room of the San Fernando Valley.

The very composition of the City of Los Angeles has banished one form of bigotry. No one ever sneers, "Why don't you go back where you came from?" because if anyone took this to heart, the whole joint would empty overnight and the only ones left would be a few bemused Indians.

What this frontier substitutes for the six-shooter is the real-estate advertisement. All of the daily papers carry anywhere from twenty to thirty pages of classified realty. This is the greatest mobility in all history within a single community. A welder from Akron moves into a $14,000 house and a month later finds he can sell it for $17,000, which he does, and buys himself a second home to live in for $15,000. He probably even has a charge account at all the newspapers' classified advertising departments—"For Rent," "For Sale," "Want to Buy." Six hundred new people come into the city every day. The welder has no trouble.

On the old frontier there were fortunetellers by the dozens. In Los Angeles, by actual count, there are one hundred and twenty-eight different religious sects, all of them going strong. Rosicrucian crosses line the hillside, and there are neon lights which proclaim the tabernacles of dozens of obscure sects and fellowships. There are also innumerable faith healers. Los Angeles is the only place in the world where a Jewish convert urges you to become a Buddhist. In addition there are thousands of people in Los Angeles who talk to the dead. Tables rock and furniture is shifted mysteriously and ectoplasm suddenly materializes. For spiritualists as well as for healers the world over, Los Angeles is the happy hunting ground.

The Jewish cemetery has billboards advertising plots with the single word, "Foreverness," and the Christian cemetery (owned by the same syndicate) advertises with a similar billboard and the single word, "Devotion." The chapels of both are air-conditioned, with fluorescent lighting in all crypts, and a Musak which plays Bach and Schubert for the Christians, Verdi and Rossini for the Jews.

In the next generation, as it has come to all frontiers, a rigid stratification will appear in Los Angeles. Mobility will come to an end and the city will take its place as the greatest single empire in the Western world.

And here, too, it is well to record that in the tempest and turmoil among faith healers and movie stars, Rosicrucians and baseball fans, I have met some of the kindest people in the world.

Quitting the job

IF YOU make $56.50 a week and one morning you walk into the boss's office and say, "Mr. Hyde, I'm leaving. I've found another job that pays sixty-five a week," Mr. Hyde will harumph and will not, in all probability, ever speak to you again. You have mortally wounded him. You are an unfaithful employee. The office staff will regard you secretly in awe and on the day you leave you will buy for the secretaries to share one of Loft's two-pound Candy Specials; and all of the secretaries will chip in and buy you a ball point pen and pencil set. But it will be the rare secretary and fellow worker who wishes you good luck. It's hard to replace a man at $56.50.

If you make $150 a week and walk in one morning to Mr. Dayton's office and say, "Henry, I'm pretty sure I'll be leaving after my vacation. I think I've a chance of catching on with Jack Sharpe's outfit," Mr. Dayton will look up and say, "Okay." And the secretaries will have a party with some doctored punch and you and some of your fellow workers may even have to kiss and pat a few of them before you catch the 6:12. Mr. Dayton does not fill you with guilt as Mr. Hyde did. In fact, Mr. Dayton will contribute to the little bounty collected by the assistant sales manager which buys you your going-away present—a leather brief case.

If the shoe had been on the other foot, you know Mr. Hyde would have fired you while Mr. Dayton would have given you a fatherly talk and told you your chances for advancement with this new merger coming up were slim. Mr. Dayton, you suspect, is a real fox. It's not so hard to replace a man at $150 a week. You'll be asked to break the new man in, of course, and very probably Mr. Dayton will start him off at $100.

If, however, you make $20,000 a year and you walk into the President's office one morning and say, "A. K., someone lit a candle last week and every neon light in town went on. Bill Kessler wants to take me in—we're going to work the Great Lakes territory and the West Coast. I'm taking the Eastern seaboard," A. K. will lean back and before he shakes your hand will say, "Well, fellow, put it on the train and I hope it gets off at Westport. But I don't want you to hurry it." When you leave, the firm will give you one year's salary, they will entertain you at one of the better banquet halls in town and A. K. will present you with an inscribed 20-jeweled Swiss-movement gold watch. Later on, you'll discover that A. K. is even foxier than Dayton. A. K. had already decided not even to replace you.

It's only the $56.50 man who's a rat.

The trouble with radar

In this wonderful California, one of my hosts was driving me to his home for dinner. As he turned into his street he pressed a button on his dashboard and, lo and behold, his garage doors, a block away, began to open. Radar, he told me. But there's always a dark cloud.

On a later trip, I was eager to see this garage radar work again, but something had happened.

It seems that the low-flying planes in this particular area throw this radar out of kilter. Something about "frequency"; and so now when this fellow presses his button, a whole flock of garage doors open up all around him, and of course everybody has stopped pressing that button. Ah, the troubles of the American middle class.

The red Kleenex

ONE must give credit to the Kleenex people. Last fall they marketed a special red Kleenex so that deer hunters could blow their noses. Red is very important to a deer hunter. It is supposedly the one color another hunter picks up and does not identify as a deer.

Why should anyone want to kill a handsome animal like a deer? Venison is not very good and steak is cheaper. The guns are quite expensive as is the whole paraphernalia.

But the red Kleenex did not work.

The hunters still managed to kill more deer hunters than deer. The deer survive. They are still with us but many of the hunters have gone to their reward, fluttering their red Kleenex in vain.

The lonely freeway

THERE is a definite correlation between the increase in practicing psychiatrists and the number of concrete miles added each year to our highway systems. As often as a new cloverleaf foliates, another driver finds himself gripped by the mysterious obsession of anxiety.

On the new freeway people drive furtively. They are constantly on guard. They sneak onto the express highway from the approaches, and keep thinking of death. The six-lane concrete turn-pike provided for our convenience is a path straight to the neuroses. You are never more alone than driving along the limited-access highway.

The field trip

SOME months ago I met Professor H. with a group of his students at the local delicatessen store. The professor is head of the theology department at one of the most noble Christian seminaries in America. He told me that they were now studying the Hebrew Scriptures and he wanted his students to get the feel of "Jewish food," and so they each ordered a corned beef and Swiss cheese combination on rye—without butter.

I can just see my old father standing on the stoop of 171 Eldridge Street stroking his beard, laughing himself sick, and repeating his favorite phrase: "Ah tee-ah-ter" (literally, "a theater," but actually, "the whole thing is one great big stage").

Ah, America!

MRS. J. L. (Polly) Pressman teaches English to a class of refugees in Charleston, South Carolina. They come once a week, but one fellow begged off every second week. He had gone through an awful lot in a German DP camp. Polly was not disposed to worry the fellow too much about his attendance but she did ask him why—was anything wrong? The refugee said no, nothing was wrong—on alternate Thursdays he goes to the Arthur Murray Dancing School.

No more parlors

No ONE uses the word "parlor" any more, and it was such a charming word. "Go play in the parlor, Hymie." On the East Side we used both "parlor" and "frontroom," and when we moved uptown we called it the "living room," which it is today, except where they have dens, playrooms, and drawing rooms. I have heard of jump-room, but haven't the faintest idea what it is.

No one says "pocketbook" any more. It is now a "bag." I once saw a huge parade with men carrying placards: "Pocketbook Workers Local No. 10." They were on strike and I remember saying to myself, so many people making pocketbooks?

Most of our other terms have changed, including "luggage"— for "satchel" or "suitcase." In the days when skirts were down to the floor they called them "stockings," but now when the skirts are 'way up from the floor, they have become very modest and insist on saying "hose."

Background everywhere

NOT the international press syndicates nor the television networks nor the radio industries are the biggest users of the telephone lines. The largest user is Muzak, the producer and programmer of background music. Muzak is heard in the Bronx Zoo, under water in Eaton's Motel Pool in Hamilton, Ohio, at baseball games in Fenway Park, and at J. P. Morgan's banking house. It is supposed to help the morale of industry workers, help fish propagate, and make a dinner more appetizing. It may well do all of these, but it has proved two things: (1) It would be nice to own stock in Muzak. (2) Americans are afraid of silence.

Un-co-operative Dixie

Down to Charlotte came a demonstrator from a nationally famous cosmetics firm. This lady had come to give a show in our big department store. She gave a half-hour demonstration illustrating the redemptive and rejuvenating powers of the cosmetics. After making herself up, she challenged the audience of Tar Heel women, "Guess my age." Up North this lady had learned they usually guessed between thirty-six and thirty-eight, then follows her punch line, "No, I am fifty." But this did not happen in Charlotte.

One of the audience immediately guessed, "Fifty-two." This was interrupted by another who said, "Aw no, forty-nine at most." The demonstrator was last seen running down the corridor; she'd had enough of the South right there.

Jack and Yonkele

If you were born in Europe and your name was Jacob, you were automatically called "Jack." But if you were born in America and your name was Jacob, they called you "Yonkele," a Yiddish endearment meaning, "little Jacob." This is the story I would like to be writing about for the next twenty years, with God's help. It is the story of our people in America—the attempt of the ghetto to be Americanized, and the attempt of the Americanized to recapture the flavor of the ghetto.

PART 2

A Glass of Warmth

Post No Bills

THE first English words the newcomer to America learned were "Post No Bills," a legend which looked down upon him from the walls of every street, alley, and tenement building.

How long does it take to become an American?

I remember seeing the students come into the classroom of P. S. 20 two or three days after they'd left the boat. The girls had shawls and wore long stockings and the boys wore corduroy pants, the seats of which were invariably too tight. They were shy and afraid. The next morning they had learned the Pledge of Allegiance and three weeks later they sat stiffly at their desks writing a poem about George Washington.

The schools on the East Side were brick with an iron fence around the playground and you lined up outside doors marked "Boys" or "Girls" and marched into your classroom.

I remember that on the first day of the fall term you had new clothes. They were usually handmade clothes, sewn together by your mother, and they were new in the sense that it was the first time *you'd* ever worn them. Very probably your brother had worn them last year and your cousin would wear them next. But all of us did get new pencil boxes. These were flat, rectangular little boxes which cost a nickel. They contained three pencils, all sharpened, a pen and pen point, an eraser and a ruler, and sometimes, for older children, a compass. We also bought a new blue-lined notebook. It was very businesslike to walk to school with this efficient sort of equipment. You felt there wasn't a fraction that couldn't be reduced or a sentence that couldn't be parsed. You had the tools.

But there were many difficulties. The most severe was of course the language problem.

The newcomer knew "Post No Bills," but often his vocabulary was quickly expanded by some wise guy who taught him all those

83

four-letter Anglo-Saxon words that got him into so much trouble. The smart aleck—an old-line American who had come over on the *Mayflower* six months before, would tell the newly arrived boy, "When your teacher says 'good morning,' you say 'sonafabitch,' and she will give you a present." This was another one of the calculated risks in the New World.

The teachers were kind and understanding. With the help of an official interpreter they explained the situation to the victim. I was not only goldfish monitor for Miss Tibbetts but also her official interpreter.

One of the impressive facts of my education was that our principal, Mr. Smith, had lost an eye in the Civil War. What a thrill it was for immigrant boys to read about the Civil War and to know that Mr. Smith had fought there, that it was not so long ago nor so remote.

"Post No Bills" . . . and by the time he entered night school, the immigrant boy was more deeply concerned with two other words—"working papers." You had to be fourteen years old to get the "working papers" certificate—in order to get a job as an errand boy, or in a factory.

But everyone knew of a friendly notary public in the neighborhood who charged you fifty cents for working papers if you happened to be *under* fourteen. Perhaps this was out of order, but it was out of order on the side of America, and since it involved work it also helped to enrich the human spirit.

Because the young immigrant boy was forever conscious of his "alienism," he looked into the faces of the Americans on the street and said to himself, "Ah, when will I talk like him, and when will I be like him?" And he did not have a moment to spare. He had to get on with the business of making good as quickly as possible. He couldn't wait till he was fourteen. He was worried about his accent, but he was conscious of the fact that if he worked hard and studied hard, it was possible to hurdle an entire generation within a comparatively few years.

America turned the face of opportunity toward you. That is why the immigrant mother, when asked, "How old are your children?" would reply with quiet confidence and dignity, "The doctor is four and the lawyer is two and a half."

Rivington Street

AT THE turn of this century we paid fourteen dollars a month for four rooms at 171 Eldridge Street between Rivington and Delancey. The rooms were on the "top floor." Everybody lived on the top floor.

There was a horse market across the street, Waller Stables, where the horses went in and out twenty-four hours a day. When the movies came in and we went to the Gem and to the Odeon to see Bronco Billy, the stables did a lot for our dreams of romance. We imagined ourselves on those ice-wagon plugs, equipped with silver spurs, chasing Indians down Delancey Street.

The Jews "segregated" themselves according to national origin. The Russian Jews lived in the vicinity of East Broadway on those first American streets named for our Presidents: Washington, Jefferson, Madison, Monroe; and they extended eastward to streets named for the British before America became a nation: Pitt, Ridge, Goerick, Scamel, Montgomery, and Hester. We Galician Jews struggled along with the Poles and Romanians on Rivington, Essex, Allen, Orchard, Eldridge, and Stanton Streets.

First there were the Spanish Jews. We never saw any but we heard of them, and they were on the top of the social ladder. Then came the German Jews. I remember seeing a big crowd outside the University Settlement house, and when I asked an elderly gent at the edge of the crowd what was going on, he put his finger to his lips—"Sh, Nathan Strauss is in there." No matter what we said publicly, every Jew was extremely proud of the German Jews. The Hungarians were probably the most orthodox in their observance, and after them the Lithuanians, known as the hardest workers, and then the Russian Jews, who were the intellectuals, utopians, poets, and journalists—the fellows who asked nothing for themselves but who wanted to give so much to the world. And finally there were the Poles and we Galicians, the mystics. We probably represented a better cross section of mankind. We produced super-intellectuals and super-bums. Max D. Steuer, the greatest lawyer in American history, and Lefty Louis, the gangster who shot Rosenthal, were both my "landsleit," all of us from the same town, too. Below the bottom were the Romanians, in a class by themselves. We reflect the habits of our surroundings and there was much of the gypsy in the Romanian Jews, especially the women. My pious mother was a Romanian and she was a strong monarchist. "Long live Karl and the good Queen Carmen Sylva" was her sentiment, and all of this on Eldridge Street. What a country, America!

On Sundays my mother took one of us along to the food market under the Williamsburg Bridge to help her carry the groceries. Like most pious immigrants, my mother was suspicious about everything in America, but mostly she was suspicious of the rabbis and their okay on kosher meat. She was never wholly satisfied but made the best of it. "You call that a rabbi, with a trimmed beard and always laughing?"

I suspect the real basis of this suspicion was that the immigrants sensed their children were waiting impatiently to throw all of this precious ritual overboard. I am convinced that they somehow knew this.

What is "kosher" after all? Does it fascinate me because the meat is freshly killed, that a prayer is said over it, that it is more expensive? Of course not. I am fascinated by the brains of those social workers who wrote the Talmud. Because kosher meat meant a ritual butcher. And a ritual butcher can work only a few hours a week. So what does he do the rest of the time? By tradition he must also be a teacher for the children, and that meant a school, and a school meant a community! What brains those Talmud fellows had! They invented all sorts of ideas with only one real purpose in mind—survival, *survival as a people.*

Rivington Street was named for James Rivington, printer and publisher of *The Gazette,* a Tory newspaper. The new nation named this street after a man who did not believe in America; as if to tell him that someday *his* thoroughfare would be the actual "entrance" for millions of immigrants from all the corners of the world, seeking political security and religious freedom.

I remember how the immigrants went up to the roofs of the tenements to listen to the music coming from the Roof Garden of P.S. 20. Under the supervision of social workers, hundreds of boys and girls were being taught to dance, and the signal for the concert to begin was the massed singing—"Oh! say can you see, by the dawn's early light . . ." And they sat on the rooftops looking toward the brilliantly lighted Roof Garden until they heard the closing chorus.

Among the landmarks which will soon be torn down is the University Settlement. This is where I acquired the habit of reading books and where I was the "king" in a pageant in honor of the city-wide Hudson-Fulton Celebration in the year 1909.

There is always one man. Dr. Stanton Coit, after a successful experiment with Toynbee Hall in London's slum district, organized the University Settlement in my New York neighborhood. The idea, Mr. Coit wrote in 1882, was, "All people . . . men, women and children in any one street . . . or any small number of streets . . . shall be organized into a set of clubs to carry out all the reforms—domestic, industrial, educational, providential or recreative . . . which the social ideal demands." The University Settlement was the bridge between the ghettos of Europe and the American civilization. I went to the public baths in the basement of the settlement house and belonged to a debating club, one of fifty such clubs which the social workers had established. In my time Charles B. Stover was the director of the Settlement. He was a continuous influence on the East Side for forty years.

The success of the University Settlement led to the establishment of more than fifty other settlement houses in New York, and by the 1920's there were more than eight hundred in the United States. The neighborhood house became the center of communal life for everyone from the infant in the kindergarten to the lonely oldsters who found opportunities for worth-while recreation and fellowship. It became the place where thousands of ardent social workers dedicated their lives to the betterment of society.

But what is all this about the memory of Rivington Street, its teeming tenements, and its terrible poverty? Why do thousands of middle-class Jews in America literally "lick their fingers" on every story I write about the East Side?

People always look back upon the "better" things in the past. But a daily sight on Rivington Street and all the other streets in those days was a household of furniture "out on the street." This occurred in every neighborhood—Irish, Jewish, Polish, and Italian. You'd pass along and see the belongings on the sidewalk. The rent had not been paid for a couple of months and they were put out.

And always on the dresser, piled high with the mattress and the two pillows, was a soup dish which contained a few coins. And all this time the man of the house, or the eldest son, was out looking all over the neighborhood for another place to stay, hoping that by the time he got back there would be enough coins to pay a week's rent in the new place. Always, there was a pushcart peddler or even the owner of a livery stable himself who carted the stuff to the new address.

Well, under such circumstances, how can you look back on the Rivington Streets as being better than what we have today?

The philosopher Eric Hoffer has written, "Our frustration is greater when we have much and want more, than when we have nothing and want some. We are less dissatisfied when we lack many things than when we seem to lack but one thing."

Red kerosene

ON HOUSTON STREET, between Cannon and Columbia Streets, was a big wide street called Union Market. The farmers from Queens and Long Island came every Saturday from April to Thanksgiving with potatoes, tomatoes, corn, peas, and beans. The boys in the neighborhood would help them and we were all paid off in produce for the two or three hours' work Saturday afternoon.

At the foot of Grand Street at the East River was Heckers' Flour Mill and Arbuckle Coffee. Across the river was a place called Greenpoint and the big sugar refineries. Boats of sugar cane came from Puerto Rico and Cuba to these refineries. The wheat came to Heckers' through the Erie Canal, Hudson River, and East River.

There was no gaslight until around 1900. Everybody cooked and did his homework and reading by kerosene. There were dozens of kerosene peddlers driving around the city in small wagons. The folks came out to the street in answer to his cry, to fill their containers with kerosene at the rate of eight cents a gallon. The legend is that one of these Italian kerosene peddlers dropped his red bandanna kerchief into his barrel of kerosene and after a while he noticed that the kerosene had turned a light red. To waste that barrel of kerosene would have meant a whole week's wages for him. So he took a chance and sold it. When the people remarked about the red color he said that it was a new process invented by the Standard Oil Company to make the kerosene burn longer and brighter, and for that he charged an extra cent. Within a few weeks the red kerosene became very popular and you couldn't give that other stuff away.

Polish and Italian funerals

No ONE on the Lower East Side was buried with solemnity, pomp, and circumstance like the Poles. A Polish funeral was the most impressive ever staged; and to have seen one is a minor distinction, because apparently the Poles today are as susceptible as anyone else to the American middle-class ethic and no longer parade to the cemetery.

The hearse was drawn by a brace of black horses, their names decked in crowns of ostrich feathers. Over their backs was draped a chenille net from which black tassels dangled. The horses' tails

were plumed and carded and a big fan of peacock feathers waved
as they pulled the hearse. All of the hearses were a shiny black
with silver fittings and many had a silver-domed roof. The sides
were glass and you could see the flowers banked around the coffin.
Often there were several victorias, each laden with wreaths and
flowers, following the hearse. And behind them was a rented limousine for the family.

But the reason the kids would follow the hearse along was the
band which led it up the streets. There was always an enormous
brass band complete with cymbals playing Chopin's "Funeral
March." They played a step at a time because the funeral proceeded slowly. The horses were trained to pace and pause with
each note, and with infinite precision they put one hoof ahead of
the other in absolute rhythm.

The entourage proceeded down Second Avenue past Stuyvesant
Square, past the house of Charley Murphy, the Tammany boss,
who always stopped to watch, resting on his umbrella and twirling
the heavy gold watch chain which stretched across the wide ex-
panse of his vest.

The Italian funerals were more festive. There was much more
emphasis on music and the band played faster. They played
Chopin's "Funeral March" but they also played "The Garibaldi
Hymn"—

> The graves burst asunder
> The dead rise to aid us.

All the little girls of the East Side skipped rope to the melody
of this Garibaldi Hymn. They had made up their own words to
that wonderful tune, which they chanted as they skipped rope. To
the best of my recall their chant went like this:

> Her first name was Annie, Annie,
> Her second name was Parker, Parker,
> A long time ago.

The names were those of the girls' schoolteachers and a girl
would go through the whole school until she missed a step and

then another little girl would start up, all keeping time to this Garibaldi Hymn.

About the time the funeral reached Stuyvesant Square, we Jewish kids left off. Beyond Stuyvesant Square lived the Irish. While someone else had taken his life in his hands, we weren't about to.

Sign of prosperity

IN THE old days the top floor always had the cheapest rent. In the six- or seven-story tenements, the walk-up was quite an ordeal, especially when the tenement had a high stoop, which was equivalent to going up the 45-degree angle of a pyramid. Add to that another six flights and you realize that going home at night was an endurance contest.

But times have changed. Checking with several real-estate people in New York, I find that more and more top floors are vacant. This follows a pattern set at the beginning of this century. The family came from Europe and rented a top floor, and as their conditions improved they put in an application for going down. This was equivalent to the poacher in the rural sections of America where the folks on the bottom land looked down on the folks up on the hills.

In the ordinary Bronx tenement today and in the overpopulated Harlem districts, four rooms on the top floor rent for about sixty dollars a month and four rooms on the first floor rent for eighty-nine dollars, which is quite a difference. It is interesting to note, however, that when people call up for vacancies today and are told there's one on the top floor, they say, "No, we can wait and get something lower down."

The triple-threat actor

DEDICATING a Yiddish theater on Second Avenue in 1911,
New York's incomparable Mayor Gaynor observed: "You Jews
are a dramatic people. Your whole history is drama, and I am sorry
to say, tragedy, too, from the days of Abraham down to this very
hour. Where else outside of your Scriptures, the Old Testament
in our Bible, is there so much exalted poetry, exalted tragedy?"

The development of the Yiddish theater was as much a successful attempt to establish a cultural value as it was for enlighten-
ment and entertainment. In those days the actor was among the
rulers of the ghetto world. After him came the poet, the dramatist,
the critic, and the journalist. Everybody else was called "the public."

The greatest of the actors were Jacob P. Adler, David Kessler,
and Boris Thomashevsky. Their names were household words,
they were living legends. All the folk tales, particularly with respect
to gastronomic and sexual prowess, going back for several centuries, were recapitulated with new characters—Adler, Kessler,
and Thomashevsky. I have never yet met an East Side Jew who
didn't have a favorite story about them, and although David
Kessler's stories remained more in the gastronomic category, Adler
and Thomashevsky were definitely triple-threat men—wherever
they traveled in the Western world. And as you would expect,
these personalities responded to the popular acclaim with a sort
of regal contempt for "the rabble." Each of them traveled with a
court of hangers-on, and when he spread himself in an East Side
café, he always had a couple of flunkies warding off worshipers
as he washed down the caviar and eggs and potato varenikis with
huge goblets of Rhine wine and seltzer.

One of the contributions the East Side made to the American
culture was the "theater party." Everyone has theater parties now,
from a Hempstead Hadassah to the Vassar Alumnae Association.
But it was invented by the immigrant Jews around the turn of the
century.

We rarely heard the statement: "I'm going to the theater," but instead: "I'm going to a benefit." "Benefit" was one of the first English words the immigrants learned, and probably one of the most important. They sold benefit tickets to immigrants as they came off the gangplank after clearance at Ellis Island. All the Jewish organizations and fraternities were based on benefits.

As a boy, I sat through many benefits. My father was president of the Mikulinczer Verein. These Mikulinczers ran a benefit five or six times a year. My father always made a speech between the second and third acts. A Mikulinczer benefit operated just like the Vassar theater party. The organization bought every seat in the house at a discount, then sold the tickets to members and friends and the net profit went to a predesignated cause.

Although Friday and Saturday matinee comprised the Sabbath, days when the strictly Orthodox Jews wouldn't leave the house except to walk to the shul, the rest of the Jewish community had fallen in step with America. There were many, however, whose conscience still gnawed them about seeing a play on the Sabbath. Sometimes they eased their conscience by heckling an actor whose part, say, called for him to smoke a cigar. The audience would yell, "Smoking a cigar on the Sabbath! Boo! Boo!"

This was my introduction to the theater and I shall always be grateful for it. I thrill to this day remembering Madame Bertha Kalich, Kessler, and a man who would have been a great comedian on any stage, Zelig Mogalesco.

Often the plays depicted the patterns of ghetto life with surprising fidelity. Basically the people came to cry at scenes which more or less portrayed their own problems and family experiences with a wayward son, an ungrateful daughter, an old-fashioned father, a cruel stepmother. *Hamlet*, *Othello*, and *King Lear* were among the productions. Occasionally they were literally translated, but more often only the theme was used and adapted to contemporary life. Jacob Gordin's *Yiddisher Koenig Lear* (The Jewish King Lear) was the most popular of these adaptations. In a Yiddish version of Shakespeare's *Hamlet*, the uncle was a rabbi in a small village in Russia. He did not poison Hamlet's father, but broke the latter's heart by wooing and winning away his wife.

Hamlet is off somewhere getting educated as a rabbi. While he is gone his father dies. Six weeks later the son returns in the midst of the wedding feast, and turns the feast into a funeral. Terrible scenes of sorrow follow between mother and son, Ophelia and Hamlet, while some of the Socialist actors got in a few ad libs at the rabbinate in general. In the end Ophelia dies and Hamlet, in accordance with Jewish practice, marries his betrothed at the graveside. Then he dies of a broken heart.

Critics? There were thousands of them. Ben-Gurion of Israel says he is the head of a nation that has one and a half million prime ministers. By the same token the Yiddish stage had fifty thousand regular critics. It was not simply a matter of seeing a show to enjoy yourself. You were a critic. You recited your criticism to everyone—in the shop, in the store, in the coffeehouse, and in the lodge hall. Most plays you said were "shmahtas." Literally, a "shmahta" is a rag, but its meaning is more explosive than that. "A shmahta" actually means "phooey."

"How did you like the show last night?" and the fellow at the workbench would shrug his shoulders and say, "A shmahta." The fellow did not know, of course, that what he had seen the night before was a Yiddish adaptation of Ibsen's A *Doll's House*. He was a big expert. To him it was a "shmahta."

There were many theaters, but the benefits took place for the most part in three of them—the People's Theatre, the Windsor, and the Thalia. The Thalia was the ritziest. You couldn't take a baby inside.

The actors hated the benefits as much as actors today hate the theater parties. They've come not so much to see the play but to see who else has come. Their attention is bad. They bring children. And they talk! Theater parties or benefits—how they talk! They talk more than the actors.

But from the audience's standpoint, a theater party or benefit is a good time. Plays never ran long, twelve days at the most, more usually three or four, so sometimes there were families that went to the theater three or four times a week. In those days, prices scaled from twenty-five cents to a dollar. It is a long way from a

Mikulinczer benefit to a Daughters of the American Revolution theater party, but only the prices have changed.

We have not really begun to appraise the influence of the Yiddish theater on the English-speaking stage, motion pictures, and radio. That crusty old Mayor Gaynor saw it even as it was happening: "You came to this land but yesterday and now will give us that learning and that culture which has produced such players as Bonne, and Von Sonnenthal, and Rachel, and Bernhardt."

The most fabulous player of the era, of course, was Adler. It was my good fortune to see Mr. Adler in the old Knickerbocker Theatre on Broadway at the end of his career. It was a benefit performance and every Broadway star of stage, opera, and the concert world came to pay homage to the great Yiddish actor. Each insisted on "going on" in his honor, and the show lasted till 5 A.M. Mr. Adler himself performed a scene from *King Lear*. I remember particularly Al Jolson singing "Vesti la Giubba" from Pagliacci, followed by Giovanni Martinelli leading the audience in "Pack up your troubles in your old kit bag and smile, smile, smile." It was a memorable evening. And I know that each of the "boys and girls" of the old days who read this will immediately think of their own Jacob P. Adler story, and so it is only proper that I tell the one I know, and if only one out of each hundred readers hasn't heard it, I'll be happy:

Adler was on tour. (In all the stories Adler and Thomashevsky were always on tour.) And before this particular performance a handsome young woman with a two-year-old child somehow got through to the great man's dressing room. Adler turned from the mirror and the woman began her story: "Mr. Adler, you remember me? When you were here three years ago you invited me to supper after the performance, you remember?" And with this she pushed the little boy ahead of her. "And this is the result—this little boy is your own son."

Adler looked at the child with real satisfaction. "That's a nice boy, a really nice boy," and reaching into his dresser drawer he continued, "Here, my dear, are two tickets to tonight's performance. Take the boy, you'll both like the show." The woman seemed crushed and began to stammer and stutter, "But Mr. Adler, this is your son, we don't need theater tickets, our problem is to eat, we need bread."

Adler was hurt; he flung the tickets back into the drawer. "Bread you need—if you want bread, you should have gone with a baker. I am an actor."

A suit for Passover

PASSOVER was really the "New Year" in everything except the calendar itself. If you bought new clothes, it was always "for Passover." And this applied to everyone, not only the kids. Your mother would say, "I think I'll have that black dress done over— for Passover." And your father would say, "We all need new shoes, but it's only a month to Passover, so let's wait a little longer." There was a far more acute sense of "beginning" on the day before Passover than on the regular New Year's Eve—and I mean either Rosh Hashanah or the night of December 31.

Finally came the Passover when it was my turn to get the new suit. I was twelve and my brother Jacob took me to Stanton Street to get me outfitted. Let me say a word about Jacob. He was older than I—and already working in a pocketbook factory. Jacob was the sort of brother who became an assistant father in America because he knew his way around so well.

My brother Jacob took me to Stanton Street to buy me a blue serge suit with knee pants and a Norfolk jacket.

Both the Norfolk jacket and Norfolk Street on the Lower East Side were named after the Duke of Norfolk, the hereditary first peer of the realm, the man who acts as master of ceremonies at the coronation of the British kings and queens. The Norfolk jacket was probably some hunting coat he used when galloping after the hounds. It had a belt around the middle.

And now on Stanton Street I was getting one, too. We tried on the first suit and it fit beautifully. This was *it*. "How much?" asked Jacob, and the salesman replied nonchalantly, "Ten dollars."

Jacob said, "Take it off; let's go." (At this point there seems to be no deviation from the procedure—everybody did exactly the same thing—the idea was not even to look at the salesman when you spoke the words: "Take it off; let's go." This established that there was no room for further negotiations whatever.)

My brother and I went out and about halfway down the block the salesman caught up with us. "Ten dollars," he said. "It's a bargain at ten dollars."

Jacob shrugged his shoulders and said, "What's the use? There's nothing further to talk about." But the fellow kept walking beside us and finally we all stopped and my brother, in a pathetically weary tone, said, "Look, my friend, you said ten dollars. Well, I have ten dollars"—the salesman's face brightened—"but for that ten dollars I've got to get him a suit, a pair of shoes, and a hat."

They talked some more and finally all three of us were going across the street and my brother and the salesman were arm in arm, palsy-walsy. The agreement had been reached. The salesman was to help us buy the shoes and the hat, and to take whatever was left for the suit. Naturally, the less we paid for the shoes and hat, the more the salesman would get for the suit, so he insisted that we buy the shoes in a place of his designation—a "wholesale house."

Everybody bought "wholesale"—a fable, of course, but none the less a psychological necessity. A man worked hard to reach the point where he could spare ten dollars from his household expenses, and consequently this wholesale idea came into being as a sort of mental reassurance that not a single penny was being spent unwisely or unnecessarily.

I got a pair of shoes for $1.25, and a cap for 65¢, and we all went back to the clothing store to pick up the suit for the balance, $8.10.

I walked home with my brother and I thought—now let that old Passover come!

The handicapped were part of us

ONE of the most pleasant memories of the Lower East Side was that the handicapped were also part of our civilization. They were not subjected to a second look when they ventured upon the street. The lame, the blind, the hunchbacked were part of the everyday world. There was no inhibition about calling attention to their deformity. The mother would say: "Run down to 'dem blinden' (the blind man) and buy a half pound of butter." Thus she referred to the fellow who had a modest produce stand under the Williamsburg Bridge, which was a long walk away. He was blind and every once in a while she thought he needed some patronage.

This same freedom of expression with no tone of disrespect to "der hoyker" (the hunchback) made him part of the community. Nor was there any inhibition about referring to an elderly person as "der alter" (the old man). "Der alter" may have run a grocery business, or been a cobbler, or worked in a bakeshop. No one thought of segregating them in any way. It may sound cruel to have identified these people thus. But the real cruelty is whispering about them or pitying them. They accepted the designation because they knew they were accepted as humans. In the ghetto complete humanity was granted to everyone.

Cooper Union

ON A RECENT visit to New York I stopped to read a new steel marker on one of the red pillars of the old Cooper Union building. Cooper Union stands on Eighth Street at the juncture where the Bowery is divided into two main thoroughfares, Third and Fourth Avenues. The inscription says Cooper Union was begun in 1853, and that it was the first structure in America built entirely with steel beams. It was named for Peter Cooper and stands as a monument to freedom of speech.

Mr. Cooper was an inventor and a manufacturer. He invented a machine for shearing rough cloth. Then he established the glue industry in America, which in turn created the furniture industry. Mr. Cooper was sort of a puttering inventor—nothing monumental like the phonograph or the sewing machine, but a thousand different things for the betterment of our daily lives. But ideas come first. Mr. Cooper will be remembered always for Cooper Union—the most notable open forum in America.

As a kid I lived about six or seven blocks from Cooper Union, and it played an important role in the lives of the people down there. The Institute part of it was small and admissions were very tough, based wholly on stiff entrance examinations in mathematics and other engineering subjects.

But its fame rests on the use of its auditorium for the great speakers, orators, and dissenters of America. From Abraham Lincoln to Colonel Robert G. Ingersoll, the agnostic; from President Grant to Eugene V. Debs, the Socialist, Cooper Union came closer to the idea of the old Roman Forum than any other institution we have. It was a sort of Bell of Atri. Whenever there was injustice you went to the square and rang the bell to gain an immediate hearing. It was here that a New York merchant by the name of Havemeyer, in halting sentences (he had never spoken in public before), protested that Boss Tweed was robbing the city blind. This led to the investigation and exposé of one of the greatest swindles in history.

I heard Charles Evans Hughes speak there during his campaign against President Wilson. I also heard Clarence Darrow and Al Smith, and all the old Socialists. The advantage of hearing the Socialists in those days was that all their great orators were usually on the platform at the same time and you made a real night of it—Hillquit, Lee, Claessens, Spargo, and others. No voice was denied a hearing. In fact the biggest crowd in its history was the one that turned out to hear a Southerner, Tom Watson of Georgia, when he ran for President on the Populist ticket. This was before Watson became a racist and an anti-Semite.

The next time you are in New York, go down to Eighth Street and take a look at Cooper Union. It will be an inspiration to you; and around the corner you have the five largest secondhand bookstores in the country. In one of those stores there is a fellow by the name of Wilkes. Dream up some hundred-year-old title of a book long forgotten and out of print and he'll scrounge around the mountain of books on the floor and pull it out for you.

Between banquets

ALL these international conferences remind me of the meetings of the lodges, vereins (fraternities), societies, and landsmannshaften (sick, benevolent, and burial societies organized among folks from the same town in the old country) that I knew in my youth. The Lower East Side was full of them. On every block there were "meeting halls." Many of these sick and benevolent societies used to call a meeting, the result of which was the decision to call another meeting.

I was captain of the degree team of Scholem Lodge No. 26 I.O.B.A. (Independent Order of B'rith Abraham). Scholem Lodge No. 26 met twice a month in those days in Proctor Hall, somewhere in the seventies. In between initiations the lodge discussed many important issues of the day, such as the forthcoming strawberry festival of Scholem Lodge No. 26; and like so many of those organizations, it was deeply concerned with banquets. The minute the treasurer announced a favorable cash balance a gleam came into the eyes of the members, and someone would get up and say nonchalantly, "Let's have a bonkett." I doubt whether there is a people on this earth who love banquets more than the Jews. And so the regular meetings of Scholem Lodge No. 26 were really business sessions between banquets, at which the officers always saw to it that each member was given the privilege to "say a few words."

But the lodge and verein meetings were of tremendous help to hundreds of thousands of immigrants who worked in the shops all day. They were able to pick up a smattering of the English language and to keep abreast of the events of the day. It gave them an opportunity for the greatest of all Jewish sports—talk. The arguments flew left and right; discussions about a favorite newspaper, a favorite poet, a favorite actor, and by all means the favorite chazan (cantor). While their sons were already steeped in the American milieu, arguing about Ty Cobb, Tris Speaker, and Packy McFarland, the older folks stuck tenaciously to the culture which they understood and cherished.

In the old country, however, there was a strict class consciousness concerning Jewish communal life, and many of the older people found it difficult to adjust to the social equality they found here. At first the immigrant could hardly believe his eyes. Then, when he saw that in America a window cleaner can become president of the shul, he went all out. Embittered by years of being the underdog—standing in awe in front of the rabbi, the scholar, and the student—these immigrants decided to get even once and for all. And up and down the country to this day they are still getting even—but good!

The big drive was to become president of the society or shul—and ah, some of those elections. The Tilden-Hayes contest was like a picnic compared to election campaigns between a wholesale butcher and a window cleaner. Candidates bought barrels of beer and there were plenty of cigars.

And all of this was to the good, in the long run. The French have a saying, "If the poor are to eat, the rich must dance," which of course means that every charity or drive must be opened with a banquet, a garden party, a raffle, or a bazaar. Many a man has given several thousand dollars extra because he was placed on the dais in the seating arrangements, and many—oh, so many—a man has soured on the whole charity ("I'll never give them another nickel") because the printing chairman made a mistake and did not put the guy's name on the program. But on to the meeting, and I'll let all the program chairmen and all the regional fund-raising directors worry about those little details.

The overcoat

A "SHLOCK" store was a cut-rate clothing store—it undersold everybody, but of course you couldn't depend upon the merchandise. Many schlock stores sold secondhand clothes.

I knew an elderly gent once who ran one of these schlock stores, and who had been stuck many years with an overcoat he had never been able to sell, and after a while he ceased trying. Then one night, just at closing time, a young fellow walked in and said he wanted an overcoat. Not just any overcoat, but an overcoat that was different from all other overcoats, one the other fellows wouldn't have, something special that cost a little more.

The proprietor looked at his wife and said, "Lena, go bring THE COAT."

Unerringly she picked out the almost forgotten coat from hundreds of others. The customer tried it on gingerly, admired himself in the mirror, then asked how much it was.

"Seventy-five dollars," said the proprietor unhesitatingly.

A broad smile creased the customer's face. He was doubly pleased. Not only was this coat different, but it cost more. He paid cash.

It happened too that this family had an unmarried daughter (it shouldn't happen) who was getting on close to thirty-five, but whenever the mother worried too much about it, her fears were always put to rest when the father said, "Lena, remember THE COAT."

The great fear—a "creezus"

THE culture of the Lower East Side of New York was completely fragmentized politically, theologically, and philosophically. In every one of hundreds of meeting halls and wine cellars you could hear the voices, shouts, and arguments of the discussionists;

pacifists, nonresistors, evolutionists, vegetarians, Tolstoyans, Daniel de Leon Socialists, Eugene V. Debs Socialists, Communists, anarchists, Tammany Hall supporters, and Republicans.

The Orthodox Jews, the businessmen, and many intellectuals were Republicans—nationally at least—and this was reflected in every presidential election from McKinley to Hoover. My district went down the line for the Tammany ticket, but during a presidential campaign it was a different story. In some of those elections the district gave 12 per cent of its vote to the local Republican and 40 per cent of its vote to the Republican presidential candidate.

There were many reasons for this Republican loyalty for the national ticket. The Republican Presidents, Grant, Hayes, Garfield, McKinley, Taft, and Theodore Roosevelt, were great "friends" in every sense of the word. Their administrations were quick to voice the protest of the American civilization against persecution. It was during a time when Romania was establishing further political and economic disabilities against its Jewish population that President Grant appointed an American Jew, the president of the B'nai B'rith, as our minister to that Balkan country. This wonderful gesture was not lost on the Jewish people throughout the world, and they never forgot it.

And of course Theodore Roosevelt! I suspect that Teddy may well have been the most beloved non-Jew in the history of our people in America. First of all the tremendous waves of immigration to America had come during the first Roosevelt's two administrations. And Roosevelt had been police commissioner and it gave him communications with the immigrants, their problems, and their hopes. During his administration as head of the police, there was an incident which demonstrated his wisdom as well as his sense of humor. A lecturer had come over from Germany, an early Nazi, and was scheduled to make some anti-Semitic speeches in New York. The Jews on the East Side, who had just escaped this stuff, were chagrined of course until Teddy made his move. He called out a squad of Jewish policemen to protect this guy, "and make sure that no one disturbs his meetings." Because of this gesture the whole thing collapsed and the entire American continent had a good laugh.

Furthermore Theodore Roosevelt was an aristocrat, and Jews always got along with the aristocrats. They understand each other. As a matter of fact we Jews are here today only because in every dark age and in every dark corner of the world there was always one aristocrat who gave us shelter, who pulled up the bridge of his castle and told the mob to go on home. Only when the aristocrat himself was in danger did he turn his back on us.

We are talking about politics and about people, and at many levels all people are the same. They are the same when you come to the real issue—parnosseh (making a living)—getting a weekly pay envelope or a fair price for farm products. All the people are interested in this one issue, to the exclusion of all others—parnosseh.

And thus the loyalty to the Republican national ticket was really based on this very idea—an identity of the Republicans with employment.

This was expressed with the most dreaded word on the East Side—"creezus" (crisis), an early term for depression. The legend was born during the Cleveland Administration. We all heard the most harrowing stories of the suffering during that depression, and the stories were passed along as each new group of immigrants arrived. And so when they became citizens they gave Tammany the vote from the governor down to the city clerk, but when it came to President, they said, "We don't want another 'creezus.'"

It was also understood that business would be good during an election year because "Morgan won't make a 'creezus' this year." This was said very seriously and was a reference to J. P. Morgan and the legend that he made or unmade the American economy at will. Some folks voted for the Republican candidate because they didn't want "to make Morgan mad."

It was not until the last two years of the Hoover Administration that the legend of the Democrats and the "creezus" was finally laid to rest. And as you would expect, the pendulum now swung too far the other way, with the Republicans solidly identified with bread lines and apple selling.

But this is a tremendous country. You have to be a connoisseur to appreciate America and understand its possibilities. And so I am sure that during the next ten years, be he Democratic or Republican, our President will continue to follow the Socialist Party platform of 1908, and expand the function of government toward a firm control of the economic cycles, so that maybe our grandchildren will no longer have to worry about a "creezus."

The witch doctor

ON THE Lower East Side of New York every barber was a sort of first-aid man in the application of several Old World remedies. One of these remedies was the use of vacuum cups called "bonkiss" in Yiddish. These "bonkiss" were about the size of a demitasse. With alcohol and flame applied inside, the cups were placed upon the patient's back and adhered to the flesh, the idea being to draw the blood and stimulate circulation.

The barber considered himself "k-maat-a-doktor (practically a doctor). Every day you'd see him walking along the street with his little black satchel which contained his dozen or two "bonkiss," his bottle of alcohol, and the tapers for the flame.

We also had the witch doctor, a sort of conjure woman. There isn't a culture on this earth that hasn't had the conjure woman, the laying-on-of-hands "healer," and the witch doctor. There was one in every neighborhood. She was an old, old woman—usually living alone in a cellar or in the back of an empty store—bent double and stomping through the neighborhood with a heavy cane and making herself as disagreeable as possible.

Her "magic" was based on a mixture of the legends of the ultra-orthodox sects of eastern Europe and the folklore of the peasants among whom those people lived for so many centuries. She was the last tie between medievalism and the New World, and it made a Jewish household rich in imagination and human interest. An old aunt always sent for the conjure woman, and in the same five-room flat, the young grandnephew was memorizing the essays of Ralph Waldo Emerson.

The moment she entered the sickroom the conjure woman

closed all the windows tight, summer or winter. This had a twofold purpose: to keep the evil spirits out and to prevent the patient's soul from being tempted to seek freedom. The old crone was very demanding and someone had to keep supplying her with tea, jam, and cookies all the time she was there. Usually she pasted bits of paper, prayer amulets, around the sickbed and then proceeded to "speak" the disease out of the patient. The illness was then considered "farshprukhen" (literally, "spoken out").

"Your disease shall go into the body of a dog," she would say. And when word came that someone had indeed seen a sick horse or dog or cat in the neighborhood, the patient knew that the conjure woman had succeeded.

The more enlightened members of the family were merely trying to please an eccentric old aunt who was sick, but they took precautions that the "alte baba" (conjure woman) did not come when other company was expected, or when the doctor himself was supposed to call. If the doctor had seen this old crone, the family would have been terribly embarrassed. They would have lost face. And one time the doctor did come unexpectedly, but it turned out perfectly all right anyway. Those were the days when all a doctor could do in a serious pneumonia case was "wait for the crisis." This doctor smiled kindly. He stopped all the commotion and the attempt to cover up for the conjure woman: "Let her sit there," he said, "at this moment I can do no more than she is doing."

Years later when I began to read about psychology and the power of suggestion, I thought back to that doctor and realized that we had been in the presence of a great man.

As with all the witch doctors going back into remote antiquity, there was some logic wrapped up in the hocus-pocus and incantations. And our modern science of psychiatry confirms the proposition that the medicine man and the witch doctor knew what they were doing. They must have affected millions of "cures" or they would not have been so firmly rooted in the consciousness of mankind through every stage of its development.

But the medicine man and the witch doctor performed a greater service to civilization than the mere administering of rudimentary psychology to a few ailing patients of the tribe. In order to maintain their status and the confidence and hopes of their people, they instinctively understood that they had to know some mysterious secrets. And so what did they do? They experimented with herbs and grasses, and they were forever handling "mixtures" and "compounds." They spent lots of time by themselves to add to the mystery, and during those periods of remaining apart from the normal activities of the tribe, such as hunting, fishing, and dancing, they struck a blow for the future of mankind's art of "thinking things out." When you have a man sitting alone, and trying to figure out ways and means of impressing his tribe, you already have the beginning of thought.

The next time you see an African jungle movie with a witch doctor, don't go shaking your head in sympathy for the poor superstitious natives. Just say to yourself that that witch doctor was the only one in that tribe who had to use his brain, and therefore he is the spiritual daddy of all the scientists, surgeons, psychiatrists, and philosophers of our day.

The wash line

ON THE Lower East Side you could tell a family's state of well-being by the wash out on the line. Whether a man was working steady or not was revealed by his work clothes. If a man's overalls or apron (as in the garment industries) was not on the wash line with fair regularity, the neighbors felt sad. They knew the man had lost his job. The wash line also revealed a family's sorrow. When a woman's wash did not appear on the line for three or four days, the neighbors began to whisper among themselves and finally went to call—to see if she were sick or what tragedy had afflicted her family. When neighbors saw a proud new array of clothes and table linens they knew the husband had got a raise. When the clothes had all been mended, the folks knew that a bill was being met or that a doctor or an undertaker was being paid.

Whether the wash line reveals as much today, I do not know,

so many of the folks have those washer-dryers. But women who do their own wash tell me it is one of the more enjoyable tasks of housework—hanging out the wash.

The "bettle"

EVERY home had a "bettle." Some folks had two and three "bettles." A "bettle" is the diminutive term for a "bet" (bed). In short, a "bettle" is a small bed. Later on, the fancy folks called it a "rollaway bed." The whole thing folded up, mattress and all, and pushed up against the wall, out of the way. This "bettle" was entirely different from the "lunch" (lounge) which I have described adequately before. But that "bettle"—oh, what heartaches, pulling it apart and making it up!

The "bettle" was a pain in the neck. You came home late at night from a meeting or a date and there was the "bettle" up against the wall or in the closet, and you had to open it up and make the bed with as little noise as possible. And if you slept on the "bettle" you had to be up at the crack of dawn because it was in the middle of the kitchen or the dining room and you had to make room for the three boarders and the seven other members of the family who were preparing to go to work.

The "bettle" served one good purpose, however. It pressed your pants. You placed a flat board on top of the springs, with the carefully folded pants between the board and the mattress. The pressure of the body did the rest. No "bettle" was complete without a pair of suspenders hanging out from under it.

Eyeglasses for a quarter

THE pushcart peddlers sold just about everything, but the Italians stuck mostly to vegetables, fruit, fish, and other edibles.

The Jewish pushcart peddlers went in more for wearing apparel, umbrellas, kitchen and household utensils.

The rent of a pushcart was ten cents a day. There were some traveling pushcarts, and the peddler would shout at the top of his voice in his native tongue, advertising his merchandise. Most of them, however, were permitted to have permanent stands on certain streets. It was necessary to get a pushcart license, but many of them evaded this requirement, and they were always in trouble.

During the administration of Mayor George B. McClellan, the police in New York were famous for their brutality and would use their clubs at the drop of a hat. The pushcart peddlers were fair game. The cops chased them from pillar to post, making wholesale arrests daily. They took them and their pushcarts to the police station and then took them to court before a judge. They were charged with peddling without a license or obstructing street corners and the judge would fine them a dollar. Most of them stayed in jail till two in the afternoon to save the dollar fine, because they couldn't earn that much in those few hours, or maybe even in a whole day. Most of the peddlers complained that while they were in court the cops ransacked their pushcarts.

Abuse of peddlers by the police was lessened considerably when Mayor Gaynor was elected. The first thing Mayor Gaynor did was to take the night sticks away from the cops. Then he discontinued arrests for violations of city ordinances, and the police now had to issue summonses. This order played hell with hundreds of Irish immigrant cops who couldn't read and write. This is when that old joke was born about the cop who found a dead horse on Kosciusko Street; he got a rope and dragged the carcass around to Third Avenue so he could fill out his report.

Later on the peddlers became powerful politically with a strong organization, and Mayor Jimmy Walker had to climb up five flights of stairs to attend a bar mitzvah—that of the son of the president of the Pushcart Peddlers Association.

Then came La Guardia and the World's Fair. He said that with people coming from all over the world the pushcarts would have to get off the streets. He built huge markets where the city charged

a weekly rental of three to four dollars, and that practically eliminated the pushcarts.

It was very hard, but it also had its tremendous rewards in experience. From these pushcarts have grown the huge wholesale fruit
and vegetable businesses. Some Italian pushcart peddlers became
great importers of spaghetti and olive oil and other products of
Italy. The Jewish peddlers became merchants, and now and then a
former pushcart peddler has been introduced to an audience, justi-
fiably, as a "merchant prince."

Just as colorful in the days of my boyhood was the familiar
character known as the pack peddler.

The pack peddler carried 129 pounds, 89 pounds strapped to the
back and a 40-pound "balancer" in front. Occasionally, however,
there was a little guy who, because he could not carry this kind
of weight, was being shoved out of existence. He was hard put,
until he hit upon the bright idea of selling eyeglasses. Ah! What a
business this was in the last quarter of the nineteenth century!
Everybody bought eyeglasses and the peddlers became known as
"glimmers."

My father, who spent most of his eighty years reading books,
bought a new pair of eyeglasses once a year. They usually cost
twenty-five cents. He bought them from a peddler who had a mirror
mounted on his pushcart. The peddler also had a variety of daily
newspapers, Yiddish, Polish, Hungarian, Italian, Russian, and now
and then one in English. His customers would stand around fitting
themselves with eyeglasses, looking in the mirror to see how they
looked and picking up one of the newspapers and testing the eyeglasses at all distances and angles. Very seldom did the peddler fail
to satisfy a customer—and everything seemed to be all right. At
least my father never complained.

I remember some peddlers who sold only rainwear and umbrellas. These peddlers did not always have to wait for a rainy
day to make money. An umbrella was a mark of distinction on
the Lower East Side, just as a gray-flannel suit or a Homburg
is a mark of distinction today. All of the "shadkhans" (marriage
brokers) carried umbrellas, rain or shine. It was a mark of the
profession. The rainwear peddler, of course, did have his problems.

His margin of profit was small and he had to be shrewd about the propitious time to replenish his stock. Some of these fellows were expert cloud readers, others depended upon begging God's favor, and some used invariable signs completely independent of the weather. I remember one who depended upon his brother who ran a cigarette stand. This peddler felt if his brother was selling packs or boxes of cigarettes, it was time to make the expedition to the wholesaler; if he sold cigarettes singly, it was not. This peddler sent both his sons to law school, so he must have had something.

There was still another interesting type among the peddlers of that era.

The customer peddler sold an endless variety of goods to the immigrant and invented the installment plan. First he sold the immigrant a "shiff's carte"—a steamship ticket for the immigrant's relative. Because of this ticket, many immigrants did not have to wait years and years before they imported their families or their cousins or their brothers. The shiff's carte paid steerage class on the Hamburg-American Line. The steerage class ticket cost thirty dollars and the immigrant paid the customer peddler forty dollars at the rate of one dollar a week. The immigrant paid for the first few weeks, then when the relative arrived and got a job, the new immigrant took up the payments.

This was only a small area of the customer peddler's business. He made a profit on the sale of that steerage ticket, but with the arrival of the new immigrant he had himself another customer.

The first item he sold to the new prospect was a gold watch and chain. The watch and chain, the customer peddler explained, were the visible marks of an American and pronounced that the wearer was no greenhorn.

The customer peddler also had the pick of the best boarders for himself and relatives, the cream of the crop. Also he carried a whole line of goods, engagement rings, earrings, curtains, and men's suits. An immigrant who found himself engaged to a girl simultaneously found the customer peddler handy with the pair of earrings, "screws" they were called because all the girls from Europe had pierced ears.

It is not hard to understand how the immigrant came to look upon the peddler as a sort of American "godfather." No problem that America offered was too great for the peddler. He was able to sell furniture to the "mochtunim" (the in-laws) and something to the "unterfuehrer" (he gave the bride away) to be given to the couple as a wedding present. Quite often this present was a bed, but until the customer peddler delivered it, the newlywed couple had to sleep on a mattress on the floor.

It was always called a seven-piece bedroom suite; the seven pieces included bed, spring, mattress, bedding, chair, coatrack, and mirror. It, too, was paid for on the installment plan.

My uncle arrived from the immigration office with an alarm clock. He had bought it from a peddler for $1.85 exactly five minutes after the immigration inspectors had cleared him.

How's that again?

THE "hard-of-hearing" clothing salesman flourished mainly on Stanton Street.

Here is how he operated: A customer was trying on a few suits and every question he asked had to be repeated three times. The salesman cupped his ear, distorted his features, trying desperately to make out what the customer was saying—"What did you say? Please repeat it! I am very hard of hearing!"

Finally the customer picked a suit he liked and now for that big moment. "How much?"

The deaf salesman yelled to the back, "Louis, how much for Number 2734?" And from the back came the voice, very loud so the customer heard it clearly, "Sixty-five dollars," and the deaf salesman with a straight face turned to the customer and said, "Thirty-five dollars," whereupon the customer pulled out thirty-five dollars, grabbed the suit without waiting for it to be boxed, and hustled off with his big bargain, while Louis and the "deaf" salesman went out to Davis's Saloon for a cold beer.

The lady and the mink

ONE morning in the early 1930's when I was manager and day clerk of the Hotel Markwell off Broadway, a handsome lady came through the lobby and went out into the street to buy herself some cigarettes. She came back and took the elevator up to the ninth floor. Soon she was back in the lobby, still clutching her cigarettes, and this time she studied the floor plan posted by the elevator. She went back up to the eighth floor. In ten minutes I heard from one of the housemaids that this lady was walking up and down between the eighth and tenth floors. Just as I was about to investigate, the lady came down to the lobby again and walked up to the desk. She seemed terribly upset. She wanted to know what room she had, because she had left her mink coat and her pocketbook, and she couldn't remember the room number.

"That's easy," I said opening the register. "Just tell me your name and we'll find your room number in a second."

She looked at me for a moment and said, "May I see you privately for a moment?" I walked from behind the counter and took her to a secluded corner of the lobby. Without looking up she said simply, "I do not know what name he used when we came in last night."

She was a charming woman. Ten minutes later the housekeeper brought down her mink coat and her pocketbook. She took a deep puff on her cigarette and said, "Thanks, thanks very much."

The New York World's Fair

WHEN New York City has a World's Fair in 1964, America will discover again what it discovered at the last World's Fair in New York City in 1939-40. There were people who came from Scranton, Bismarck, and Phoenix who never got as far as the exhibits at Flushing Meadows. They were in the middle of the greatest World's Fair ever planned—New York City—and there they stayed.

It is an enormous challenge for a staged exhibition to overcome. The times being somewhat different, let us hope that the experience of the New York World's Fair of 1939-40 will not be repeated. For that fair, as practically all of us who had an interest learned, was a commercial flop. We found that you cannot call people to this city, which is the Seventh Wonder of the World, and then tell them to travel eleven miles to Flushing Meadows to see a baby in an incubator. You cannot call them away from the Empire State Building and Radio City to go out and look at a papier-mâché Trylon and Perisphere.

Along about 1938 all of us hotel managers in New York City began rubbing our hands in anticipation of the big rush. Except it never came.

We had raised the rent of all the permanent guests in the hope that they would move. They obliged us. They left. Most of the show girls and actors on Broadway fled to the Upper Manhattan rooming houses, vacating their eight-dollar-, ten-dollar-, and twelve-dollar-a-week rooms. The hotelkeepers thought they would get this rate once a night instead of once a week. But after the World's Fair had been going for three months, they even promised to help move these actors and show girls by taxicab if they'd only come back and take their eight-dollar room again.

In the Hotel Markwell we had a lady tenant paying nine dollars a week for a nice outside room. Her name was Hazel and her room rent was paid by Frank Costello. Of course who paid her rent did not concern me much. Frank Costello was a gentleman as far as my hotel was concerned. He never went upstairs in all the years that I gave him receipts. He came in every Monday, paid the rent, and talked to Hazel over the house phone. She would come down to the lobby and Costello gave her an envelope. I suspected that Hazel was the widow of some fellow who had worked for him, but this was only a guess. You didn't ask Costello any questions.

A few months before the World's Fair opened I told Hazel that her rent would be raised to twenty dollars. The following Monday, Frank Costello came in to see me. We argued a little and finally made a compromise. I was to transfer Hazel to a smaller room which ordinarily let at seven dollars a week and charge her twelve dollars.

Soon after the Fair opened, Mr. Costello said one Monday, "Hazel, she tells me that her olda room is stilla empty." Costello was right. The room from which I had chased Hazel to make way for the rush of Fairniks was unfortunately still unoccupied. Each Monday, Mr. Costello repeated this altogether sad fact.

About the fifth time that this fact was called to my attention, I said, "All right, Mr. Costello, tell Hazel to move back into her big room." Mr. Costello smiled from ear to ear as he phoned Hazel. "Hazel, go backa to the biga room, and at the olda rate, too." He said this last very loud so that I'd hear it and, wisely, I nodded agreement.

That was the story of 1939-40 in the greatest metropolis the world has ever known.

What is it that gives the city its unique quality? The fact that New York has dozens of weekly and monthly newspapers in Yiddish, Turkish, Spanish, German, and Arabic. The fact that no one who has ever lived in New York City has ever been able to visit all its museums, museums from the Frick collection in the *fin de siècle* mansion on Fifth Avenue to the Guggenheim Museum in the new Wright-designed building only a few blocks away.

The story of New York is not only its dozens of different ethnic and racial groups. The story of New York is the complete story of America.

Now if you want taxi drivers to know you as you step into the cab, New York is not for you. If you want to nod to your friends when you go to the store, New York is not for you, either. One New Yorker is anonymous to another, but not on that account unfriendly. New York, as a matter of literal definition and pointed fact, is the friendliest of cities. No one is as unfriendly and cold and impassive as the clerk at the suburban supermarket. But New York is a city of small businesses in multiples of thousands. The shoemaker smiles at you, as do also the grocery clerk and the milkman. And your neighbor does not say hello—because his wife has no gossip about you.

New York City is a series of small towns continuous from the Atlantic to Spuyten Duyvil.

New York has every appurtenance of civilization including the supremely civilized monuments of our mercantile society—R. H. Macy, Gimbels, B. Altman, and Saks Fifth Avenue.

New York City is also food, the only city without an endless chain of neon-lit drive-ins serving badly fried chicken and burnt steaks. New York serves every conceivable dish from shish-kabob and smorgasbord to corned beef and cabbage and kasha varnishkas. It is one of the few cities in America where a man can sit down and have a drink before his dinner. New York is one of the few American cities without bootleggers.

And despite the greedy mistakes of realtors and the criminal ignorance of city planners, New York has survived them all as a city of inexpressible beauty. It is quiet and romantic and bawdy and daring and efficient and hurly-burly by turns.

At this very moment there are twelve million youngsters in our country who dream of someday going to New York.

May they meet there in 1964.

The Grand Street boys

WALK through the headquarters of the Grand Street Boys at 106-108 West Fifty-fifth Street, and you can live the history of New York for the past fifty years. On the walls are photographs of men like Alfred E. Smith, James J. Walker, James A. Farley, Otto Rosalsky, Herbert Lehman, and the late Sir Samuel Stirling, who went from the Lower East Side to England and was knighted for his charity, but never forgot.

The Grand Street Boys is a fraternal organization with its roots in the East Side. Over it all presides Judge Jonah J. Goldstein— Jonnie Goldstein to thousands of New Yorkers—a man who has devoted his life to public service and in one of the most turbulent eras of big city politics has emerged after a half century with flying colors of integrity.

As a member of the Grand Street Boys, I am particularly proud of its most important project, the Maintenance Scholarship. There are many of these awarded each year to students and they help at least relieve some of the surface poverty. And the idea behind this is that those boys will someday do for others what the Grand Street Boys did for them.

The emblem of the Grand Street Boys shows three barefoot ten-year-olds, one of whom holds a small piece of cake which he is about to share with the other two. The cake is a piece of gingerbread, not much bigger than a man's hand. It is called bolowa and it used to cost a cent on the East Side forty years ago. Judge Goldstein tells me that the emblem does not signify any "share the wealth" plan, but represents common sense.

If the boy with the bolowa wants any of it, he had better give some to the other two, otherwise all three boys, and the bolowa, will end up in the gutter.

Evil Eye Finkle

HERMAN MELVILLE catalogued all the words for whale in the different languages of the world, and now Dr. Edward S. Gifford has done the same for the evil eye in his book *The Evil Eye: Studies in the Folklore of Vision*. The Italians call the evil eye *mal occhio*, the Germans *böse Blick*, the French *mauvais oeil*, and the Indians *drishtidosham*.

Whether or not the evil eye exists in the realm of fact is immaterial. People believe it does, and people act on what they believe, not on what is or is not true.

The eye is the first part of the organism to spot misfortune and to feast itself on sin and lust. And it is quite possible that a malignant mind may translate its malignancy through its eye. Thus with Evil Eye Finkel. Evil Eye Finkel was a prize-fight second, but he was possessed with a wide, staring orb. Managers used to hire Evil Eye Finkel to put the hex on opponents. Evil Eye Finkel would sit in one prize fighter's corner and stare malignantly at the other with his unblinking orb, and, sure enough, he'd put the hex on him and the fighter lost. Evil Eye Finkel made a good living this way, but he came to a bad end when someone discovered that in some professional bouts he was selling his services to both fighters.

A glass of warmth

"A GLEZL VARMS" literally translated from Yiddish means, "a glass of warmth," but actually it means, a glass of tea—a glass of very hot tea.

A peddler standing at his pushcart all day in the freezing weather would step into a cafe and ask for "a glezl varms"—or a friend would visit your father and your mother immediately brought him "a glezl varms."

Thus "a glezl varms" went back to its literal meaning. It was more than a glass of tea. It was "warmth," "fellowship," and "talk"—but mostly talk, good talk.

Unforgettable quartet

UP ON East Houston Street was the Little Hungary, the most famous restaurant on the East Side. We kids used to watch the "swell" people come out of the Little Hungary, and one night after midnight three of us were standing on a corner singing when a carriage from the Little Hungary stopped in front of us. It was occupied by a stout gentleman and a beautiful woman. The portly gent motioned for us to come to the edge of the curb, and he led us in the harmonizing of "Darling, I am growing old, silver threads among the gold." He was Victor Herbert, the great composer.

A solid foundation

ON THE Lower East Side of New York at Grand Street and the East River there stands today the wonderful East River Housing Project. It is twenty-two stories high, and the first four floors are reserved for the Orthodox Jews so that they will not have to ride the elevator on the Sabbath. This strikes me as the right sort of thing to fling in the teeth of progress.

East Side aromas

No AROMAS can equal those of Houston Street, in particular the aromas that came from Katz's Delicatessen with the big salamis hanging from the hooks and the corned beef and the pastrami and the Jewish frankfurters (specials) that have made Katz's a gastronomical heaven. Equaling the delight of Katz's were the Jewish pastry shops with the hot challahs and the Jewish rye bread. The dairy delicatessens emitted smells to make a gourmet swoon. A friend wrote to remind me of the aroma that came from the old Jewish grocery stores—a combination made from the large open barrel of pickles, the herring, the dried apricots, and the corned beef. He says he has opened a campaign in company with the descendant of a Jewish groceryman who now runs a supermarket chain of eighty stores. They are trying to petition Proctor & Gamble to re-create the odor in chemical quantities for the air-conditioners of the stores. Good luck to them.

The Fourth of July

I NEVER think of the Fourth of July that I do not remember a song that was popular for a year or two when I was growing up:

What's the matter with Johnson?
He's all right.
What's the matter with Jeffries?
He can't fight.
It was on the Fourth of July
That Johnson knocked out Jeffries' eye.
What's the matter with Johnson?
He's all right.

This song described the heavyweight championship fight which took place in Reno, Nevada, on July 4, 1910. Jack Johnson was the heavyweight champion, perhaps the best Negro athlete to step inside a prize ring. Jim Jeffries was the former champ and he came out of retirement for the bout, but Johnson knocked him out in the fifteenth round.

More than the fight, the song allies itself in my memory with July Fourth on the East Side. Because we were immigrants, it was only natural that we overcelebrated. Everybody had a flag. Flags hung from every window and from every fire escape. Workmen carried them in their pockets and peddlers displayed them on their pushcarts. I have never seen so many flags before or since.

The noise on July Fourth started early, as soon as the sun peeped over the tenement roofs. We had torpedoes which cost twelve for a penny, little round balls that you threw on the pavement. And firecrackers that came in long strings and you lit the first one and the string writhed and squirmed along the street. And rockets that we set off from the roof. This bombardment never let up. And at night the East Side was a strange enchanted city whose inhabitants waved sparklers as they trailed through the streets.

In every neighborhood park there was a city-sponsored band concert. And there was always an oration by a Tammany sachem with the medallion and sash of his status adding to the color of the occasion.

Times have changed a lot, and now we seem intense and nervous about our patriotism; we are not as relaxed as we were when we sang:

What's the matter with Johnson?
He's all right.

"Holding the book"

WE KNEW many a girl who "held the book" for her "intended." "Holding the book" meant that the girl was working in a factory and helping to finance her feller through medical school. During the evenings she helped him study by "holding the book," bringing him hot tea, and resting his eyes every hour or so with a damp cloth.

Occasionally we had what was the most poignant of all ghetto tragedies. When he finally became a doctor the "difference" between his new status and the factory girl now seemed to be insurmountable; with a terrible climax of weeping and sorrow, he took a bride from "uptown," a manufacturer's daughter.

No. 8721

OUR "society" doctor when we lived on Rivington Street was a great man, Dr. Julius Frankel. Dr. Frankel had worked his way through medical school as a window cleaner. There are many men today, surgeons and scientists and comptrollers and lawyers, who worked at anything to gain their education. They sorted rags, they ran errands, they were subway pushers at the Thirty-third Street stop of the IRT.

I sat in the office recently of an elderly lawyer who commands huge fees and directs over thirty younger lawyers. We discussed the life on the East Side that each of us had lived many years ago. In the middle of our conversation this gentleman rose and walked toward his safe. From inside he extracted a little box, and coming back to me with a pleasant smile, he opened it and let me look inside. It was an old badge with the big number 8721 on it— a pushcart peddler's license issued to him in 1910. Like a couple of babies . . . we both cried, a little.

PART 3

Affairs of the Heart

The beautiful women

WOMEN have been immortalized in sonnets, made forever permanent in marble, and tinted magnificently in oils on canvas. But what is it that makes them beautiful and loved? It may be perfection of physical form; it may be the degree of sympathy, intelligence, and compassion they can express. It is certainly nice for a woman to have all these things, but this is not necessarily why they are beautiful and loved. Hollywood women, the most beautiful in the world, are often cast aside by several men. The most compassionate women are often old maids and the Mona Lisa smile may well have been the result of adenoids.

Disraeli loved and honored his wife and thought she was beautiful because she called him "Dizzy" and greeted him every evening when he came home from Parliament from the top of the stairs in a red bathrobe.

What really makes a woman beautiful and loved is—a man. The moment a man chooses her for his own, she automatically enters the hall of fame of the beautiful and the loved.

Important events

PEOPLE ask, "What will be the most important event in the next ten years?" This is a big and important question.

In ten years' time I am quite sure we will be on the moon. We might have war. Or we might achieve a lasting peace. Science might conquer the degenerative diseases.

Each of these will be important. But the most important event of any decade for most of the people will be getting the kids ready for school.

Just imagine if the car battery doesn't work on the morning

when it is your turn for the car pool. It is Tuesday. Ten families are dependent upon you. Yet the car absolutely refuses to kick over. Your daughter is in tears. In the science class this morning she's scheduled to read a report on photosynthesis. And now you have to make ten telephone calls to ten different mothers. Taxis scream from their garages. The community fashion show will be delayed as ten mothers scurry with ten other children who will be reading similar reports. Some of the mothers will even have to take the lunch to school for the kids. Will anything be more important in the next decade than this? If we're going to worry about one thing more than the moon, science, or war, it must be whether the battery will work tomorrow.

Test of sovereignty

THERE is no culture without the gal with a heaving bosom and a plan.

The idea of sex certainly is older than the idea of prostitution, but only by a few minutes. Sex has always been put to more uses than procreation.

England levies no income tax on its ladies of the evening and America has its hundred-dollar-a-night call girls. It is interesting that one no longer hears any gossip about how prolific Russian women are, which only proves what most of us thought about Russia anyway. In uncivilized countries promiscuity abounds— except the anthropologists don't call it that, they call it one of the cultural mores.

Israel is only twelve years old but she is no longer a baby sister among free nations. She is as sovereign as any nation can be. In Tel Aviv they just arrested a former policeman who has been found deriving benefits from the earnings of a prostitute. The fellow got five months. Which is an interesting story, if you consider that this Jewish panderer was arrested by a Jewish cop, tried by a Jewish jury, and sentenced by a Jewish judge, all be-cause of a Jewish prostitute. The test of sovereignty is recapitulated in this simple, age-old story, though prostitution, in itself, is no proof of either sovereignty or civilization. But sovereignty and civilization are real and must be saluted once a nation can sadly say its prostitutes support its pimps.

But of course there are no special villains. Sex has influenced decisions at every level of the human drama, including secrets of empire and betrayal of country. (Many a fellow, without an ideology in his head, joined a Communist cell in the early 1930's because of the prospect of a less inhibited sex life. Years later he paid the penalty for it before some Congressional committee, but even at that crucial moment in his life he could not reveal himself. This is the one thing we do not talk about under any circumstances. Silence, from childhood to old age).

The importance of sex in our lives is based on the fact that it is an "affirmation of life"—and it also involves man's greatest quest, the need to prove himself. And this need to prove himself is so intense that he must remain forever unconvinced of his prowess. It is not only biological. It is also sociological and political. Sex involves that single moment when you make your own rules. A few moments later you fall into step with time clocks, and sales, and forms to fill out, and appointments to be kept. And we find that the tighter those "outside" rules are in a given period the greater the sex drive becomes. The great sex literature and pornography were produced in the eras where the rules outside your bedroom were the most strict. Interestingly enough the American literature of the Revolutionary period is almost completely free of sex overtones. The need for "making your own rules" was almost wholly absent. The age of Franklin, Jefferson, and Washington was probably the moment of the greatest political relaxation man has ever known on this earth.

The Old Testament, stern though it is, is much more lenient toward prostitutes than we American Puritans. The really bad sexual offense in the Old Testament is adultery, and it deals pretty hard with the married adultress who is, after all, an amateur. The reasoning is that if a man sweats in the fields he ought to sweat for children of his own flesh and blood.

Prostitutes, the professionals, include some of the kindest people in the world. I remember that chapter in Lecky's *History of European Morals* where he speaks of the noble prostitute who helps make our daughters and sisters decent women. That famous Mayor William J. Gaynor put his finger on it way back in 1911. A group of civic leaders called on him with a demand that he chase the prostitutes out of New York and he told them that if he exiled all the professionals, there wouldn't be enough police officers to protect the decent sixteen-year-old girls, and, "You fellows would help the other men make five thousand new prostitutes during the first year."

Once reformers brought him a list of hotels where prostitutes plied their trade. The Mayor studied this list of third-rate hotels and asked, "Why isn't the Waldorf on this list?" When silence greeted this remark, he continued, "Do you want to bet?"

On another occasion, he told a reform committee, "If I close the brothels, the prostitutes will move in next door to you. They will be scattered throughout the city in the fanciest apartments. They will make the best tenants. They will give the janitor a dollar everyday, while you give fifty cents once a year at Christmas. And they will flourish."

Mayor Gaynor was more than a philosopher. He was a practical man and a prophet. For what he warned against is precisely what has happened. I respect the professional, but I have no use for the amateur who has chased the professional out of business; the so-called call girl who does it for money but who poses as a model, an actress, or a housewife. These are the lowest tramps in the world and they are not worthy of the compassion the philosophers of the world have shown toward that saddest woman of our civilization, the prostitute.

Prostitution is the same as juvenile delinquency. It is caused not by willful sinning, but by social factors. There is less prostitution in Charlotte than in any city I have ever known. It is worth studying the reasons for this.

Charlotte is a distributing center for thousands of firms and its social classes are stratified to an alarming degree. You can have fellowship and association with members of the upper middle class for twenty years and never once see them "uptown" during the evening. The entire social life in Charlotte evolves around the home and the private club.

There are very few factories here and the floating population made up of traveling salesmen is not enough to support a bookie palace or prostitution on any substantial scale.

For years I used to see the same three prostitutes who did work in Charlotte. I met them through some mysterious underground grapevine which relayed the information that I would go their bail when in trouble. These prostitutes used the local post office for their headquarters. This fact reminded me of the de Maupassant story about the prostitute in the Parisian cemetery. She picked out the headstone of a man who had died one or two years before, placed flowers on his grave, and stood there weeping inconsolably. Soon a stray man would try to comfort her.

Well, something must have happened to the prostitutes who clung to the Charlotte post office for I haven't seen them in several years. In this society the post office provides the only real opportunity for a streetwalker. For she can wait there, writing a post card, able to size up each man covertly. The traveling salesman comes in with the telltale brown envelope, his report of sales made that day in Gastonia, Columbia, or Greensboro.

The prostitute then approaches him and asks for change of a dime or maybe even for the time.

But now even these three women are gone. Their departure is evidence of the increasing stratification of the Charlotte society.

A "first" brings luck

SHAKESPEARE wrote: "You take my life when you do take the means whereby I live." Next to God, family, and country, the most important thing in a man's life is earning a livelihood. The Jews call it parnosseh, and I doubt whether there is a more expressive word in any language. It means having a place to go to in the morning—a job—but it means more than that.

It also means survival as a man, as a family, as a people. Parnosseh suggests the time when Jews were prohibited by law from tilling the soil, from entering the professions, and from engaging in trade, and then parnosseh came as my mother expressed it in Yiddish with an old ghetto proverb, "The Jews climbed the straight walls with their bare hands." And helping others to parnosseh was a noble deed. People would go without because some woman who sold the product depended upon that sale for parnosseh. I saw that thousands of times on the East Side of New York.

It was also good luck to give a peddler or a merchant a "first." A "first" was the first sale in the morning when the merchant opened his store in the town or his stall at the market. After many of the customers had made purchases at various stalls, there may have been one peddler left who had not yet made a sale and he would announce it: "Balabusten, balabusten (housewives, housewifes), I haven't yet had a beginning." And of course someone would be sure to make a purchase.

The first brought good luck to both parties involved: for the merchant it meant a good day; for the customer it meant a special divine merit in the book to be opened on the Day of Judgment, because as a matter of fact there is nothing more important in the eyes of God than earning a livelihood—parnosseh.

War's terrible secret

CLEOPATRA had just ordered her servant to kill Pothinus, the leader of her opposition, and the soldiers of the opposition were storming Cleopatra's palace for vengeance.

And in his play, *Caesar and Cleopatra*, written before World War I, George Bernard Shaw has Caesar say: "Do you hear? Those knockers at your gate . . . You have slain their leader; it is right that they slay you. . . . And then in the name of that right shall I not slay them for murdering their Queen, and be slain in my turn by their countrymen as the invader of their fatherland? Can Rome do less than slay these slayers, too, to shew the world how Rome avenges her sons and her honor. And so, to the end of history, murder shall breed murder, always in the name of right and honor and peace, until the gods are tired of blood and create a race that can understand."

Shaw understood, and someday most of us may. Meanwhile, there are many things you will tell your best friend, a few additional revelations to your husband or wife, and perhaps you'll go a little further into your intellect and memory with your clergyman, doctor, lawyer, and psychiatrist. But you never totally reveal yourself. No one ever strips himself bare. And one of the best kept secrets of all is the "love" of war. It is a great leveler—all wear the uniform—and it releases one from all responsibility. Man dreads making decisions. In war all the decisions are made for you and you do not have to worry about food, rent, and taxes, and you laugh out loud when the invoice catches up with you in some camp or foreign post. War also involves the movement of population. It relieves boredom. You work in a factory, and one day is the same as the day before. Suddenly you find yourself in Brest, France, or Saigon.

It also means prosperity of a sort and a release of sexual inhibitions. "He was scheduled to leave tomorrow so what else could I do?" she tells herself the morning after.

And all of this secret "popularity" of war is because the average man is not yet a philosopher. Since we have always known war, it is as yet hard to visualize how really good it would be to have an absence of war and an absence of the threat of war. Ah, if we only knew the joys that await us—the expansion of knowledge, the vast cost of war diverted to education and health and what the Greeks called "the good life," and the joy of knowing your sons will grow into manhood and have sons of their own someday, and that they will live out their lives without wheel chairs or beds in a veterans' hospital.

A day for the "help"

In CHARLOTTE there's an independently owned parking lot near the post office where the owner has a novel system of paying a bonus to his attendants. To supplement their earnings, he turns the lot over to them on Sundays, and the gross income on that day belongs to the employees.

This recalled to me the time when this system was used in a less honorable endeavor.

It was part of the testimony that came out during the Seabury investigation into the Magistrate's Courts of New York. In one night court which concerned itself mostly with streetwalkers, the magistrate had inaugurated a novel system. A large part of the graft came from the women who paid certain fees to be let off. This "income" went to the higher-ups . . . but one night a week the "business" was turned over to the lower echelon. The entire take that night went to the attachés, clerks, bailiffs, and policemen who were in on the deal. A lawyer would plead: "Your Honor, there are one hundred reasons why this girl shouldn't be held," and when His Honor shook his head, the lawyer leaned toward his client: "Can you raise another fifty dollars tonight?"

Then he would say, "Your Honor, there are a hundred and *fifty reasons*," etc. It was done as crudely as that. A more subtle method was pounding the counsel table for emphasis, and each rap was equivalent to twenty-five dollars. And so as the counsel spoke of the virtue of forgiveness and told of the woman's sick mother, no one was listening . . . everyone was counting.

What makes women tick?

When Judd Gray and Ruth Snyder confessed to the sash-weight murder of Ruth's husband, Albert Snyder, hundreds of women crowded the courtroom to cheer Judd Gray and hiss Ruth Snyder. The mousy corset salesman, who in the end kept whimpering, "*She* made me do it; *she* was the cause of it all; *she* picked up the sash-weight and finished the job after I hit him twice only; *she, she, she* . . ."; this man actually had the overwhelming sympathy of the women, from factory workers to Park Avenue housewives. If the jury had been composed of twelve women, good and true (God help us), I am sure they would have sent Ruth Snyder to the electric chair, and sent little old Judd Gray back to his corsets. (Both, however, were executed.)

What makes women like that? Every jail warden will tell you that all his murderers (especially wife-killers), receive mash notes from women all over the country; they send flowers, candy, Bible tracts, and marriage proposals.

The most glamorous of all bank robbers was a fellow by the name of Hamby. I caught a glimpse of Hamby on the day he was arrested in the early 1920's at the old Hotel Navarre on Seventh Avenue. Tall, handsome as a movie actor, Hamby refused to reveal a single detail of his life, and there was nothing on file anywhere. He robbed a bank with an accomplice and when they returned to their appointed rendezvous to cut up the swag, he killed the accomplice and went out looking for a fresh accomplice for the next job.

A legend was built up around him by the newspaper boys. Some said he was the black-sheep son of a United States Senator. Others said he was the son of a famous multimillionaire. Anyway Hamby wouldn't tell. The Hearst press offered him five thousand dollars, or at least offered to give it to any relative or person he would designate, if he would talk, but Hamby went to the electric chair without revealing his "identity." It is my guess that he didn't write his story because there was nothing to write; that he was just a plain, ordinary, garden-variety hoodlum, and that he had enough sense not to explode the legend. Hamby received so many presents from women that the warden of Sing Sing had to give him a list every morning of the stuff he received. The women of the world sent candy, flowers, love letters, and marriage proposals by the hundreds. The warden supplied two Salvation Army units with the stuff, but burned the sex-mad, love-ridden letters. What is this about women? Does anyone know?

What makes women tick? This is the mystery of mysteries.

The groceries of the poor

For three years I lived in a neighborhood of lower-income groups. In this prestige society, the word "poor" is too tough a pill to swallow so we say "lower-income." The men worked in mills, bakeries, garages. They were construction workers and truck drivers. Their women worked in the mills and in the factories. These folks were forever buying groceries. They bought the groceries at the supermarkets and they carried these bags home and I saw them go by my window. They bought often—each day was a brand-new operation.

It is because the poor are always buying groceries that they never start a revolution. Their every effort is spent to obtain the necessities of everyday living: enough fuel to get through the next morning, one dollar's worth of gasoline to get them to work and back, an extra job at night to buy shoes for a child. The poor are not happy being poor, neither are they pleasant, but they are not the troublemakers.

The Age of Feudalism was the stablest of all ages in the history of Western society. It was composed of only two classes: the nobility and the peasants. Feudalism ended with a centuries-long revolution. But it was not started by the poor. Historians tell us the feudal society started to end when gunpowder and manufacturing showed up. The aristocracy had invented both but it controlled neither. A new man began to exploit these two developments: a man who was neither a peasant nor a lord. He became the man of the middle class—the man who would eventually own Europe and America. The word "villain" in fact comes from the early French word *villein,* the man of the village, the merchant, the entrepreneur. Revolutions begin when the poor are a little better off than poor, when they have a little more time to look things over and they begin to think of luxuries like the right to charge interest, to gain political liberties, and to redistribute land.

But when the poor are carrying groceries—on the top of which the last purchase, the toilet paper, is always visible—things are safe from overturn.

Women never tell all

THE popular magazines have been suggesting that the sexes are fusing, that the American woman (in addition to controlling the purchasing power) has become the dominant force in our society.

Women have always been the dominant force in most of the civilized societies of mankind. She may be less subtle about it today, which gives the impression that her influence is a new development. Women have always been smarter than men. They have always understood human motives better, and, what is even more important, they have known how to exercise power and still create the illusion that the big he-men were sweeping them off their little footsies.

Only on rare occasions has the woman found it necessary to show her hand—to drop the play acting and settle an issue on the spot. As in the case of Lysistrata, for instance. Athens and Sparta, the two dominant world powers, are at war. The women of Athens open negotiations with the women of Sparta and come to an agreement. No more sexual relations with their men, until the dopes stop killing each other. The big shots home on furlough, first take it as a joke, then they begin to fuss, and finally they go stark raving mad. The only break in the agreement was that a weak sister here and there cheated, but even women are human. The Greek Aristophanes who wrote his play knew all about womanpower.

But do women tell the whole truth about women? I doubt that this has ever happened. Not even Jane Austen dared do it.

Ellen Glasgow once threatened to do so, but in the end she told her friend James Southal Wilson that she didn't dare. Men of course have told on each other and that is why their books will remain on the shelves longer. The list is a fairly long one too, with Shakespeare, Dostoevski, Proust, and Rolland near the top. The fact that women will not tell all about other women is evidence of one of our "big lies," and one which men, who invented it, dearly love to hug to their breasts. This big lie is that women cannot be trusted with a secret. This is an old technique—attaching to someone else (as a symbol of prejudice) the trait which you hate most in yourself. Men of course blabber all over the place—among themselves, and to the wives, mothers, children, and sweethearts of their best friends; but women—*never*. Women never tell on each other. It is part of the "united front" against men, which women have had since antiquity and long before antiquity. The woman, novelist or shopgirl, has not yet appeared who would dare violate the unwritten rules of this million-year-old alliance.

Hamlet utters a paradox, "Frailty, thy name is woman," probably to hide his own indecision, his own lack of power.

There was nothing "frail" about Lady Macbeth, or the wife of King Agamemnon, or the wife of Hercules, or Joan of Arc, or Portia, or Lillian Wald, or Eleanor Roosevelt. Thomas Randolph in his poem, "In Praise of Women in General":

> . . . yours was the nobler birth,
> For you of man were made, man but of earth,
> The son of dust.

Clytemnestra, the wife of Agamemnon, took over a man's world without the slightest hesitation. She managed the city in her husband's absence. Like most women who know their own strength, she called herself "a mere woman." This is one of the strongest weapons in the arsenal of womanpower, the disarming statement par excellence, and there never lived a woman who hasn't used it with telling effect. In her determination to act as freely as a man, Clytemnestra took a lover, a sort of "womanish" man. Not unlike many army wives who attached themselves to 4-F-ers while their husbands were away at war. When she flatly refuses to obey her husband the king, the great Agamemnon appears broken and helpless.

The towering bravery of Lady Macbeth leads her even to utter the word "coward," a word that no man can endure from another, still less from a woman, and least of all from a woman he loves. She removes all obstacles and silences all arguments. In one scene we see her commanding intellect and tremendous spirit and, I may add, her complete honesty with respect to what they were about to do. All men say exactly the same thing when planning to commit a crime. To the accomplice they say, "Suppose we fail?" And every accomplice gives the same answer: "Aw, we can't fail, the thing is foolproof, there's nothing to worry about." But not Lady Macbeth. "Suppose we fail?" asks her wishy-washy husband. And Lady Macbeth answers: "We fail—but keep up your courage, and we'll not fail. You can become the king and I can become the queen, it is a risky business, but it's worth it, and if we fail, we fail, and that's all there is to it."

Lady Macbeth understood the superiority of women, but there was no lack of respect for her husband. That is another secret of womanpower.

I observed this often among the Jewish people on the East Side of New York. It was a patrism—the father was the *big* man. We never sat down to the table unless he was there; and the mother carried her respect for him to the breaking point. She never betrayed her power, which of course was supreme. When a family was confronted with a major decision, she made it, she made all arrangements, and then told the master all about it— privately. At the supper table, she said: "Children, your father has something important to tell you," and she drank in every word of his wisdom as if she were hearing it for the first time.

To the graduates

A HIGH-SCHOOL graduating class is the toughest audience in the world.

They are polite enough to listen to any amount of platitudes without coughing or stirring. But they are all smarter than I am. They see things more clearly because they are more ready to accept them. And they are stronger. Some of them already, and all of them within the next year or five years, will make a decision that would leave me and my fellow adults weak and nervous. They are going to decide what to do with their lives while the rest of us are wondering what we did with ours.

For this reason, and because it was before one of the four or five most important institutions of my own city of Charlotte, I looked upon my commencement address at Myers Park High School as the most crucial speech I made last year.

But one happy event made the prospect of my talk a little less terrifying. When I was in Los Angeles I met Ozzie and Harriet Nelson, and I took Mrs. Nelson aside and asked if she would urge her son, Ricky Nelson, an idol of teen-agers, to come over for just a minute. Harriet Nelson is a kind and understanding woman and five minutes later in came David and Ricky. We had a quiet talk about books, and when I said goodbye I shook Ricky's hand, and I showed this hand to my graduating audience in North Carolina, and swore to them I hadn't even washed it.

The students applauded and laughed and after that things weren't bad at all.

When I was graduated from New York's East Side Evening High School in 1920, I remember that the commencement speaker was an Annapolis man who had sailed with Dewey into Manila Bay in 1898. As I composed my speech I kept trying to remember what this fellow talked to us about, but I couldn't. All that stood out in my mind was this handsome, gray-haired naval officer, trim and smart in his commander's uniform. And one phrase. He told us that before Dewey had beaten the Spanish fleet, Manila had been spelled with two "l's." But Admiral Dewey, he said, had knocked the "l" out of it.

I told this story, and I wondered, will it be my fate that forty years from now this graduating class will remember of its commencement speaker only the same joke he remembered of his? I am willing to bet that this will be so.

The world the Annapolis commander left me was a nicer world than the world we are leaving them, but these high-school seniors were generous enough to skip all that.

They will have to make their decisions, too, in a world in which they find themselves a scapegoat of the moment.

The scapegoat is the teen-ager. To ease the pain of our own frustration, to justify our own shortcomings and our own failures, we have shifted the burden to the teen-ager and we think we can now rest easily. The other day in our own North Carolina Legislature a fellow introduced a bill to allow the teacher to spank the students. A Daniel come to judgment! New York and Michigan have been toying with the same bit of nonsense. And so we are doing everything to help create two illusions: first, that we are doing something noble, and second, that we do not have any responsibility in the matter. This is a stupid procedure, which these graduates will learn in college when they study the history of human behavior. They will find that we, all of us, are the result of the conditions to which we were exposed. Some day these graduates will be clergymen and doctors, and businessmen and teachers, and they will be these things because of the classmates met, the friends made, the people who came to their home, and the language and ideas they heard expressed. Each of us is a reflection of the society which surrounds us, and the entire teen-age culture, where it has given us concern, reflects the frustration, the tension, and the rootlessness of our highly mobile adult world. A "spanking" law will not solve it any more than you can cure cancer with an aspirin tablet. It reaches down to the rootless world we have created in the wake of our tremendous industrialization.

You are fifteen years old and you live in Harlem in New York and you hear your mother and father enter into a conspiracy. They are conniving; you hear your mother whisper to your father— "Let's tell the renting agent we are Spanish, not Puerto Rican" —and you are thereby cut off from history and tradition and a sense of belonging, and you must belong. You must belong to something. So the teen-ager goes downstairs and gets himself a black leather jacket with the word "Pirates" on it and now he belongs.

What do you want this teen-ager to do, jump for joy? He has been deprived of dignity and this is the most tragic of all afflictions.

A human being can go without food longer than he can go without human dignity.

And this human dignity involves the graduate's own future. He will someday look into a mirror and ask himself, "Do I have a mature mind?" and I quote to him from all the great minds which have left us the heritage of the English-speaking civilization, that there is only one way he can answer that affirmatively. You have a mature mind when you respect new ideas, when you respect all your neighbors, and when you respect yourself. It is utterly impossible to respect yourself unless you respect ideas.

Mankind has advanced only when it succeeded in fighting off its book burners and book censors. Ideas. In first-century Rome you couldn't walk a hundred yards without seeing two or three handsomely uniformed legionnaires. It was a gigantic empire with tremendous political and military power. Then along came a little bald-headed Jew from the East who didn't even have pockets in his pants. The graduates whom I addressed call him St. Paul and this St. Paul had a Book and an Idea and because he had a Book and an Idea, he conquered the whole empire, lock, stock, and barrel.

When a society begins to fear ideas it means that the nation has lost confidence in itself and that it can no longer meet the challenge of the world.

These were some of the thoughts that I secretly hoped these graduates would retain beyond the stories of the Annapolis commander and Ricky Nelson.

And, speaking for my generation, I made so bold as to pronounce an old Irish prayer over this graduating class, and for all the high-school graduates everywhere in our country:

> May the hills rise up to meet you,
> May the wind be ever behind you,
> And may God hold you in the palm of His hand.

No more dragging them

OUR sociologists have not paid sufficient attention to one of the truly important changes of centuries-old habit and tradition. I refer to the fact that the long-haired woman has just about disappeared from the scene. Most girls and women now wear their hair very short and the trend is toward even greater extremes. Eventually there will be no difference in the cutting or care of the hair between men and women.

This is a far-reaching change since the female symbol of long tresses goes back to the dawn of recorded history. This sex symbol was so universal that the use of false hair to supplement the natural tresses was known to all cultures and societies. A bride would have her picture taken with her long hair flowing over her shoulders. Sometimes she would braid her hair and hold the long braids in front of her so that they might be seen. Often when a boy called on a girl for the first time a sister or a friend, at a prearranged signal, would playfully undo the ribbon or pins holding the hair in place and the tresses would fall down the blushing girl's back. She would act coy and blush while the boy began to stammer and perspire. But you can be sure that the drama of it and the memory of the hair made a lasting and favorable impression. Today the women are getting to look more and more like boys; the time when you could drag them by the hair is definitely over. And all of this took place within the last twenty-five years. Amazing.

The Over-40 Club

IN CHARLOTTE, as in other cities, there is an organization known as the "Over-40 Club." It is directed by a few public-spirited volunteers who conduct an employment service for men and women over forty years of age.

It is rather sad to realize how difficult it is for people over forty to get jobs, and a little ridiculous, too, when we look at a few facts of life. For instance, Justices and Judges Felix Frankfurther, Hugo Black, and Learned Hand, all well past middle age, are still among the best judicial minds in our country; Carl Sandburg and Bernard M. Baruch are in their middle eighties; Lord Bertrand Russell still furnishes us with the most profound insights into the natural sciences, and Arturo Toscanini conducted his most creative interpretation of music at the age of eighty-five.

Many live way into their eighties so they can have the satisfaction of saying, "I told you so." Herbert Hoover, Field Marshal Montgomery, Harry Truman, and I'm certain our President, God willing, will have long life, and for the same reason. In all of this we may have the clue to the better and happier life in old age.

In the science of geriatrics (the field of medicine which deals with the hygiene of old age) the answer may be in the area of a wider outward interest in the affairs of the world.

My father lived to over eighty and I remember how deeply interested he was in the affairs of the world right up to the very end. When he entered my house he never asked, "How are things?" From the moment he opened the door he was pulling newspaper clippings out of his pockets, and without a "hello," he dived right in: "Look at this stupid editorial, let's answer it!"

I have a hunch that the well-being of the aged depends, in a large measure, in his attitudes and ideas with relation to the world outside of himself. I have watched elderly folks sit on the benches in the park or in the resort-hotel lobbies, and it is a great pity to hear them: "My son, he should enjoy good health, hasn't called me since last Mother's Day." "You think you have suffered, let me tell you the trouble I have had with my leg for the past eight years." This constant inward attitude may very well be connected with most of the unhappiness and disorder of the aging.

As we get older we must expand our horizons and keep thinking of the arguments we will use someday when we are old enough to say, "I told you so."

But in America we worship youth, and it is not all based on the intense sex drive. It goes much deeper into the Western culture.

One of the many reasons for this Jewish "survival" we are always discussing is reverence for the aged through all the centuries. I remember in my own day on the Lower East Side of New York when an Orthodox couple got married they would often stop off at the Jewish Home for the Aged to ask a blessing of the old folks.

In fact you automatically referred to elderly people as "sheyneh mentschen" (beautiful people). An old man or an old woman was referred to as "beautiful." You rarely see this expression in the literature of the English language.

This reverence carried with it a sort of reverence for the "activities" and "talents" of the aged, as opposed to the "feats" of the young. Thus a pin-up I remember which hung on many walls was a picture of an elderly man reading the Torah. And all of this resulted in the ambition to emulate activities such as learning, concern for the social sciences, and so forth.

The worship of youth in the Christian civilization goes back to its foundations in the metaphysics of the Greeks. This culture was rooted in the stories of youth—Venus, Adonis, Diana, and Apollo; and how the heroes fought on the field of battle to decide who would win the beautiful Helen of Troy. King David's campaign in the Rephaim Valley against the Philistines is studied in the famous war academy in France, and his image is engraved on the façade of West Point. But the Jews, to whom he belongs, rarely mention his battles. They revere him only for his poetry:

> The Lord is my shepherd; I shall not want.
> He maketh me to lie down in green pastures: he leadeth me beside the still waters. . . .

All of this added to the sense of ambivalence which confronted the Jewish people in the Western world, the drive to identify themselves with a culture of which the folk heroes were St. George fighting the dragon, and Roland and Oliver on the field of Roncesvalles. And even in the stories of the American culture's two greatest men, it was necessary to emphasize the fact that George Washington had thrown a silver coin across the Rappahannock, and that Abraham Lincoln had won a wrestling match.

I am willing to say that I believe the symbol of the Christian world is Joan of Arc, significantly a young girl; and I would balance this off with the symbol of the Jewish culture—Job, significantly an old man. The matriarchy of the Great Mother embodied in youth, and the patrism of the Jews in the form of the thundering "aged."

Primitive man, of course, concerned himself only with youth— the hunter and the warrior; and for many centuries he actually killed his aged. As civilization advanced he no longer killed his old people, but he either turned them loose to shift for themselves or kept them in the tribe in a social position below the young women and children. But there was one old fellow who continued to fool around with a few stones which he had always kept hidden when the warriors were in the village, and finally one day this old fellow decided that he was about ready. When the young men returned from the hunt on this particular day the old man held it aloft for all of them to see. It was a sharpened spear with a long handle he had whittled from the splinter of a tree. Thus began a new era in our intellectual advancement. Humanism was born when it was realized that the old fellow, or the cripple, could sit at home with his legs folded under him and *think*, and thereby actually contribute to the success of the hunt, or even win a battle against an enemy far away.

And all of this carries over into our day-to-day living. In the "youth-worshiping" culture the old folks are not only ashamed of their age as if it were some kind of a crime, but they are terribly ashamed when they have to accept help from their children. In the Jewish culture "it's coming to them." An elderly parent will say, "My children do everything for me," or "My daughter doesn't let me put my hand in cold water."

And so as the Over-40 clubs continue to grapple with their problem of trying to place these "old" people, it would be well to go back to Cicero. He wrote a magnificent essay called, *On Old Age*. It is a dialogue in which Cato, who is eighty-four, is being visited by friends, the general Scipio, who is thirty-five, and Lealius, who is thirty-six. They argue all night, and Cato says it is not really a matter of how young or old you are, that "the unhappy and the

discontented find every age a burden." The argument is summed
up in an agreement to leave it all to the final determinant, Nature.
"Nature," says Cicero, "is not a careless playwright."

The lucky break

THERE is an American myth about the lucky break. I am
as much for luck and hope as the next man, but the sad thing is
that many people forever depend upon chance. They wait for the
telephone to ring and a voice to say, "If you guess the name of
this tune, fifty thousand dollars is yours."

There's an element of luck in success, but all of us know,
secretly, there's not one-hundredth as much luck as there is hard
work.

The sourdough who brings in a pay lode risks his life against
the malignancy of natives and the greed and cunning of fellow
prospectors. And the blonde who's "discovered" on the drugstore
stool has studied dancing and voice since she was five and acting
since she was six, and for the first two years she kicks back half
her salary to that talent scout anyway.

I do not say that there have not been men who made a lucky
investment.

But the luckiest break I ever heard of happened when I was a
desk clerk in the Hotel Markwell. We were "carrying" an actor
and his wife and son. And the actor just couldn't find work. He
was desperate.

Well, one night the actor stopped at a drugstore to make a
phone call. He was down to his last nickel. In the phone booth,
he found a doctor's satchel, and inside, instead of a stethoscope
and scalpels and pills, he found stacks of money. He took the bag
filled with money back to the Markwell. He and his wife counted
over thirty-seven thousand dollars, all in ten-dollar bills. They decided to keep the money.

But during the night his conscience raged. And in the morning,
broke though he was, he told his wife they had to report their

finding to the police. There wasn't any reward. Every bill in the satchel was counterfeit.

I hazard the guess that the actor was lucky. He was lucky because he saved himself a lot of trouble and he discovered something very few of us ever do: that he was basically an honest man.

Enter palsy-walsy—exit respect

WE ARE now well into the third generation. I refer to the great mass of immigrants from 1880 to 1920 who created the fabric of the American Jewish community.

During the process much more than the names have changed. There is the matter, for instance, of the relationship between fathers and sons. It has been adjusted to reflect the society in which we live, and that includes this business of being a pal to your sons. Many fathers go at it hammer and tongs, even to the wearing of the same color shirts and pants, which of course is very cute.

There is this business of doing things together—going fishing together, building things together—and being a real pal, as it were. Are we sure all of this is what it is cracked up to be? It seems to me that the reverence with which sons of immigrants remember their fathers is entirely absent in the children of today. There was a different pattern when I was a boy. No function in the home could begin until your father came home. Today it is just another door opening; someone else shuffles in and the kids do not take their eyes off the TV set.

Your father once enjoyed tremendous respect. It was more or less an aloof relationship. He never told you how much he loved you and rarely, if ever, kissed you, except perhaps on your bar mitzvah or your return from war or from a long trip. All the demonstrative affection belonged to the mother, and of course she went all out. When the father returned from shul, all the children ran toward him, helped him with his coat, made way for him to the table to give the blessing. There was no "going fishing with

Dad" business. It was definitely not a palsy-walsy relationship, yet I know that I speak for thousands when I say that it was the most unforgettable relationship of our lives.

No one spoke till he spoke. He said, "Goot Shabos," or "Good evening," and he looked very stern. Then suddenly his face wreathed in smiles and that was the signal. The kids and women-folk all began talking at once.

This pal business may work out all right, but I have my doubts. Under such a program the father must of necessity boil over into too great an intensity, and that can do the boy far more harm than letting him go fishing alone.

The united fund

THE City of Detroit with its United Foundation claims to have pioneered the idea of combining charities into one fund drive. The City of Denver might also have a good claim to this honor, and the original Federation of Jewish Charities of New York could point out that nearly a half-century ago it put into operation many of the ideas now employed by United Fund appeals.

But if we are looking for the real pioneer of our United Appeals we must go to the Book of Leviticus:

> And when ye reap the harvest of your land, thou shalt not wholly reap the corners of thy field, neither shalt thou gather the gleanings of thy harvest.
>
> And thou shalt not glean thy vineyard, neither shalt thou gather every grape of thy vineyard; thou shalt leave them for the poor and stranger.

And to emphasize the importance of this law, the Deuteronomist defines charity in these terms:

> When thou cuttest down thine harvest in thy field, and hast forgot a sheaf in the field, thou shalt not go again to fetch it: it shall be for the stranger, for the fatherless, and for the

widow: that the Lord thy God may bless thee in all the work of thine hands.

The idea behind these laws was the humanitarianism that a person who needs help should not be shamed by actual contact with his benefactor. You leave the corners of the field partly unharvested and retire from the field and let the needy come and take what they must have, or as we do it today, leave it to trained social workers to handle the funds.

The idea involves the dignity of the individual. Our father Abraham haggled with God, perhaps there are three men worthy of saving in the city, suppose there is only one man worth helping? Here we laid the foundation of our culture—the importance of one man, the importance of any one man or woman anywhere.

Birth control

DOES anyone think that the controversy about the "population explosion" will seriously affect the number of children born?

I am not prepared to explain why we don't need a massive world-wide program of birth control. For the moment I'm only concerned with this circulating nonsense that if we don't institute this program, we will suffocate ourselves through too many people crowding on the planet.

The world faced this problem once before—and solved it. When man was only a predatory animal hunting game for his food, he began to deplete his resources. There were too many hunters. If, at this point in history, man had instituted a program of birth control, there would be sixteen million hunters still living in caves. But man removed the danger of starvation by inventing agriculture.

Let the earth explode with people. Let the planet have ten billion inhabitants. It will be better for it. Just as man invented agriculture at the right moment, so he will invent new nourishment for the hundreds of millions yet unborn.

Why are we so terribly smug about our laboratories when it comes to an atom bomb or a new-style refrigerator, and yet are willing to give up completely when it comes to more people? Why do we insist the only way we can prevent hunger is to prevent people?

Here we are, a highly literate, technologically competent race of men about to launch an investigation of outer space, declaring that our future rests upon Hindu, Puerto Rican, and Amazonian mothers. When a young Hindu girl finds out what we expect of her, that we are depending upon her to save us, she is going to be scared to death.

This does not look familiar

YEARS ago we had a newly arrived cousin from Europe staying at our apartment on the East Side. Naturally, during those weeks, he made other trips—to his job, to the lodge hall, and to other relatives—but in order to go to each of these other places he had to come back to our tenement house and start from there. If he was visiting in one place and had to go to another maybe only a block to the left or right, he couldn't make it; he had to double back a mile or more to our address and start out fresh. I do the same thing. In order for me to go anywhere in town I have to come back to the big hotel in the center of the city.

I am terrible on directions while driving a car. Occasionally when I get lost driving home from a friend's house, I try to find a high point in the road; there I get out and look for the beacon light on top of the city's tallest building. And I drive toward that light, which always reminds me of the command of the Seventh Cavalry in the Civil War—*"Charge to the sound of guns."* I always charge to that beacon light.

On longer trips often I'll be driving along for maybe an hour or an hour and a half, and suddenly I'll look around and in an admonishing tone of voice I will say, *"This does not look familiar —this does not look familiar at all."* It's happened many times, yet I always seem to register surprise. The next thing I do on these occasions is to sing, "*This does not look familiar,*" to the tune of the quartet from *Rigoletto*—all the parts. "*This does not look familiar.*" That's the tenor. Then comes the soprano, followed by the contralto, and finally the baritone, "*No, this does not look familiar, no, it is not familiar at all.*"

When I am through with that part of the trip, I either go back or maybe turn at the next crossroad. It's a funny thing, but in the end everything is all right.

Prayer, love, and food

WHILE all the world's a stage, all the men and women do not read their parts exactly alike. The roles, however, remain the same and the plot rarely varies. We are children, parents, and grandparents. It is at the moments when we think and say the same things that we know everyone in the world is in some way our neighbor.

Not every expression is reserved for one nationality. The English say, "God helps them who help themselves," and the Spaniards say, "God helps him who gets up early." And I have found that when two strangers start to become friends, they start by asking the question, "Are you a married man?" This is the first personal question one man asks another.

Throughout America, February second is Groundhog Day. If the groundhog sees his shadow, he will back up into his burrow and sleep for another six weeks—and we shall have winter.

Now the Chinese believe that the dragon raises his head on the second day of the second lunar month (which happens to be February). The Chinese women don't sew on that day, lest their needles pierce the dragon. With this safeguard the dragon raises his head, and spring begins.

One neighbor may not like another nor necessarily hold in respect things in which his neighbor believes. But all men hold another man's prayers in some degree of awe. Prayer and food are the delays we allow a condemned man.

The entire Judaeo-Christian ethic has for its foundation the supper table, the Feast of the Passover, the bread and the wine, the Last Supper.

The first words to come from one language to another are the words for food. Our language as well as our diet is enlarged by words like spaghetti, pizza, chow mein, blintzes, smorgasbord, pastrami, sauerkraut, bologna, borsch, hors d'oeuvres, and canapés. Speaking of hors d'oeuvres and canapés, they are not inventions of the French. The Egyptians, in fact, put them into the tombs of deceased kings.

I am always amused when I see "spoon bread" on a Southern menu. The girl at the cafeteria counter serves the hot soft corn bread with a large spoon and it is very good with gravy or butter. The spoon bread of the South is the same as the mammaliga I knew as a boy in New York. Romanian corn bread. My mother made it often. Instead of serving it with a spoon, our people sliced it, soft as it was, with a thread. The great fascination was when your mother pulled a hair out of her head and divided the portions. It was a game.

As the Southern boys were waiting for the spoon bread to come out of the oven, other boys five thousand miles away in a Jewish village of Walachia or Bucovina were pleading with their mothers to cut the mammaliga with a hair instead of a thread—just one more time please, mama.

All people laugh and cry in the same way and daydream and hope in the same way.

But I think it is prayer, love, and food that give men a share of a common humanity.

The pin-ups

THESE pin-up girls are just about as sexy as statues in an art museum. Most of them are Narcissus worshipers, fearful of normal sex lest it disturb the contours of their bodies; afraid of the consequences lest it destroy their careers. Most of them, in fact, are completely sexless, wanderers in a sort of no man's land, loving nothing quite so much as their own bodies and jealous and fearful of all its normal functions. That is why they go from husband to husband, looking for something and afraid to find it. Millions of adolescents will continue to pin them up on their walls as their sex fantasies, but if it were strictly a matter of virile, normal sex, all the pin-ups combined are not equal to one spinster schoolteacher with eyeglasses.

Common ground

CONCEIVABLY, if United States Senator Eastland of Mississippi, and Roy Wilkins, head of the NAACP, were to find themselves alone on a desert island, they would be two Americans who would talk only of home.

The marriage of Dick Tracy

SAMUEL BUTLER wrote that he never gave religion his complete credence because God wrote all the books. I am somewhat of Mr. Butler's persuasion as regards marriage. I am wholeheartedly in favor of marriage but lately I have begun to think we are loading the dice against the bachelors. It has come to my attention that all of the adventurous comic-strip heroes are now married. Dick Tracy is married. Smiling Jack is even a widower and Li'l Abner is hitched to Daisy Mae. What makes me a little doubtful of the wonders of marriage is this: do we really need this kind of a crusade? Did we really have to sacrifice the last of our bachelors? Pretty soon, at this rate, we will have crossword puzzles marked "His" and "Hers."

Public sorrow

I REMEMBER riding in a subway once and seeing opposite me a woman sobbing. It is the strangest of all sights, I think, to see a public display of unexplained grief—almost harrowing. Yet the lady who leaves Loew's Poli, a handkerchief dabbing her eyes, is part and parcel of the passing scene.

The bride's secret

WHEN young brides first learn they are pregnant, they never announce it, but instead confide this as though it were a secret. "We're going to have a baby next June," they say, "but please don't tell anyone." "Don't tell anyone"—this is their favorite phrase. I guess that this is part of a ritual we play out.

But the young mother-to-be finds toward the end of her pregnancy that she's on the other end of the boomerang. At the eighth month she finds all the friends and relatives she's whispered her secret to gasp when they meet her out and about and ask, "Aren't you in the hospital yet? I thought you said in June. Oh, you mean the end of June."

I suppose all of this is related to the never-ending awe we feel at the miracle of birth. I've never given away a young bride's secret—if secret it is—and I've never asked them why they weren't in the hospital, but sometimes I suspect I'm disappointing them.

A clinch with a dame

SHAKESPEARE did not have Julius Caesar and Mark Antony achieve only fame and fortune. They went into a clinch with a fabulous dame every so often to the cheers of a hundred generations of audiences and to the end of time. Fame and fortune aren't enough for anybody except for the editors of *The Wall Street Journal*. Without Cleopatra the lives of Julius Caesar and Mark Antony would be pages in *Who's Who* and not in *What's What*. Shakespeare knew *what's what*.

My line-up of drinkers

DOES occupation or trade have anything to do with drinking—the quantity or the ability to hold it? The fellows up at Yale who have been working on an alcoholic survey these many years have not yet published any findings along this line, but from my own observation I am sure occupation has something to do with it. My line-up would go something like this: The lead-off man would be an upholsterer; the number two fellow, a coal miner; in the third important slot, I'd put a printer; and in the clean-up position, a steelworker. Ah, what a team!

The little girl

THE managing editor is smart who uses a picture of a dressed-up little girl as often as possible.

A little girl stands in the center of a room and she can keep winding a bit of ribbon or string around her finger, and she winds and winds endlessly—while a little boy, the moment you take him out of the play-pen, makes a beeline for the doorknob. He wants to get out, and *out* as soon as possible. And therein you have as much to The Story as you will find in a hundred novels.

Courtroom scene

HERE is a scene played out in a thousand juvenile court-rooms every day of the week. Three kids are brought in for some delinquency, each boy brings his mother, and each mother makes out a convincing case before the judge. Her boy would have been all right if only he hadn't fallen in with "bad companions." The three of them are standing there, seriously blaming the "bad companions" and no one sees the humor in the situation at all.

Family development

THERE is one development in family relationships that has become universal. It has come probably as the result of a century of mother-in-law jokes. Wives don't want their husbands to say, "My mother-in-law." The protocol now is, "My wife's mother."

A human mystery

IN THE ghetto there is a proverb: There is always enough money for the shroud.

In my time I have spoken to dozens of men in the Tombs and in the Federal House of Detention (awaiting trial or sentence), and many cases followed an amazing pattern: "I could have squared the rap if I could have raised three hundred dollars."

The family and friends who wouldn't give the fellow three hundred dollars to "square the rap" were now spending one thousand dollars to defend him.

Families who could not raise twenty-five dollars to pay a month's rent and thus avoid having their furniture placed out on the street were now receiving money from all sides because it was for—a funeral.

A mystery of mysteries in our study of human behavior.

Conversation in Rome

In rome I met two lovely Brooklyn ladies in the bar of the Hotel Flora. They were well bred and both were quite handsome. They work for the General Electric Company and they had saved their money religiously for two years in order to make the Grand Tour in style. They had even taken dancing lessons at Arthur Murray's. They told me they had been through France, Switzerland, and Italy. "Not a man did we meet," they said. "Not even one pinch. The only men we came face to face with were the Pope at our audience and Harry Golden at the Flora."

Future of the Jews

When my generation (1880-1914) of immigrants and sons of immigrants finally passes out of the picture, the Jews of America will have lost their tomm (the best definition for this wonderful Yiddish word is "glamour" or "charm" or, better still, what Renan called "the salt in the stew"). By the year 2000 half the Jews will look like Barney Baruch and the other half like Texans, and they will comb the highways and the byways looking for some surviving elderly gent with a beard so they can sit him up on the dais and "enjoy." A survivor with a very heavy accent will command fees of five thousand dollars for a single lecture.

PART 4

Bagels, Bourbon, and
Madama Butterfly

Personal memories

In *Rain*, Jeanne Eagels, as Sadie Thompson, stands in front of her tent on the island of Pago Pago. She is soliciting passing Marines. Coming from her tent is the sound of a tinny phonograph with a terribly scratched record, playing "Wabash Blues." She is wearing high-button shoes, and she is keeping time with one toe and a long-handled umbrella. *This was the most memorable moment I ever experienced in the theater.*

The greatest spontaneous ovations I ever witnessed were those for: (a) President Franklin D. Roosevelt walking down the ramp in Madison Square Garden on the night of his "Martin, Barton, and Fish" speech, and (b) Enrico Caruso singing "La donna è mobile." Despite the ironclad rule against encores at the Metropolitan Opera House, the folks kept up the cheering and shouting, and he had to sing it again; and still they did not let up, until finally Caruso turned his back toward the audience and just stood there with arms folded till things quieted down. Call Caruso an opera singer if you will, but he was a great actor, too, and thousands of people went to the Metropolitan not only to hear him but also to see him walk across the stage, and thousands who heard and saw him have remembered the event all their lives.

Walter Hampden and Ian Keith alternated in the roles of Othello and Iago, and it was a great pleasure to see the play on successive nights. Mr. Hampden was wonderful, and his fencing scene in *Cyrano* is of lasting importance in the annals of the American stage.

I remember, too, Walter Huston in *The Barker* when his only son leaves with the carnival tart, played by Claudette Colbert. John McCormack standing on the banquet table at the Hotel Astor singing, "Oh, How I'll Miss You, Dear Old Pal of Mine"—his final farewell. Ethel Merman marching across the stage singing, "I Got

Rhythm." Fritz Kreisler at Carnegie Hall, the audience rising as he enters.

Rex Harrison, Julie Andrews, and Robert Coote performing "The Rain in Spain" from *My Fair Lady.*

Paul Robeson singing "Shenandoah" for an encore after a Town Hall concert. He tore your heart out with it. Robeson lost these past twenty years, espousing Communist causes. But America lost, too.

John Barrymore delivering again the curtain speech he made after a 10 A.M. performance of *Richard III.* "Shakespeare," he said, "will some day have a theater of his own on Broadway."

There have been some thrilling moments in the movies, too. When Victor McLaglen is standing in that cellar before the Irish patriots, trying to squirm out of the accusation that he had betrayed his best friend to the Black and Tans, in *The Informer*—that was probably the greatest single moment in motion pictures.

The *Lambs Gambol* was usually held at the Metropolitan Opera House on a Sunday night each year. The Lambs Club is the famous actors' fraternity which does not permit women to membership or into the clubhouse. The *Gambol* was the annual benefit for the actors' fund. Along about 1926 or 1927 I saw the first public experiment with television. The television screen at the *Lambs Gambol* showed Gloria Swanson sitting in her suite at the Waldorf-Astoria, saying, "I am the first woman to appear on a *Lambs Gambol* stage." All the great actors did their stuff. Will Rogers was the master of ceremonies and as the night wore on, he would announce the train schedules for people living in Connecticut, New Jersey, and in the suburbs. The *Gambol* usually lasted till about 5 A.M., and then everyone went out and had breakfast. Of all the performances there, from John Barrymore to Spencer Tracy and Al Jolson, the most memorable was a mere recitation by the cowboy actor, William S. Hart. He recited "The Shooting of Wild Bill Hickok" and acted it out to the climax when he pulls his two guns. It was so terrific they tore the house down with applause from the leading professional actors of the world. At one *Lambs Gambol,* Will Rogers enticed old John Philip Sousa to step up and take the baton. I remember that old white-bearded gent waving his arm up and down at his side as the orchestra played "The Stars and Stripes Forever." Everyone was standing, and most people were bawling like children.

The funniest of all "single" acts was not performed on the stage, but at a theatrical banquet at the Astor Hotel many years ago. Most of the guests were associated with the theater and motion-picture industries—producers, directors, agents, and many famous actors and actresses. It should be emphasized that many of these people were Jews, from the Shuberts on Broadway to the Zuckers of Hollywood; that is the whole point of this story. Will Rogers was the master of ceremonies. After the dinner everybody settled down to listen to a talk by that famous cowboy humorist. Chewing on his gum and in that famous Western drawl of his, Rogers delivered his entire speech in Yiddish. He started off: "Mein tierer schwester and brudder . . ." and never once faltered. In good Yiddish he told them that he was about to reveal a secret—that he really was a Jew. He went on to say that he was born in the Ukraine and joined a troupe of wandering gypsies at the age of seven; and that Morris Gest found him, brought him to America, and taught him his rope trick.

Later it was revealed that Eddie Cantor had written out the speech in phonetics and Will Rogers had memorized it perfectly.

And when Ethel Barrymore, as the Welsh schoolteacher, read from her miner-pupil's homework—". . . and when I walk in the dark . . . I can touch with my hands where the corn is green"—this, too, became an unforgettable experience.

The best speak-easy of the old days was called The Deauville Club on West Fifty-seventh Street. It was operated by a big fellow by the name of Charlie Hansen who had refurnished the home of Isadora Duncan and made it into a beautiful café. It was probably the only place of its kind where you actually needed a card of admission. The food was magnificent—out of this world—and the more or less "respectable" people in public life went there to eat, as much as to drink the refreshments which Mr. Hansen served to you in coffee cups with saucer and spoon. Mr. Hansen, very popular, was married to the screen star of the silent movies, Lillian Walker, and was being "chased" by most of the beauties of the day. A little over ten years ago I saw Mr. Hansen. He was a bartender in a Sixth Avenue beer saloon.

Sports in Israel

TENSION is relaxing in Israel and the country in its moments of leisure is beginning to take to sports.

Its sports are universal because all its peoples are immigrants. They have golf courses outside of Tel Aviv and many swimming pools are in the last stages of construction. The South African and British immigrants have introduced bowls and cricket. American immigrants have introduced baseball and a stadium is being built where some enthusiastic Israelis foresee a Trinational World Series among America, Israel, and Japan.

The Israelis are trying on many sports for size, but the national game is soccer. And what could be more natural? Israel is made up of flat spacious plains and a warm climate. Its young men are hardened and healthy and need a game where they can shout and run and kick. Soccer is probably the oldest game in the world. It started, I suppose, when some primitive savages began kicking an empty skull around a field.

I have no doubt that eventually soccer will be the game all Israelis play.

The two great indices of a national character are always reflected in sport and art: art because it is so self-conscious; sport because it is so un-self-conscious. A man may write good poetry because he has conscientiously studied the great poets, or because he has hit upon a happy rhyme scheme: but he goes to a ball game because he played it as a boy and he understands it thoroughly. In sports a nation, like a man, can be utterly honest with itself.

On the Lower East Side, for instance we did not play soccer because there was no space in the street. We knew it was called "Gaelic football" and that Irish teams played occasionally in the Polo Grounds, but the sport held no interest for us.

Nor did we play much baseball. We played a variant of it, called "stickball," with a broom handle and a five-cent rubber ball and the diamond was from fire hydrant to fire hydrant with the manhole cover, second base, in between. As a consequence Jewish ballplayers did not start wearing the uniforms of the big-league teams until the late thirties. Sid Gordon and Hank Greenberg were Jewish ballplayers, but the Jews never produced a Babe Ruth or a Willie Mays.

The great sports heroes the Jews produced were the basketball players and the boxers.

For many years the East Side Jews had a monopoly on all of the great basketball players. Although the Jews did not invent the game they took immediately to it—for the same reason they took to boxing, because it was an indoor sport. The city Jews produced Nat Holman and Benny Leonard, two of the greatest of their kind.

We were also notorious handball addicts, which we played constantly, using the side of a building until the janitor or the cop on the beat chased us.

The city Jews also produced some football players, but never in great quantities. We do have some all-time greats and they are invariably passers. They get the ball and run far back and toss a long, long lob downfield, the way an infantryman tosses a mortar shell. The Texans and the Southern boys throw short bullet passes all over the field, but a city street does not allow this type of passing. You have to run back and throw the ball high and long so that the fellow who's going to catch the pass can outrace the trolley car as well as the opposition. This is the way Sid Luckman used to throw.

These same city boys, now grown to maturity, are trying like mad to introduce these sports into Israel. But the Israelis aren't interested. Who wants to play handball in a city block when a whole countryside is waiting for someone to kick a soccer ball around? The reluctance of the Israelis to adopt these indoor sports enthusiastically causes some tears in the eyes of rich Jewish businessmen, but the Israelis know what they are doing, just as the East Side boys knew. They are making the best of what they have.

Verdi's surprise

GIUSEPPE VERDI in Italy, like Victor Hugo in France, fought for the freedom of the human spirit and the dignity of the individual. Like Hugo, he too was exiled by a dictator in his land. He never compromised with his libertarianism and rationalism. When the Russian czar commissioned Verdi to write an opera he knew that Verdi was likely to use an embarrassing theme based on an autocratic tyrant, so he urged him to use some other country, not Russia, for his setting, and that's all. This was the opera, *La Forza del Destino*, which Verdi obligingly set in a Spanish background. When he was well over seventy Verdi was commissioned by the khedive of Egypt to write an opera to commemorate the Egyptian coronation. Verdi wanted to get out of it so he asked for the unheard-of fee of a quarter of a million dollars. The Egyptian court accepted without any hesitation and Verdi wrote *Aida*, the first performance of which was produced at the base of the Egyptian Pyramids. These "opening nights" harassed Verdi all his life. A new opera requires weeks of preparation and rehearsal. This means that you are working with at least ten artists; soprano, mezzo-soprano, contralto, tenor, baritone, basso, etc., as well as about two hundred others; orchestra, ballet, chorus, stagehands, directors, prompters, scenery designers. These people go home every night and mingle with friends and relatives. So what happens? By the time opening night rolls around, all of Italy is singing and humming the opera. They are as familiar with the music as though they had heard it all their lives. This always made Verdi mad as hell. He would take his place before the orchestra on the evening of the "grand opening," and behind him his fellow Italians anticipated every movement of his baton and some were even prompting the singers. But what could Verdi do about it? Finally he had his inning. When he rehearsed his masterpiece, *Rigoletto*, he withheld the famous tenor solo, probably the most famous tenor aria in all Italian opera, "La donna è mobile":

How fickle women are,
Just like an evil star,
Light as a feather gay,
False as an April day.

On the morning of the grand opening at La Scala in Milan, Verdi
called together the members of the orchestra and his principals
and gave them each the music of this great aria carefully arranged
for each instrument. Then he locked all the doors and told the
tenor to keep at it all day long. That night the Italians, as usual,
were all smiles and kept time with Maestro Verdi's every movement. Then came the end of the second act—and suddenly the
tenor sitting in the darkened inn opens up with this tremendous
"La donna è mobile," and as the audience of three thousand Italians
sat there open-mouthed, old Verdi put down his baton, turned
around to the audience, and put his thumb to his nose.

The night I felt like Oscar Hammerstein

IT ALL started one day some years ago when I read that
Margaret Webster was on tour and I had a hankering to see *The
Taming of the Shrew*.

So I brought Miss Webster to Charlotte in one of her Shakespeare productions. I packed every nook and cranny of the huge
Charlotte Armory Auditorium—for Shakespeare.

My sortie as a producer was so successful that Sol Hurok's office
sent down an investigator to find out what I had done. I explained
the important fact that the Mecklenburg County (Charlotte) English Teachers Association had won permission for me to sell tickets
in the classrooms.

At the start, I called the Hurok office and agreed to the stipulated
cost of fifteen hundred dollars for a one-night stand. I thought it
would be easy to sell that many tickets and by my one little phone
call I had proved myself a responsible, community-minded citizen.

Where in the world I got the idea that this large troupe of

players, this freight car of electrical equipment, this half acre of costumes would be routed to Charlotte in the hope that I'd sell enough tickets that night, I'll never know. Because the next communication I received not only asked for the advance payment of the fifteen hundred dollars, but additional cash and surety bonds for insurance, union stagehand salaries, promotional advertising, a deposit for an electrical contractor, and the costs of printing tickets and programs.

What to do? I didn't have the money. I couldn't sign a check for fifty dollars unless I did it in the spirit of adventure. I never opened the bank statements. I kept them unopened and sent them to the accountant every six months. If there was nothing in the checking account, I didn't want to be annoyed worrying about it. If there was, well, it was all to the good, like a bonus.

So I went to one of Charlotte's leading citizens—George M. Ivey, owner of the J. B. Ivey Department Store. Without blinking an eyelash he told his secretary to draw a check in the huge amount I needed. I sent the check off to the Hurok office and we were in business.

On the afternoon of the performance I went out to the Auditorium with six tickets I was bringing along, reasoning that there'd be some folks rushing up at the last minute. When I got there I found a line already halfway around the block. I sacrificed lots of money that evening because I'd brought no change. People wanted two tickets which came to $4.40. They gave me a five-dollar bill. I'd peek at that long, winding line behind them, shrug, and give back a dollar for change. After a while I just threw the money on the floor. I found this a better system. I could serve the customers faster.

And still they came. I had reserved the balcony for forty seats I'd sold to the Johnson C. Smith University (Negro). At the last minute, two buses from the fashionable girls' school, Winthrop College, pulled up under the marquee. There were no more tickets left for the orchestra. I told the chaperons the only seats available were in the balcony alongside these Negro college students. The heroine of this story was one of these lady professors who said without hesitating, "Of course we'll take them." Upstairs they went. Nothing happened.

I did not look at the play at all. I walked up and down the foyer, opening the door every five minutes to look at the audience. I had a big cigar. All I needed was the high silk hat to make me feel like Oscar Hammerstein I.

The day after the performance I knew it would be dramatic if I returned Mr. Ivey's money straight from the box-office till—the crumbled fives, tens, twenties, and bagful of change. But you'd be surprised how cumbersome it is to carry that much money in small bills. After some thought I decided the inconvenience would outweigh the drama, so I paid Mr. Ivey by check.

Where are the poets?

When Edna St. Vincent Millay sneaked out of her college dormitory and spent the night with her Bohemian friends in Greenwich Village, she sat down next morning and wrote a poem about it. Now that's what I call poetry!

Today the narrative poem, the epic, the verse that tells a story, is a thing of the past. Each of our poets is obsessed with the idea of writing for "posterity" and afraid to mention a contemporary event or personage lest it lose its meaning for lovers of poetry in the year 2060. This thins the ranks of those who can understand their poetry in the year 1960. And you must be either a trained psychiatrist or a subscriber to the *Partisan Review* to understand the poems of T. S. Eliot, E. E. Cummings, Ezra Pound, Delmore Schwartz, and others. The average man can read them upside down or sideways with equal results.

With all the tremendous events of the past thirty years, unparalleled in all of human history, we have not had a single story poem. With the exception of those gifted Negroes of Jamaica who greeted Winston Churchill with a ballad which sang of his political triumphs, our poets seem to lack a sense of history. Isn't it a function of the poet to teach us history, to give us a sense of time and place?

> Listen, my children, and you shall hear
> Of the midnight ride of Paul Revere!

Except for Stephen Vincent Benét and Carl Sandburg, who has written anything like that in our generation? There was a battle at Balaklava during the Crimean War, and Alfred, Lord Tennyson sat down and wrote a poem about it. He taught us that Britain and Russia were natural enemies, because it was part of British policy to keep Russia behind the Dardanelles. Lord Tennyson did not tell us all of that in his poem, but we found out soon enough.

> Half a league, half a league,
> Half a league onward,
> All in the valley of Death
> Rode the six hundred.
> "Forward, the Light Brigade!
> Charge for the guns!" he said;
> Into the valley of Death
> Rode the six hundred.

Who hasn't thrilled to the Lord Byron lines on the Battle of Waterloo?

> There was a sound of revelry by night,
> And Belgium's capitol had gather'd then
> Her Beauty and her Chivalry, and bright
> The lamps shone o'er fair women and brave men.

And then Lord Byron gives us the details. The young men rush off to meet Napoleon, with courage, heroism, and death.

> Last noon beheld them full of lusty life,
> Last eve in Beauty's circle proudly gay,
> The midnight brought the signal-sound of strife, . . .
> The earth is cover'd thick with other clay,
> Which her own clay shall cover, heap'd and pent,
> Rider and horse,—friend, foe,—in one red burial blent!

The great poets of the past spoke their minds. Robert Browning in 1885 wrote, in "Why I Am a Liberal":

> But little do or can the best of us:
> That little is achieved through Liberty.
> Who, then, dares hold, emancipated thus,
> His fellow shall continue bound? Not I,
> Who live, love, labor freely, nor discuss
> A brother's right to freedom. That is "Why."

And Lord Byron spoke of life, and its problems with an eye everlastingly on the passing parade!

> One of the two according to your choice,
> Woman or wine, you'll have to undergo;
> Both maladies are taxes on our joys:
> But which to choose, I really hardly know;
> And if I had to give a casting voice,
> For both sides I could many reasons show,
> And then decide, without great wrong to either,
> It were much better to have both than neither.

Lord Byron—what a man! After uttering his name, you must show proper respect and wait at least ten years before speaking the name of T. S. Eliot or Evelyn Waugh, the poor imitator of that poor imitation, Hilaire Belloc.

Where are the poets of yesteryear?

What about the P.T.A.?

THE country has some monumental problems in education. What can we do about the sixty thousand teachers who leave the profession for private industry and by death and retirement every year? How can we qualify the one million teachers we will need in the next five years? What shall we do about the P.T.A.?

This last, I think, is quite important. While everyone has talked thoroughly about education, very few, if any, have discussed the

P.T.A. Ostensibly the Parent-Teacher Association was formed to help protect the child in the classroom. Since its formation, however, a goodly number of teachers have been badly knifed in the classrooms. Three teachers were killed, two others died of wounds, and at least ten were so badly incapacitated that they had to be retired. There has not been a single student casualty.

Yet despite these figures, the P.T.A. devotes its energies to protecting the child in the classroom. And they keep badgering the teachers to insure an even greater security. But it would seem the kids are safe enough, and it is time now for the P.T.A. to turn to the great work it can do in the field of elementary and secondary school education.

If the P.T.A. changed its course, it would remove some of the dehumanizing and degrading elements it has fostered upon the teachers. "The P.T.A.," brags one of its members, "gave the teachers a new sofa in the restroom." But to get that new sofa the teachers had to beg and implore the P.T.A. in a succession of bitter night meetings for over a year. And why should the P.T.A. have had anything to do with the teachers' restroom? The restroom is part of the educational process. It is a direct responsibility of the taxpayers. A women's restroom is part of the newspaper game and no employee has to quarrel for a year with a publisher to get it.

When the P.T.A. assembles for its first meeting each fall, thousands of parents confront outnumbered teachers with questions like: "Explain what you will expect to teach." "How much homework?"

There is nothing unkind in these questions. Nor does the P.T.A. mean to be offensive. Nor does the P.T.A. mean to be thoughtless when its members telephone a schoolteacher six times during the dinner hour. But to deny that the P.T.A. introduces an area of intimidation into the educational structure of a local school system would be stupid.

The insurance executive who accompanies his wife to the P.T.A. meeting and asks the teacher sternly why she gave Johnny a C instead of the B Johnny needs to get into college does not realize he is intruding upon another person's professional competence. The insurance executive wouldn't tolerate a question about company investments or officers' salaries from an insured, but the teacher is supposed to answer his questions because for your taxes you get to bully teachers.

Education is a business only between teacher and student, not between parents and teachers. The proof of this is the fact that there is no P.C.A. (Parent-Composer Association), no P.N.A. (Parent-Newspaper Association), no P.T.V.A. (Parent-Television Association). Richard Rodgers, John Knight, and David Sarnoff wouldn't dream of sitting down once a week with a lot of grumbling mothers. No parents are clamoring to "help" Rodgers, Knight, and Sarnoff work out their problems; and music, newspapers, and television are as much part of their children's lives as school.

The work of the P.T.A. is ahead of it. What the Farmers' Grange did for the farmers, the labor unions for the workingmen, and the N.A.M. for the manufacturers, the P.T.A. could do for education. Will they leave the teachers alone and direct their activities toward the State legislature and local school board?

Of bagels and bialys

Is THIS the time to write about bagels? Statesmen discuss the fate of the world, the Russians have hit the moon, a crucial national election is almost upon us, and there are a hundred points of tension on the planet. Some might question the wisdom of an essay on breakfast rolls.

But let us consider the wonderful world of rolls.

The English muffin is becoming increasingly popular, and so is the blueberry muffin, and the French brioche. And up in the Hotel Congress in Portland, Oregon, they serve a traditional hard roll, shaped more or less like a football except it is flat on the bottom. It is the best roll of its kind in America, with a very crisp, brown crust. This hard roll is delicious with butter and a hot cup of coffee.

On the Lower East Side we had the "shtongle," or, as it was more properly called, the "zaltz shtongle." It was a long thin roll, about six inches in length, and its crust was covered with salt and caraway seeds.

The Italian breadstick was much thinner, measuring about the circumference of a finger. It was superb for dunking. The American culture, too, has developed some fine rolls—the hot biscuits served under strawberry jam in New England and dripping with honey in the South. We shall have to include the Parker House rolls, and the "white-mountain" roll which is sprinkled with flour after baking. The American home-fried doughnut, while sweet, has to be numbered among our cultural achievements.

From Europe the immigrant brought the Vienna roll. It has a hard crust, liberally seeded, and bakeries in New York City still bake thousands of them Saturday night for that big Sunday morning breakfast. Similar to the Vienna roll was the smaller and not quite so thick Kaiser roll which the Lower East Side immigrants called a "zeml." For a long time many of us school children looked forward to a lunch consisting of two zemls and a father-sized cup of coffee. There was also the magnificent "platzel," a flat onion roll. The platzel was made by baking onions into the soft dough. Toasted and loaded with cream cheese, the platzel makes breakfast or lunch the supreme moment of the day.

Most famous of all Jewish rolls perhaps is the bagel. The bagel is the size of a doughnut, hard, glazed to a shine, and serves best as the base for a sandwich made of cream cheese and lox. The delicacy is world-renowned and because of this the word bagel has long since entered into the American language. But this is only because the "bialy" (pronounced bee-olly) has not had such good public relations nor so good a press as the bagel.

The bialy is named after the city of Bialystok where Gregory Ratoff was born. The bialy follows the idea of the bagel, having a hole in the middle, but it is soft and shapeless and, like the platzel, baked with onions.

Its unique qualities derive from the ability of master bakers to time to the precise second how long the dough can stand. In other industries these bakers would be emotionally, temperamentally, and physically equipped to construct precision Swiss movements in watches or to split eighty-carat diamonds accurately and easily.

I think it is important in these days that I write this tribute to the bialy. Personally I believe that toasting spoils its tantalizingly sour taste. Just cut the bialy carefully, cram it with cream cheese, take it with hot tea or coffee, and enjoy! enjoy!

Ethel's finest hour

ETHEL BARRYMORE belonged to the Royal Family of the American stage. She never had a written contract with Mr. Frohman, her manager (can you imagine anyone not keeping an agreement with Ethel Barrymore?). Miss Barrymore had no "grievances." She was on the top, ready to go into rehearsal for *Déclassé*, her greatest triumph. The world of art was at her feet.

It was 1919 and the actors had gone out on strike! Then this great lady made her statement:

"While my entire theatrical career has been associated with but one management from whom I have received only fairness and consideration, I feel that . . . traditions of my family . . . and I therefore associate myself with the members of my profession in the Actors' Equity Association . . . and shall join the picket lines. . . ."

Hundreds of hungry actors literally wept for joy as they heard Miss Barrymore's statement. People cried and hugged each other and on the day Ethel Barrymore walked into the Equity headquarters, the striking men and women all tried to kiss the hem of her skirt.

Out of that strike grew Actors' Equity Association, one of the best and most admired trade unions in America. The president of Equity does not draw a six-figured salary nor does he live in a union-supported ranch house and talk every day with a union-paid broker. The president of Equity is an actor and the incumbent is that fine gentleman Ralph Bellamy. The executive secretary who runs the business of this union is, of course, a professional man, but almost all other officers of this union are working actors. The strike which led to the formation of Equity was a bitter one. For months the proprietor of the Algonquin Hotel, Frank Case, fed the hungry actors, and thereby earned their undying gratitude, and made the Algonquin a New York landmark.

The actors' terms were simple: eight shows and no more a week; a minimum wage for any speaking part; the management to furnish costumes and rehearsal pay.

For many months there was only one play running on Broadway and that was *John Ferguson* by St. John Ervine (who a few years ago wrote that wonderful biography of George Bernard Shaw). The newly formed Theatre Guild had produced this play and were the only producers to meet the demands of the actors. For many weeks the actors lived in the hope of making one more dent and it was the old actor Frank Bacon who finally turned the tide. Frank Bacon was starring in a play called *Lightnin'* which he had also written. The play was doing wonderful business and everyone thought Frank Bacon would not surrender the acclaim he had sought for so long. But at one of the strike meetings he stood up and said that he had spent forty years in cheap hotels drinking cold coffee, and he guessed if he stood it that long he could always go back to it, and he would honor the demands of the other actors and not cross the picket lines. The next day and every day thereafter there was the cast of *Lightnin'* in a horse-drawn wagon parading around Times Square with the slogan "Lightnin' Has Struck!"

At the time, the managers stated publicly that a strike by the actors would destroy the theater. Yet this proved untrue. After the formation of Equity we had Eugene O'Neill and the great realistic plays like *What Price Glory?* and the golden age of the twenties with Ziegfeld, Marilyn Miller, the Astaires, Al Jolson, Eddie Cantor, and Jeanne Eagels. We began to get better actors for the simple reason that actors could concentrate on their craft. Before the strike actors and actresses had to go to the Little Church Around the Corner to get married because no other New York church thought them respectable. Actors occupy an honored position in our society now, our colleges have departments of drama, and no major newspaper is without a drama critic.

The *Evening Graphic*

DADDY BROWNING was a wealthy old man who one day legally "adopted" a teen-age girl. A little later they were married and shortly thereafter divorced. The divorce proceedings afforded a field day for the scandal sheets. But no one made hay out of the divorce suit like Bernarr Macfadden's *Evening Graphic*. When Peaches told the jury Daddy had bruised her, Macfadden's paper said he beat her and ran a four-column picture showing a woman disrobed before a jury. It looked like Peaches had bared all, but all the *Graphic* had done was to superimpose Peaches' face on another photo.

Up in the fancy schools of Westchester County the garbage collectors were bootlegging copies of the *Graphic* to the students at a dollar a copy. The girls of the 1920's slept with the *Graphic* hidden under their pillows just as their grandmothers of the 1890's slept with French novels under theirs.

What a paper the *Graphic* was! There was an old joke that went around that described it precisely:

Out-of-town visitor: And what are you doing in New York?

Reporter: I work for the *Evening Graphic*.

Out-of-town visitor: Isn't that interesting!

Reporter: But please don't tell my mother about it when you get back.

Out-of-town visitor: Why not? What does your mother think you do for a living?

Reporter: My mother thinks I play the piano in a whorehouse.

Yet there is something pleasant about the memory of the *Graphic*, the memory of a time when the most important thing to occupy the American consciousness was Peaches and Daddy Browning. I'd much rather worry about Daddy Browning's marital relations than about fallout from the hydrogen bomb which shrivels the bones. I'd rather have Peaches Browning and the *Graphic* warm my bones.

Bernarr Macfadden sold seven million copies of all his publica-

tions every week. He started the true-confession type of magazine
and the magazine *Liberty* made physical culture a national phenomenon. But he was so dedicated to physical culture, that in the
end it betrayed him. Macfadden started the *Graphic* to help him
win the nomination for Governor. But since Macfadden had much
publicized his own health program—sleeping on the floor, doing
two hundred pushups in the morning, never touching a drink or a
sweet—the party bosses shied off. People may tolerate reforms, but
they'll never tolerate a build-up-your-health regime.

When Bernarr Macfadden died a lot of wonderful nonsense vanished from the world.

The ghetto of Rome

For three days I lived in the ghetto of Rome. Through a
rabbi I arranged an introduction to a young man who agreed to my
plan. I would send his wife and two children to the seaside resort
of Ostia where I would rent a room and a kitchenette for them.
As soon as they left on their first vacation, I moved in with the
husband. The ghetto is crowded and it is only by some such arrange-
ment that an American tourist could live there.

I moved into a two-room apartment with my friend, a thirty-two-
year-old man as handsome as Robert Taylor. The Italian Jews, like
their non-Jewish neighbors, are probably the handsomest men in
the world.

While the Porta Judeorum, the Gate of the Jews, is still there,
the ghetto is a voluntary ghetto. Even so, it is not simple to enter
the open society in Italy. Classes are stratified both as to income
and religion.

The ghetto however was not always voluntary. In fact, it was
one of the first compulsory ghettos founded. Pope Paul IV founded
it by edict in 1556. He made it against the law for Jews in Italy
and Rome to live for longer than a month in any place that did
not have a synagogue. Once the Jews had collected around their

sanctuaries, he walled them in. Prior to this time Jews had lived in ghettos as a matter of convenience. From this time on the ghetto, however, became compulsory and so it remained until Napoleon started the revival of political liberties. The last of the restrictions were struck away when the secular power of the popes ceased with the ascension of King Victor Emmanuel II, who made Jews complete citizens in 1870.

When some Jews of the ghetto leave it for the open society and enter the mainstream of Italian culture, more usually than not they break all ties with the Jewish community. This is also true in France. Only in America, Canada, and the United Kingdom of the Western world has it been feasible for a Jew to participate at every level of society while maintaining complete identity as a Jew.

Seven churches, built in the Middle Ages, surround the ghetto. These churches were built primarily to convert the Jews they surrounded. Enforced attendance at these churches was a law. Jews listened to three or four sermons every week about Christianity. It is interesting to note that the seven churches are relics today, while in front of the synagogues within the ghetto peddlers swarm about selling cameos, tourist plans, and post cards.

In the Rome ghetto there are two sanctuaries—one for the Sephardic (Spanish) Jews and one for the eastern European Jews. My friend followed the Sephardic rituals but spoke Yiddish fluently because his mother had been a Polish girl.

Poverty, unsanitary conditions, and the general neglect are all too evident in the ghetto. The residents shrugged about this, but boasted that in the ghetto there is no prostitution—and this is surprising in a city where the streetwalkers outnumber the tourists. But this distinction is small comfort in a situation of such poverty and lack of sanitation. I asked my host about himself and the hundreds of other strong, handsome Jews I saw scavenging for rags, peddling, and hawking. Why not go to Israel? If not for themselves, for their children? I asked it of other ghetto residents who entertained me. Their replies were always ambiguous.

I asked the rabbi why so many Italian Jews endured the listlessness and the poverty of the ghetto instead of emigrating.

Israel, said the rabbi, means work. The ghetto corrupts. Men, he said, simply get used to doing nothing.

Despite this, I hope someday to return to the ghetto of Rome— with its great synagogues, its Catholic churches, its filthy courtyards fronting the tenements without plumbing, the sound of a phonograph somewhere playing Verdi and Mascagni—all overlooking one of the fountains of Rome built by Bernini himself.

Madama Butterfly at the Met

AT LAST we Verdi, Puccini, and Rossini lovers are coming into our own. For years the snobs had us at great disadvantage. "*Traviata? Butterfly?* Ehe," they'd say, "that's for the organ grinders."

But see what's happened. First Mme. Callas performed a *Traviata* such as no opera lover had ever heard. Mme. Callas brought something back from the golden age of opera—excitement. After this the Met produced *Madama Butterfly* with a Japanese stage director and handsome Mme. Antoinette Stella. They came right back with Verdi's *Otello* with Leonard Warren and Mme. Victoria de Los Angeles, which the critics acclaimed as the best *Otello* ever produced in New York. The record stores report they cannot keep Renata Tebaldi's recordings in stock.

So we Verdi, Puccini, Donizetti, Rossini, and Mascagni boys need no longer suffer insults from the Stravinsky, Bartók, Buxtehude, and other "Water Music" snobs. The trouble with the "Water Music" fellows is that they never listened to the music. I suppose Spohr and Purcell *aficionados* identified great opera with robust Italians, women with huge breasts, and tenors who pinched the soprano during her rendition of "Mia Patria" in *Aïda*. They sought gentility. But they missed the point.

Why did immigrants love the "Sextette" from *Lucia* and the "Intermezzo" from *Cavalleria?* At the Sweet Sixteen party there was always a girl who sang the "Sextette":

Softly chimes the hour of parting.
One more kiss before
We part again.
Ta ra ra-ra ta ra ra ra ra ra-ra—

And from a thousand tenement stoops on a warm summer's evening you'd hear the boys practicing the "Intermezzo" on a mandolin. The reason is, I suppose, that you can sing these arias right along with the basso and the diva. You do not need a musical education to appreciate "Un Bel Di Vedremo."

If *My Fair Lady* can run forever, why can't *La Traviata* and *Otello* and *Madama Butterfly* run on alternating evenings for at least six months? This would end that deficit the Met is always worrying about.

This repertoire business was based on the assumption that only the very rich could support opera. They purchased their loges and boxes at stiff annual fees and, in return, expected a different opera for each of their subscription tickets. Thousands of people today would reserve seats for all three operas during their winter vacations in the big city. It would be an event, and indeed a memorable one.

Bourbon whisky

MANY wonderful things have come out of Pennsylvania. The first oil, the ancestors of many of my Presbyterian neighbors of North Carolina, and bourbon whisky. Bourbon is whisky which is at least 51 per cent corn. The manufacture of bourbon began when Pennsylvania farmers had a problem moving grain to the markets. The wagons moving from western Pennsylvania to the East took a terrible beating over mountains and impassable roads. Since these farmers were already distilling corn into whisky for their own use, they reasoned, why not distill it for public consumption?

One fifth of a bushel of corn (eleven pounds) makes one gallon of whisky. This meant fewer wagons, fewer trips, and more money. But the Federal Government under Alexander Hamilton cracked down on them. The Government levied the whisky tax. The hardier spirits among these Pennsylvanians said to hell with it and moved their families, possessions, and distilling skills westward into Kentucky. I mean no direspect to all my friends in Kentucky, but this fine bourbon came out of Pennsylvania.

Test of civilization

JOHN CROWE RANSOM, the poet and literary critic who has taught for nearly fifty years at Vanderbilt and Kenyon, once edited a little primer for college freshmen. This book has long been out of print, but one day last year a big trucking operator came to visit this gentle professor. He had this little primer with him. The trucking operator wanted to go to court to challenge a decision the Interstate Commerce Commission had once handed down against his concern. He visited Mr. Ransom and showed him the decision and pointed out the paragraph, all in a single sentence, which prohibited him from using a certain route in another state. He asked this teacher if this sentence made sense. Mr. Ransom studied the sentence and parsed it. It was filled with adversative clauses and subjunctive clauses and but-for clauses, and Mr. Ransom discovered it also lacked any objective clause. This was all the trucker needed. He went to court and introduced only one expert witness—John Crowe Ransom.

The high-water mark of civilization is when a people can listen to one of their own poets.

The seven horsemen

MR. HERMAN SHUMLIN and I were waiting backstage in the Cort Theatre on the night of November 19. It was 7:55 P.M. and we could hear the opening-night audience quiet as the stage manager brought the house lights down. There was a moment of breathless silence, then the stage manager said, "House out. Curtain!" Mr. Shumlin raised the curtain and we could hear the audience applauding the set. At the first line Mr. Shumlin started for the stage door on his way home, his work done. I said, "Mr. Shumlin, what do you think?" Mr. Shumlin turned back, stared at the set a moment before he answered, "It's all in the hands of the seven men."

Mr. Shumlin was talking of the play *Only in America*, which he had produced and directed. The seven men were the seven dramatic critics of the New York daily press.

After the third-act curtain had descended and well-wishers had deserted backstage, Jerry Lawrence and Bob Lee, the authors of the play based on my book, and I met at the Lee apartment to wait for the reviews.

Lawrence and Lee, who have seen many of their shows open on Broadway, have a friend who telephones them from each of the morning newspapers as soon as the review is set in type. The phone rang and we listened to the first review, in the *Herald Tribune*: "There is, I believe, a notion in the trade that Broadway success can be guaranteed by quite a simple formula: you grab yourself a best-selling book, and just add water. In this instance, the water—a veritable Niagara of false emotion and stretched-out jokes—drowns everything."

It wasn't long before the other votes started to come in. Some were what the trade calls "mixed." But it was no go and we knew it.

It might seem that bad reviews, which often herald the closing of a play and the loss of money to the backers, loss of work to the actors, and a loss of prestige and time to the producer, authors, and directors, would result in bitterness. But the opposite is true. Bad reviews are not welcomed, but everyone connected with *Only in America* knew what he was doing and was morally prepared. A play is presented for the critics' scrutiny and the risks are understood.

People are willing to accept these risks for the simple reason that these critics represent our last bastion of integrity. They can neither

be bullied nor seduced into writing good reviews nor will they hold
a grudge against any play until they've seen it. The one wonderful
thing about reviews is that you don't have to wait long. You are
not dragged through the lower courts and you do not become old
and weary waiting for the final decision. What makes the theater so
exciting is this very thing—you are spared the greatest of all
tragedies of dying, the *lingering* death.

A play takes up a year of heartache to get to Broadway, but the
critics render the decision within an hour and fifteen minutes, and
it is a major decision, one from which there is little appeal. The
theater is probably the only business in the world where a major
decision is made so quickly, with so little fuss, bother, or delay, and
with so much celerity and honesty.

Watching a play being born and making the long trip from Charlotte to New York to Philadelphia to Broadway is worth it, and
when bad reviews come your way, you can be excused for thinking
these seven critics look a little like some desolating, scything horsemen, laying waste before them. Indeed, they are no less than the
Seven Horsemen of the Apocalypse, and may their tribe increase.

The weekly press

THE weekly press is regaining the prestige and influence it
had at the turn of the century. After the first decade of the 1900's,
the weeklies around the country began to slide downward. The
reason was William Randolph Hearst. Whatever one may think of
Mr. Hearst's life and politics, he put a new vitality into his papers
around the country. He applied the personal touch; he made contact with the people and kept it for thirty years. The people in
the cities, in the counties, and in the country grabbed his papers.
Gradually the weekly press took a back seat, and coming out of
the Depression, the weeklies were associated mostly with the lists
of delinquent county taxpayers, or the medium used by lawyers
for divorce notices and other legals to make sure that no one
connected with the case would see it. But all of that has changed.

As fast as the weekly press continues to go up, the daily press is going down. I do not mean down necessarily in earnings. The dailies made mistakes during the wave of prosperity and easy advertising dollars. The major mistake was that the daily lost contact with the people. Into this breach the weekly press jumped with both feet.

The vigor of the daily press is slowly disappearing, and in its place we have what is known now as "objectivity," a virtue which the weekly press most wisely has not embraced. The weeklies are informing their readers; they are not so much obsessed with the idea of entertaining; and they are providing food for thought with every paper that rolls off the press.

Where is Charley Ross?

IF YOU mentioned Philadelphia around the turn of the century, no one thought of the Liberty Bell. People thought of Philadelphia as the place from which Charley Ross mysteriously disappeared. And they were likely to wonder: is he living now?

If Charley Ross is alive today, he is ninety years old. But around the turn of the century he would have been twenty-five, and if he were alive then, he was a young man with no idea of his antecedents.

Charley Ross disappeared on July 1, 1874, the victim of the first modern kidnaping. Charley Ross was four years old on that July day, and he and his brother Walter were playing on the lawn of the mansion their father Christian Ross had recently built. Mr. Ross was a well-to-do Philadelphia merchant, and he looked out of his window at noon and smiled to see his two sons so happy. When he went back to his office, he noticed the two boys were gone. He didn't think anything of it, since they might have been playing around a neighbor's house. When he didn't find six-year-old Walter or four-year-old Charley in the yard that evening, he became worried. He notified the police and with neighbors set out calling their names.

Christian Ross found Walter, alone and crying, in downtown Philadelphia. After they quieted him, they pressed the boy hard: where was Charley? Still sobbing, Walter confessed he didn't know. Two men in a buggy had offered him and Charley some candy and when they accepted it, the two men took them for a ride in the buggy. Walter said they told him they were going to visit a certain "Aunt Maggie" who had cookies, but when they kept riding he began to cry and the men put him out. But they had kept Charley.

Two days later the strange disappearance was revealed for a crime when Christian Ross received a ransom note asking $20,000.

Kidnaping, however, was a new crime and no one was quite sure how to deal with it. Christian Ross, in fact, had several meetings with the kidnapers on lonely roads and he refused to hand over the money until they handed over his son. He wanted and insisted on a simultaneous exchange. The kidnapers refused.

But now the police had their first clue. An anonymous informer named William Mosher and Joseph Douglas as the kidnapers. Douglas, who had recently been released from jail, was placed by police investigation in a rooming house nearby the Ross mansion in June. Fearful the kidnapers would harm Charley Ross, the police hesitated in making an arrest. It was a fatal hesitation.

For while the police held back, Douglas and Mosher tried to burglarize a Philadelphia home. The owner, armed with a shotgun, shot both men down, killing Mosher outright and severely wounding Douglas. Douglas was removed to a hospital where he started to sink fast. The police questioned him. He confessed to the kidnaping, and explained that Mosher had the infant Charley Ross with some friends to keep the boy out of sight until the ransom was collected. Who these friends of Mosher were, Douglas said he didn't know.

Douglas died the next morning.

Hunt and scour as they might, neither Christian Ross nor the police were able to locate Charley Ross. For the next thirty years people wondered: was Charley Ross still living? Cranks and adventurers came forward to announce they were Charley Ross but all were proved frauds.

Around 1920 interest in the mystery began to wane, although even now old-time natives of Philadelphia will point out the Ross mansion as the home from which little Charley mysteriously vanished forever that bright July day.

The gentle heart

WHEN I see the weekly column conducted by Fulton Oursler, "Dear Friends and Gentle Hearts," I think immediately of America's immortal troubadour, Stephen Foster. The man who left us the greatest heritage of folk music died in Bellevue Hospital on January 13, 1864. They found in his pockets exactly thirty-eight cents and a piece of paper on which was written, "Dear friends and gentle hearts."

Perhaps this was the title for a new song, but whatever it was, it described accurately the man who added "Old Folks at Home" to the spiritual riches of the world. Oursler's newspaper column, full of obscurantism, superstition, and miracles, is not in the tradition of Stephen Foster, who sang of the soil and who expressed the speech of the primitive and the simple. It is an amazing coincidence that both the Caucasian Sirdar March and "Old Black Joe" start off with the identical musical phrase:

> Gone are the days
> When my heart was young and gay,
> Gone are my friends
> From the cotton fields away.

Better times

GENERAL CAPUS WAYNICK, the Adjutant General of North Carolina, wrote to me about his memories of the day of the Johnson-Jeffries fight on July 4, 1910. Johnson, the great Negro heavyweight, battered Jeffries to a pulp. General Waynick was stationed in Washington, D.C., when the news was flashed that Johnson won.

As soon as the fight was over, the general says, he saw Negroes fleeing, hotly pursued by whites, and many of these pursuers were in the uniform of the armed forces. At Second Street, a Negro barber emerged from his shop and expressed himself vigorously to the mob on their disgraceful conduct in sight of the nation's Capitol. A bottle narrowly missed his head and crashed into his window. Hoodlums attacked streetcars in which Negroes were riding and the general saw three Negro musicians in silk hats battered as they rode unsuspectingly in an open trolley.

I wrote General Waynick that things are getting better. I remember when Joe Louis won the heavyweight championship from Jimmy Braddock. I watched the Negroes of Harlem parade all over New York and the whites laughed, cheered, and applauded. And even Southern whites felt a deep dismay when Ingemar Johansson unloaded that right on the jaw of Floyd Patterson, a native North Carolina boy. Things are not perfect, but they are getting better.

Alexander the Great

IN THE battle of Arbela in which he smashed the Persian Empire and became ruler of the world, Alexander the Great lost four hundred soldiers—Darius left one hundred and twenty thousand dead Persians on the field of battle.

I have often thought that an interesting novel could be based on Alexander's invasion of Palestine. Why he did not lay siege to Jerusalem is still a great mystery, and probably involved a woman. Incidentally it was too bad that there was no Alcoholics Anonymous when the conqueror settled back in Babylon to rule his world. Steady, hard drinking killed old Alexander, or I should say, young Alexander, and the military genius who conquered the world was himself conquered by whisky—or whatever they called the alcoholic stuff that went into the "cup of Hercules."

Holapchkis

I CAN go on for at least one hundred pages on what's good to eat, but for the moment I'd like to call attention to one of the finest results of our Jewish culture—my favorite, holapchkis. For those unlucky people who are not personally acquainted with this wonderful work of art, let me say that it is best with good chopped meat and rice, and all sorts of exotic spices, rolled into a beautiful sheet of cabbage and made into sizes of about three inches long and two inches around. Then it is cooked in a specially made sauce with chopped cabbage and raisins. The only true way to eat this food of the gods is with a hefty piece of rye bread in one's hand, with which to keep sopping up the delightful juices, while working away on the holapchkis themselves. Right now I'd give a thousand TV Westerns for just one holapchka.

Health insurance

THE first health insurance plan (such as had been proposed by former President Truman) was put into operation by that great, creeping Socialist—Prince Otto von Bismarck, chancellor of the German Empire. It was put into effect in the year 1884 and was in operation right up to the time of Hitler. Adolf told them they no longer needed health insurance, they would soon become masters of the whole world anyway.

The mother country

FROM 1815 to 1915 America looked to Britain for the key to its foreign policy. Now we administer a spanking for the slightest infraction of the rules we have established. And just as we tried so hard to reflect the looks, talk, habits, and attitudes of the British, the process will now be reversed right down to the home and family. We called Britain the mother country, but she was more accurately a father image. The father has always dominated British life—the headmaster, the regimental commander, and the member of the nobility who was replaced only by the eldest son.

Now the American "child" and the British "father" have exchanged places and America will become, in fact, the mother country. The British woman will soon come into her own in wake of American foreign policy, and Colonel Blimp will become Caspar Milquetoast: "Jim, put that newspaper down this minute and listen to Susie recite her poem."

The casualty list

NEITHER the Romans nor the Greeks published casualty lists. You either came back or you didn't. With all their philosophy and greatness they never thought in terms of people—individuals, John Doe and his wife and his children. The Romans and the Greeks were annoyed with their old, their blind, and their cripples. The Greeks sent them outside the city of Athens. The Romans made no special provision for them to get their grain rations. You had to come and get it or go without. The Jews put it in their Law. The aged, the cripple, and the blind were the guests of honor at the Sabbath table. A new idea in human relations.

"A room somewhere"

IN *My Fair Lady,* Eliza begins her wonderful song with the words, "All I want is a room somewhere." This is sheer poetry. The song is as poignant and emotionally precise as my old favorite, "After the Ball is Over." Mr. Lerner's lyrics are poetry because he understands the real obsession of our civilization. We need to get back to the time when we looked out the window and discarded the demands of being ever-busy. All we really need is "a room somewhere."

PART 5

Would You Want Your Sister To Marry A Governor Faubus?

Governor Faubus and Little Rock

When the Federal Courts ordered Central High School of Little Rock, Arkansas, to integrate, Governor Faubus called out the National Guard to ban the nine Negro children from entering the school. Thus, Little Rock and Governor Faubus became the joint symbol of resistance against integration, and were so proclaimed throughout the entire world. Much was written about Governor Faubus. He appeared on nationally televised programs and every pronouncement he made was carried in 24-point headlines on newspapers throughout the world. His political history was outlined as well as his personal background. He won re-election on the platform that he had staved off integration.

Less is known about Little Rock. It is a beautiful city with a salubrious climate. It has a medical center and a growing population. From 1950 through 1957, forty new industrial plants located in Little Rock, bringing a total value exceeding $8,000,000 to the State and providing 2,378 new jobs. In 1957, with the help of Mr. Winthrop Rockefeller, eight new plants moved to Little Rock bringing $3,000,000 in industry and 1,000 jobs.

In 1958 and 1959, the years following the now famous Little Rock Story, no new plants opened in the city, no new jobs were created. Little Rock became an arrested city. It is static. It is probably one of the biggest suckers in history, since new industry is still pouring into Georgia, Alabama, Tennessee, and the Carolinas.

The complexity of protocol

"Seek simplicity," said Oliver Wendell Holmes, "but distrust it." The simple thing is the one that works. It would be a lot easier to live day by day if everybody in the United States were accorded the same how do you do in the morning, the same choice of seats on a bus, and the same choice of attending a public school.

Look at the complexity of segregation in its relation to the great American accomplishment—the automobile.

When a husband or a wife drives out to pick up the colored maid, tradition decrees that the maid sit in the front seat. The back seat of the car is reserved for guests and friends of the family. The car works at principles contrary to the bus. In the military services the back seat is reserved for the colonels and the generals. The first impulse in the heart of a Southern car-owner, then, is to put the Negro maid in the front. The Southern driver doesn't want people thinking his maid is a colonel.

But then it doesn't look exactly right to be seated next to a Negro girl. This problem is solved by putting all the children in the car when the driver leaves in the morning. Thus when the colored girl is picked up everyone can be relegated to the back seat and the colored girl passes not for a colonel or distinguished guest, but for a maid.

But what if there are no children? A family cannot be expected to propagate simply to drive the domestic to work. And what if, instead of one domestic, there are two? This is a real problem: three people can't sit in the front or that's real integration. And if the two domestics sit in the back, then the white driver looks like a chauffeur.

The easiest way out of this quandary is to have Detroit build bigger cars. But just last fall, Detroit started to build smaller cars.

Segregation is highly complicated. It is like diplomatic protocol where one is forced to do unnatural things. At a state function, the men precede the women. The ladies are dismayed. It seems to them there's a simpler way of getting a lot of men and women around the table than to follow the *de rigueur* seating arrangements of the Middle Ages.

My readers on Mars will never believe any of this.

Montgomery sells its zoo

THE city fathers in Montgomery, Alabama, faced a tough problem. They had a nice zoo in Montgomery, but it was segregated. Montgomery's Negroes, who had won the famous bus strike, had gone off to the courts with a petition asking that the zoo be integrated. The United States District Court ruled for the petition. The zoo, a public institution, had to be integrated. The ruling was interpreted to mean not the animals who lived in the zoo, but the children who came to see the animals.

The city fathers ran hither and thither for advice. They wrote to eminent zoologists, they listened to lawyers and committees. Finally they came up with their answer. They sold the zoo at auction. They sold the animals to other zoos, to motel owners who wanted an attraction, and to people who liked strange pets. The city fathers had consulted everyone—except the children and the animals.

They didn't ask the children whether they would rather feed the elephant in the company of children of another race nor did they ask the elephant whether he would rather look at white and black children with peanuts or pace back and forth in a small cage outside a Jacksonville motel.

The city fathers of Montgomery have managed to sell off the city to avoid integration. Montgomery has no public swimming pools, no park system, no tennis courts, and now no zoo. Pretty soon Montgomery won't even have Montgomery.

What the city fathers could have done is keep the polar bear for the white children to look at, the black panther for the Negro children, and a mixed-color panda for both. It would have taken a lot of devious legal reasoning to put this over on the court, but at least Montgomery would have a zoo.

Token integration

IN NORTH CAROLINA there are eighteen Negro students in what were previously all-white schools.

The State has 319,613 Negro children of school age.

At this rate, it will take 17,756 years for North Carolina to comply with the Supreme Court ruling of May 17, 1954.

Yet many of us refuse to understand what this is all about. City officials insist on referring to white schools, when in fact they are public schools.

It is well to remember that North Carolina is considerably more advanced than the other Southern States of South Carolina, Georgia, Mississippi, Alabama, Louisiana, and Florida. These States are anxiously bestirring themselves to write school-assignment laws similar to the pupil placement procedure the North Carolina legislators wrote. The law provides a school board need not take action at all. It merely must refrain from discriminating when individuals seek to assert their rights by applying for school assignments without regard for race. Judging by its imitators, the law works. It circumvents the Supreme Court ruling.

In other words, we put it over on them.

But what did we put over?

Is it equity to place so heavy a burden on Negro pupils and parents? In order to escape the humiliation of segregation, a Negro must submit to public interrogation and face the hostility of a white school alone. North Carolina has established a precedent which is dire in portent, for it agrees to restore civil rights only after it has denied them. The compliance the Supreme Court asked for clearly demands positive action. We have established a principle for our young—you can beat the Supreme Court, you can disobey the law of the land, all you need is a gimmick.

Moreover we have continued the process of wasting human resources.

Oil strike at the country club

In los angeles the Wilshire Country Club restricts its membership against you-know-whom; and so the middle-class Jews out yonder built their own, the Hillcrest Country Club, which they proceeded to restrict to five hundred "exclusive" members. Ah, the troubles of the American middle class.

Now they have discovered *oil* on the land of the Jewish country club, and the Gentile country club is very sad, which serves it right. The Jewish country club has leased out its oil interests, but there is yet another problem. The exclusive members of the Jewish country club cannot afford to make any more money, so they are trying desperately to set up some sort of a charity foundation to take up the slack, which is estimated to be at least one million dollars.

But there is still another condition. The Hillcrest folks insist that the oil companies slant-drill, so the golf links will not be disturbed. Amerika goniff.

My advice to all the Gentile country clubs is to give up this nonsense about "restricting" your membership. You'll never bring in a gusher until you do this.

A book on the schwartzes

Jewish merchants, principally immigrants from eastern Europe, followed the mills of New England to the South, and by the first decade of the twentieth century there was a "Jew store" in nearly every city and town. These merchants dealt in soft goods, mostly ready-to-wear apparel. In addition, the pack peddler (cloth, needles, notions) was doing business in the rural areas; later came the clothing peddler, the eyeglass peddler, and finally the peddler with jewelry. Incidentally, there was a fellow in each State who handled mattresses. He called himself the "matritz man," and thousands of Negro sharecroppers used the same Yiddish pronunciation.

These Jews did three things that helped elevate the Negro of the South to the status of a man: (1) he was the first white man to permit the Negro to try on ready-to-wear merchandise before he was required to buy it; (2) he was the first white man to write a life insurance policy on the Negro; (3) he was the first white man to extend credit to the Negro.

What the Jewish merchant did was completely devoid of politics, idealism, paternalism, and charity. He was interested only in making a profit and expanding his own business, and those motives are the very foundation upon which rests the self-esteem imparted to the Negro.

The peddler started in business with a little merchandise acquired on credit. His lack of capital, the language barrier, perhaps even his strange appearance made it almost impossible for him to compete with the established merchants for the white trade. Furthermore he felt at home with the Negro. How were the Negroes different from the peasants he used to trade with in Poland and the Ukraine?

When the merchant visited his relatives in the North and was asked how he was doing, he would reply, "I have a book on the schwartzes," which meant, "I am doing a credit business with the Negroes." This credit book may have been for clothing, usually at the rate of fifty cents a week. It may come as a surprise to many people who do not associate Jews with the grocery business to know that around 1905 there were hundreds of Jewish grocerymen in the South, taking advantage of the fact that the white Gentile grocer was not yet interested in the Negro trade. In Durham, North Carolina, alone, there were as many as ten Jewish grocers, each with "a book on the schwartzes." The Duke family were the first people in the State to employ Negroes in industry, and so for the first time the Negroes were receiving a more or less comparable wage in an urban community. They stripped the tobacco leaf, and there was no discrimination.

In the areas where the Negro was a sharecropper or a farm hand, the Jewish merchant extended the credit but kept the ac-

count on a ledger sheet under the name of the Negro's white
landlord or employer. The merchant charged 10 per cent for ex-
tending credit. The Negro usually brought his cotton crop to the
merchant and made his settlement at the same time. In the 1890's,
when all of this began, cotton was selling at about eight cents.
Thus he would be credited with an average of fifty-six dollars. He
would pay off the book out of the proceeds and usually buy some
more merchandise; shoes were a dollar a pair, bacon twelve cents,
a felt hat a dollar, and a shirt seventy-five cents. Often the merchant also dealt in mules and farm equipment.

The Negroes sent the children to pay on the book, a Saturday
evening ritual. The book was about three by five inches. The
Negro had his wages of about twelve dollars for the week. If the
book showed a debt of seven dollars, the customer would usually
send five dollars on the account. On Saturday afternoon the merchant laid out his own books on the counter. He made two entries,
one in his ledger and one in the book, which he returned to the
children with the balance brought forward. He then reached into
the two barrels under the counter and gave the children hard
candy and assorted cookies. The merchant made it a point to
keep the account alive. Even if the children brought the full
amount of the debt he never marked it "in full." He left fifty cents
owing to him. The Jewish merchants called this "the carry-over."

As more and more Negroes left the farms and came into the
cities for jobs, the jewelry merchant came along about 1909, and
he also sold on credit. The Negro women did all the buying. (The
Negroes of the South are a matriarchy. Only now do we see some
slight change for the better in the status of husband and father.
But during all these years the Negro woman has been the head
of the household. She was more secure in her job, and her earnings, as a domestic, were far more consistent.) The first thing the
Negro woman bought from the Jewish jewelry salesman was a
clock—one of two styles, the "Half-an-Hour Strike" or the up-
right banjo-type. The clock cost ten dollars and the installments
were twenty-five cents a week. She was getting four dollars a week
in those days, and her fixed charges included twenty-five cents for
the clock, twenty-five cents for the "matritz" (rebuilt), twenty-

five cents for the fleur-de-lis watch which she wore on her bosom to church, and twenty-five cents a week for the wedding band.

Let us note that the Negroes did not go in for frills or useless articles. This is a pattern which runs through all of history. Her place in society was set in those days, there was neither the opportunity nor the need to prove herself.

And during that era you would be almost certain to hear the Negro woman say, "That clock man is so nice; but that collector man, he's mean."

And now the story is entirely different. Today the maid gets twenty-five dollars a week, her husband gets forty-five dollars, and they are buying the same things the whites are buying. Now there are plenty of sterling silver punch bowls. We've all gone through this. From their combined earnings of seventy dollars to eighty-five dollars a week, they are paying fourteen dollars in installments, plus the sixty dollars a month to the CIT on the car, and like everybody else they have plenty of tsores (worries).

Negro voting

WHILE Negro leaders and white civil rights allies are trying hard to win the right to vote for the Negro in the South, they have encountered two serious problems. The first are the obstacles segregationists have erected against Negro franchise. The second, perhaps more serious, is Negro apathy, apathy because they have no choice between primary candidates.

Alabama is perhaps the extreme example of the barriers a white community can put in front of its Negro citizens. Charles G. Gomillion of the Tuskegee Institute reports that while Negroes represent 30 per cent of the State's population, they comprise only 6 per cent of the registered voters. Negroes do not vote in Alabama, for the most part, because they cannot get a certificate of registration. To obtain this certificate, an applicant must fill out a questionnaire with twenty-one questions, and most of these questions are tripartite in form. The fact that some of the applicants read and write slowly prevents others from completing the questionnaire during the registration period. Often if a Negro applicant makes any mistake, his application is denied and he is not given another chance or opportunity to appeal.

In many Alabama counties the registrars work only a short day. If there is a large body of Negroes applying, only one registrar will appear for work and Alabama laws require that two be in attendance to accept or certify applications. When this does not dismay Negroes and the registrars exhaust their sick leave, they begin to retard the process by holding lengthy conversations.

But of the Negroes who win the certificate of registration only a small percentage votes. Some fail to vote because they cannot pay the poll tax, some because they are not notified of the Negro polling hours, some because they feel "one vote doesn't matter." The majority of the Negroes who do not vote, however, are usually intimidated. Either they are made aware that they will lose the good will of the whites if they do, or that they will lose their jobs, or what is even more common, they will be denied bank credit, the lifeblood of the Southern agricultural community, white or black. There are other Negroes, who work for whites, who are not allowed the time off to go to the polls (in direct contravention of the Federal laws). And there are many Negro businessmen in the smaller cities and towns who are cruelly forced out of business by the simple expedient of having wholesale dealers cut off all business with them.

The Alabama State Legislature in 1957 gerrymandered four hundred Negro voters out of the city of Tuskegee to prevent them from voting in a municipal election, and the Alabama politicians are still trying to figure a way of reducing the eleven hundred registered voters who are left.

There are other States where the situation is just as bad— notably Georgia and Mississippi. In Mississippi Negroes vote freely in only six of the State's eighty-two counties. In Georgia, where one million Negroes are of voting age (eighteen is the legal age), only one hundred and sixty thousand Negroes vote and most of these are in Fulton County (Atlanta).

At least five counties in northern Florida threaten Negroes

whenever necessary to keep them from registering. Although there are sixteen thousand Negroes old enough to vote, a scant one hundred and ten have been able to register.

Of course we must remember that the matter of apathy is closely related to the difficulties encountered by the Negro in registering. Yet in the larger cities where there are no difficulties, the white politicians have no fear of a Negro majority. They know that not enough Negroes vote to worry about. It has in fact been suggested that there is more energy expended in discouraging white mill-workers from voting than in discouraging Negroes.

Nor should any of us overlook the fact that the white voter in the South, and in the North, too, has a bad voting record for the most part. Negroes do not have the only claim to apathy. Half of New York City did not vote a short time back for either Halley, Reigelman, or Wagner for mayor.

But now Negro leadership has come up with a strategy (a Golden plan) to correct this indifference among Negro voters. They recognize the fact that the Negro often has little choice in the Democratic primaries, for the candidates never put the integration-segregation issue at stake. Since the Democratic party controls the South and in many instances elections are only a ritual, it is in the Democratic primaries in May when all issues are laid before the voters. Never do Democratic candidates (by mutual agreement probably) discuss plans for school integration or even oppose Jim Crow. Such a policy leaves the Negro voter unaffected and the primary does not elicit his interest. The new strategy will try to educate Negro voters to "beat down seniority." If two candidates include in their platforms a plank for continued segregation, the idea is to vote against the incumbent, and to keep voting against the incumbent, whoever he may be, until the incumbent decides to say something (which he will do soon enough). Spread around the South, such a strategy might well resolve the problem. In all Democratic primaries the plan is to vote against the fellow who's in.

Atlanta's Standish

WHAT a wonderful name this man has—Standish Thompson—and here's the story:

Brother Standish is the tax commissioner of Atlanta and he is a man with a problem. Brother Standish sent out the tax forms in only one color—the cards were all printed on white paper—and hundreds of people saw in this gesture a move toward the complete mongrelization of the Anglo-Saxon race.

Brother Standish made a public statement: "These white cards will not affect segregation according to the way the law stands." The tax commissioner wanted it understood that this tax form printed on white cards for all citizens was "not a step toward integration."

Previously tax bills for white citizens were on white paper, and those for Negro taxpayers were on yellow paper. The beleaguered Brother Standish summed it all up: "The new procedure is purely economic in intent, but separate windows and lines for returning of taxes of white and Negroes will continue to be maintained."

But I do not envy Brother Standish's position during the next few months. Even John Alden couldn't help him.

Flowers for Wilberforce

IN ENGLAND I went to the grave of William Wilberforce, buried in Westminster Abbey on July 29, 1833. His birthday had been celebrated a day before I arrived in London. The flowers which covered the grave were still fresh, including the small wreath from *The Carolina Israelite* of Charlotte, North Carolina, and I read the inscriptions from the others—the Methodist societies of course, the Quakers, and the embassies and consulates of most of the African countries.

And I thought about my theory of the influence upon history of one man. One man out of two and a half billion people who inhabit this planet is nothing. On the other hand, he is *everything*.

He is William Wilberforce, who became obsessed with the idea of ending Negro slavery.

William Wilberforce was born in Hull, England, August 24, 1759. He belonged to the upper class, and followed the not unusual sequence of Cambridge, the best clubs, a mistress, gaiety, and a seat in Parliament about the year 1780. In Parliament he remained silent for three years, but his brilliance was patent, despite his gay life. Pitt sought him out as a close friend and adviser. Madame de Stael once declared that Wilberforce was the wittiest man in England.

One day, however, he heard a Methodist preacher by the name of Whitfield who changed his life.

"If Billy turns Methodist," said his mother, "I shall cut him off." Said Mr. Wilberforce to Pitt, "I laughed and sang and pursued gaiety and now I say to myself, 'What madness is all of this.' " Pitt, the prime minister, tried to talk him out of becoming a Methodist but finally said, "If this is madness in Billy, I hope he will bite us all."

Wilberforce became a reformer, but a different kind of a reformer. He did not shout, "Give up John Barleycorn! Refrain from the women of Babylon!" Instead he went after the slave trade, "an issue worthy of his greatness" reads the inscription on his statue.

The opposition was fierce. Famous members of Parliament rose to dispute Wilberforce. They said that Britain's mastery of the seas was due to the slave trade, that is how the British seamen received their training. "The save trade," said Wilberforce, "is not the nursery of the British seamen, but his grave."

On the first go-round Wilberforce lost, even though he had Pitt and Burke on his side. The planters of the West Indies and their powerful allies, the users of American cotton in Manchester and Leeds, were too much for him.

What finally won for Wilberforce was that he succeeded in making slavery a religious issue. Here Wilberforce succeeded where Thomas Paine had failed. In France, Paine and the Jacobins had made it a *political* issue. If you were against Paine on another issue you did not follow him on the slave issue, even though you might have shared his views in this respect. Wilberforce did not leave a loophole. "You believe in Christianity? Now tell me how you can support the slave trade?" The only personality involved, he said, was the *Founder* of Christianity.

William Wilberforce never relaxed pressure. A month after his death in 1833 came final victory, the end of the slave trade in England and in all its colonies. Throughout the world eight hundred thousand slaves became free.

Wilberforce had intended to come to America the very year that he died. He had conducted a voluminous correspondence with Methodists in the United States. It is thrilling to imagine what might have happened if Wilberforce had come here twenty-eight years before our Civil War. But he established a great moral principle, "The greatest trait of a man is to fight desperately, especially for something which he himself does not need."

And as I walked into the London sunshine I felt a thrill myself, from the Lower East Side of New York, the son of Jewish immigrants, now living in North Carolina, to see the day when I could place a flower on the grave of William Wilberforce, the great Methodist of Westminster Abbey.

The Negro D.A.R.

EXCLUSIVE: Several Negro scholars have been working quietly on the formation of a Negro Daughters of the American Revolution. I understand that they have authenticated the qualifications of some four hundred and ninety Negro "Daughters," whose ancestors fought in the Revolutionary War.

The first man to die in the Revolutionary War was Crispus Attucks, a Negro, who led the charge against the British on March 5, 1770, the day of the Boston Massacre.

Rhode Island made all Negroes free men who enlisted in the regiment commanded by Colonel Christopher Green. Connecticut also sent off a black battalion commanded by Colonel David

Humphrey. Massachusetts enlisted a company of Negroes, designated "The Bucks," who won a banner from John Hancock for valor.

Most of the colonial Negroes fought with General Washington during his Long Island campaign and others fought in the South Carolina campaign of De Kalb. Some of the "Daughters" live in New York, California, and Michigan, but over half of them reside in Virginia, Georgia, Alabama, and Mississippi.

Negro D.A.R. leaders estimate conservatively that there are over eight thousand lineal descendants who qualify for membership.

A Golden plan

HERE it is, my friends, The Golden Plan to Eliminate Anti-Semitism:

First I must have the co-operation of the three rabbinical associations representing the Orthodox, Conservative, and Reform congregations of America; the American Jewish Congress, the American Jewish Committee, the B'nai B'rith, the Jewish War Veterans, the Jewish Labor Committee, the International Ladies' Garment Workers' Union, and the Workmen's Circle. The first step in implementing the plan is for all these organizations to issue a joint declaration as follows: "At the very first sign of any overt anti-Semitism in the United States, we shall recommend to our memberships that all the Jews in America become Christians, en masse, overnight."

Now here is what would happen. The Jews of America are now mostly in the middle class or upper middle class. Naturally the majority would seek membership in the Episcopalian and Presbyterian churches. The prospect of five million Jews applying for membership in the middle-class Protestant churches would be the greatest social threat in all history. The result: the Episcopalians and the Presbyterians would organize a strong Anti-Defamation League. They would go from door to door whacking anti-Semites on the head: "Sh, you don't know what you're saying."

The price of academic freedom

THIS is the story of Dr. Chester C. Travelstead, dean of the School of Education at the University of South Carolina.

On May 2, 1955, Dr. Travelstead wrote a letter to Governor George Bell Timmerman, Jr., of South Carolina. He wrote as a private citizen, using personal stationery and his home address, challenging the governor on a speech defying the Supreme Court's desegregation decision. Dr. Travelstead's letter said in part:

> You said in your speech, Governor, that "the opinions of the Supreme Court of the United States in the school-segregation cases upholds for the first time in judicial history that equality of treatment is discriminatory." It is my considered judgment, Governor, that it was not the intent of the Court to say that "equality of treatment is discriminatory." Rather did it say in effect that segregation is in and of itself discriminatory and therefore in violation (of the Constitution) . . .
>
> It is my opinion, Governor, that many men of great stature are sincerely convinced that the Supreme Court's ruling was both timely and sound.

On May 31 the president of the University, Donald Russell (who served as assistant secretary of state under Secretary Byrnes) called Dr. Travelstead to his office. While Dr. Travelstead was not told to desist from writing such letters, Mr. Russell remarked: "Let us do everything possible not to make the politicians mad."

On August 2, Dr. Travelstead spoke in Drayton Hall on the campus before approximately four hundred summer-session students and faculty members. His speech was entitled, "Today's Decisions for Tomorrow's Schools"; in it he enumerated eight major educational problems facing America. The last problem was integration in the public schools. Said Dr. Travelstead:

> It is my firm conviction that enforced segregation of the races in our public schools can no longer be justified on any

basis and should therefore be abolished as soon as practicable,
even though as a white Southerner I have since my early
childhood taken for granted the practice of segregation . . .

Three days later President Russell told him that he had received
several complaints that the part of the August 2 speech dealing
with segregation "cuts our throat with the Legislature when we
request funds for the university." On August 19 he received his
dismissal: "The executive committee of the board of trustees is of
the opinion that it is not in the best interests of the university to
renew your appoinment as dean of the School of Education."

A member of the committee said: "*A person should have enough
common sense to know what he should and should not discuss—
without any clear-cut policy about such matters.*"

Thus South Carolina lost one of its ablest educators, the rest
of the faculty was effectively silenced, and the University of South
Carolina became a beleaguered fortress of academic freedom in
what Governor Timmerman called "The War of Northern Aggression." Meanwhile, Dr. Travelstead has been appointed dean
of students at the University of New Mexico.

An eye for an eye

MANY leading Southerners have been saying that the Supreme Court, in ruling against racial segregation, acted on sociology
instead of law. Even *Time* magazine, which has been consistently
correct on this issue, once wrote that the unanimous ruling was
based on the work of Gunnar Myrdal. It is quite true that in its
decision the Supreme Court quoted from Myrdal's great sociological treatise on the Negro, *An American Dilemma.*

But what is more important than the fact that there are twenty-
four million Negroes who have some stake in this matter? This
indeed is sociology. For there would only have to be one Negro
living segregated to enforce the moral legislation the Supreme
Court proposed.

The argument that the Supreme Court acted on sociology is specious. For this argument makes the presumption that any law once erected is inviolate. The Supreme Court corrected itself in the legal-tender cases and history corrected the Supreme Court in the Dred Scott Decision. If law was inviolate, a pedestrian who lost two teeth in an auto accident would have the right to knock out two of the driver's teeth. "An eye for an eye and a tooth for a tooth" was a humane law in its time. If we no longer enforce it or want to enforce it, it is because of a broadening concept of justice, and because our experience has shown us that it is a useless deterrent.

Injustice at lunch

EVERY city has a "City Club," or a reasonable facsimile thereof, with substantially the same rules and "gentlemen's agreement" about its exclusiveness.

I know that the folks in Charlotte, Minneapolis, Cleveland, Toledo, Rochester, Norfolk, Mobile, New Orleans, San Diego, and St. Louis will identify it at once.

In Minneapolis I sat with a businessman in the "Jewish" luncheon club. Now Minneapolis celebrated its hundredth anniversary recently, and my seventy-year-old host was born there. Thus he was a pioneer; he watched the city grow from a village and helped it achieve its metropolitan status. Yet he was never welcomed into the "City Club," or the "Minneapolis Club," as they call it there.

You will say that the "City Club" is not a tax-supported institution, therefore it comes under the category of a private preference. But does it really?

In our society the deals are closed across the lunch table. At lunch the contracts are made, the *planning* is agreed upon, the sales manager is hired, the new freeway takes shape, the political situation is discussed, the school building program is proposed. Across the country it is in the "City Club" that the decisions are made which govern the city—our city.

Is this a private preference or an arbitrary exclusion of an influential segment of the business, professional, and cultural community? If you subscribe to the exclusive club, you are arbitrarily eliminating competition—free enterprise, as the saying goes—because it is here that a businessman takes a shine to a young lawyer or likes the way a young doctor handles himself. Furthermore it eliminates many worthy men who deserve promotion, and does an injustice to some of our greatest national business concerns. I checked with three of our mightiest companies. They do not promote a Jew to a position of regional manager or agency director in a distant city because he would not be welcomed into the local luncheon club and this absence of communication in the local community would be a handicap.

Moreover, I know of a dozen decisions made in our own City Club which affected the welfare of our city.

The point at which public right ends and private preference begins is not a very clear one, and neither is it established by law, but in the case of the "City Club" there is no doubt that its exclusiveness is unfair.

John Marshall! John Marshall!

Up in Richmond, Virginia, the neon sign on the best hotel keeps blinking, "John Marshall . . . John Marshall . . . John Marshall." It blinks this message every five seconds despite the fact that the political bosses of Virginia are ready to close down all the schools, if necessary, to prevent a handful of Negro children from sitting in the same classroom with white children. These political bosses would destroy their civilization.

And what a civilization is this Virginia!

Virginia and North Carolina are the only two States in the South with an intellectual aristocracy. In Virginia, however, the intellectual aristocracy is also the social aristocracy. The key to the integration matter is the State of Virginia, the Mother of Presidents. When Virginia desegregates, the entire South will fall in line.

The Virginians made these rules in the first place—the rules of our democracy. The Virginians gave us the ballot and the free public school, and the Virginians were the first to enunciate the principle that *no man is an intruder in a public institution.*

I wonder what Senator Byrd thinks—what do the massive resisters think when they walk under that blinking neon sign? I am at a loss to understand why they have not changed the name of the hotel. The Herman Talmadge or The Orval Faubus or The Pitchfork Ben will do, not The John Marshall. It was John Marshall who laid down the rules upon which our United States of America has thrived and prospered. This is what he said:

> If any one proposition could command the universal assent of mankind, we might expect it would be this: that the government of the Union, though limited in its powers, is supreme within the sphere of its action. . . . "this Constitution, and the laws . . . thereof, shall be the supreme law of the land . . ." Being supreme, the federal government must have the right to select the means to effectuate its legitimate purposes.

The black rabbit and the white queen

You know the fighter is going to lose the bout when he walks groggily to the corner at the end of the fifth round.

The white supremacists are walking to the wrong corner. Groggily the Florida House of Representatives passed a bill to appropriate $500,000 to finance an advertising campaign to "sell the North the South's viewpoint on segregation." The entire American press, one must imagine, with a high percentage of Negro readership, is eagerly awaiting those full-page ads which read, "Racial Segregation is Good for the Soul." What out-of-work advertising man sold the Florida Legislature this bill of goods?

At the same time the State agency that serves Alabama's libraries placed the book, *The Rabbits' Wedding,* on the reserve shelves. The book was written by Mr. Garth Williams and is for children between the ages of three and seven. Mr. Williams, who said he was only trying to write a story of soft and furry love, had a white rabbit marry a black rabbit. While an Alabama librarian says there are no political implications in removing the book from the open shelves, anyone who wants it, nevertheless, is going to have his or her name recorded—that's standard library practice.

Not to be outdone by this, David Hawthorne, a Miami segregationist, is asking the Florida Legislature not to stop with an advertising campaign, but to ban the *Three Little Pigs.* Hawthorne wants the children's picture book banned from the State's bookstores because it pictures the black pigs as superior to the white pigs. The big bad wolf eats the white pig and the dappled pig but cannot contend with the brick house the black pig has built. "The book follows the same old brainwashing routine," Hawthorne said.

Of course Alabama and Florida and Mr. Hawthorne are all missing a good bet. In Savannah, Georgia, I watched a game in which I saw a black knight take a white queen. I can only imagine what these fellows will do when they discover chess.

Anti-Semitism

THE accumulated literature on anti-Semitism would fill several warehouses. Yet none of it has established the social pattern of anti-Semitism. Anti-Semitism is a virus that cannot be isolated. To cure a disease, a scientist must establish the circumstances and conditions which cause it. No one is certain about the circumstances and conditions of anti-Semitism. Anti-Semitism erupted in the Dark Ages, in the Middle Ages, and in the Renaissance. It has coursed through the feudal system, through the absolute monarchies, through the dictatorships, and it has afflicted democracies and republics. It has occurred both when Jews achieved wealth and prestige and when they lived in the ghettos in abject poverty. Anti-Semitism has spread its virulence in communities where there were large numbers of Jews and in communities where there were no Jews at all. It has occurred in cities where Jews pushed in the subways and in the cities which had no subways.

No Jew who calls for an honest discussion of remedies can be called oversensitive. To say that Jews are oversensitive is a roundabout and craftily subtle way of silencing condemnation. It is a low-grade fever of anti-Semitism.

The one thing we know about the anti-Semite is that he is sick. The anti-Semite is obsessed with a social pathology. This argument also is used to still protest. There are pathologies all of us must learn to live with. But the fact that anti-Semitism has been a constant in Western civilization does not mitigate or lessen the affliction any more than supposing that because malaria was a constant people were healthy. The anti-Semite has a blind, unreasoning hatred not only for the living, but for children as yet unborn and for people long since dead: witness the truth that many incidents of anti-Semitism take place in cemeteries where gravestones are overturned or defaced. In short, the anti-Semite is psychotic—insane. Psychotics are made by abnormal degrees of anxiety and frustration. The teeth ache, the ear runs, a man is sexually impotent, a woman frigid.

In the twentieth century, long after the influence of Jefferson, Franklin, the Constitution of the United States, and the Bill of Rights had been asserted, long after the invention of brass plumbing and the movies, the world witnessed the systematic slaughter of six million men, women, and children for no reason other than that they were Jews or that one of their grandparents had been a Jew.

The Jews have a religious holiday in which they grieve for the horrors of the Spanish Inquisition. The eminent Catholic scholar, Carleton Hayes, estimates that the number of Jews killed during that time was between seven and twelve thousand. Another one hundred thousand Jews were made homeless and expelled. In the early part of this century, in the Russian city of Kishinev, Cossacks swept down upon the Jewish Pale of Settlement and left forty-seven Jews dead. The world stood aghast.

But how can you set aside a day of mourning for six million dead? How can public opinion be effective against the process whereby the Germans shaved the head of a victim to use his hair for mattresses, pulled out his gold fillings to send to the Reichsbank, and gathered up the toys of his dead children to use in the German Winter Fund Drive?

Oversensitive indeed!

The swastikas on the synagogue walls admittedly have been painted by hoodlums, delinquents, and pranksters. The response that swept the world after the first had been smeared on a West German synagogue is akin to the response that "Kilroy was here" ignited in the United States Army in World War II and the response the hula hoop elicited two years ago—with this difference. It is not an innocent response. The swastika is a symbol of mass murder, and the man who paints a swastika on a synagogue has murder in his heart.

But curiously anti-Semitism always fails on its own grounds. It is never enough. The slaughter of six million Jews between 1940 and 1945 does not begin to satisfy. Yet people seek some sort of relief in anti-Semitism. If the crops fail, if a depression envelops the economy, if half the population is unemployed, if inflation wipes out savings, shifting the burden by punishing the Jews brings relief from guilt and an easing of tension—for a while.

Why the Jews? You can shift a burden onto anyone, make anyone nearby a scapegoat. Why Jews? It is a complicated reason why the Jew is chosen, as complicated as history itself. Part of the reason is that the Jew is as old as recorded history—the Jew bears an identity with all of history, its upheavals and changes, its guilt and hope. The Jew, in fact, is subconsciously identified as man—man in the abstract—man incarnate. The charge that Jews desecrated the Host in Stuttgart in 1092 and the charge that the Jews push in the subway in 1960 are valid charges in that man does all these things. But the anti-Semite is a-logical. And logic cannot prevail against him. The Germans, for instance, who, Thomas Mann says, were catapulted into Christianity without a Renaissance, have always been the most anti-Semitic of people. The lure and adventure of Wotan and Valhalla were never banished by the conversion to Christianity. When the Christian ethic binds them too tightly, when the primitivism and atavism of Valhalla sounds, the Germans lash out against Christianity by persecuting the Jews, the precursors of Christianity.

It is for this reason that one can always say anti-Semitism is a Christian problem. When it appears, countries have largely abandoned the Christian ethic and owe only a nominal allegiance to the ethical and social laws imposed by the pulpit and the Bible. Freud, in his little monograph published at the end of his life, *Moses and Monotheism*, said that Judaism was a father religion and Christianity a son religion. Anti-Semitism, he claimed was always a reaction to Christianity, a form of Oedipal guilt. Anti-Semitism remains incurable as long as Christianity does not recognize it as an attack upon itself. Responsible Christian leaders have always condemned it. But Christians have been cerebral about anti-Semitism where they need to be emotional. They should treat it as they treat heresy—with shock and despair. Shmarya Levin, the Jewish philosopher wrote, "Friction begins where planes meet." Judaism and Christianity are planes that met long ago. If every Jew disappeared at 11 P.M., Christianity wouldn't last until midnight. The Jews are the living witnesses to Christianity—and this only the psychopathic anti-Semite really understands.

The conduct and actions of the Jew are irrelevant because the anti-Semite proceeds on a priori assumptions. The feature story in the Sunday paper may describe the accomplishments of the boy who woke up at 4 A.M. to milk the cows, put himself through college, and is now head of the local Coca-Cola bottling plant. This is a success story. But it is not a success story when it involves a Jew. The motion-picture tycoon who helped evolve one of the largest industries in the world is nothing more than a former Jewish pants-presser. The Jewish textile magnate is an ex-peddler.

What is a virtue elsewhere is less than a virtue in Jews. The anti-Semite accuses, "They stick together." Probably the greatest virtue of mankind is that it has achieved a communal unity, yet against Jews this noble concept is an accusation. The men who offer a Masonic funeral to a departed member of the lodge stick together, but this is their virtue. Ah! If Jews only had all the virtues the anti-Semites say they have!

But the Jew of course is not without his protection. A new sort of civilization protects us. Barring some titanic catastrophe—such as an all-out hydrogen war with the Soviet Union or a complete economic collapse after a runaway inflation—political and economic anti-Semitism is impossible in the English-speaking world.

The anti-Semitic movements which start with the creation of economic and political disabilities and end with pain and humiliation and often death for Jews take place in the monolithic state suddenly made directionless by a political vacuum. But since the Constitution of Charles II, the newly coronated monarch of England promises protection to each of the minority groups that swear allegiance to the crown. For anti-Semites to begin a pogrom of even the mildest sort would mean overthrowing the Crown, let alone gaining control of Parliament.

In America the anti-Semites would have to tear up the Constitution. In addition America has fifty States—fifty governors, fifty State legislatures, fifty attorneys general, fifty State constitutions. It is a little saddening that this great democratic idea of States' rights has become identified with the race question. States' rights is the greatest protection a free people ever had. Fifty governors, fifty lieutenant governors, thousands of legislators—that's a lot of people who would have to go along. A demagogue may gain wide acceptance in one State, or in three or four; he may have literally millions ready to follow him, but he can be arrested for vagrancy over another State line twenty miles away.

The Crown, the Constitution, and fifty States are a protection against the recurring malady of anti-Semitism. The pinpricks of Greek-letter fraternity rejection and country club exclusion are not impressive worries. The devices of legal equality and the tradition of freedom alleviate these discomforts in the English-speaking world as long as the major disease remains under control.

I urge Jews to direct all resources to defending civil rights wherever they are abused.

The battle that gave the Jew civil rights was fought by good friends, improbable allies, and Jews themselves. I speak here of Roger Williams, Thomas Jefferson, Benjamin Franklin, and the Presbyterian minister Reverend Tennant in America, Lord Macaulay and Lord Shaftesbury and Arthur Balfour in England, and Emile Zola and Georges Clemenceau in France. Jews can help others win now.

Paradoxically this is the true integration into the American milieu. What a moral thing if the Jewish community of America fought for the rights of the Mexican wetback, for instance, for the end of racial segregation in the South, and for the Negro and the Puerto Rican with their terrible housing and employment discrimination. No matter where civil rights are threatened, we should be there! When you are worried about others, you are fearless. When you fight for *others*, you build an impregnable wall of security around *yourself*.

Musical chairs

A GOOD experiment is to get on the bus in the very best residential section, along about 8:30 P.M.; the servant girls have finished cleaning up after dinner. On every corner one or two Negro women get on the bus, which begins to fill up from the back toward the front. Then, one by one, the whites get on, and they congregate in the front of the bus and are mostly standing until the Negroes in the front seats begin to stand up and walk toward the back as the Negroes begin to get off. Sometimes you feel like saying, "Button, button, who's got the button?" It's a game. The thing changes color two and three times as the bus

wends its way through traffic. Often the bus driver, according to the law, says: "Get up from some of the front seats and let some of these white people have seats." Often, of course, white and Negro will be sitting on the same seat. This is legal—the law says two races may occupy the same seat when all other places are taken. Once I got up from a seat to make room for a Negro woman because seats from the back were filling up. A white man said to me, "Don't get up, there'll be more white people coming on soon." The whole situation changes in a few minutes; where whites sat a few minutes before, Negroes sit. Once, while the Negroes and whites were thus busily engaged making the minute-to-minute adjustments and readjustments, front and back, I saw up front in the white seats a team of baseball players from Puerto Rico, and each member of this team was a whole lot blacker than any of the Negroes in the back.

That fine old aristocrat, the president of the University of Virginia, Mr. Colgate Darden, once called this bus business "a game of musical chairs." I wish I had said it.

The secret of interfaith work

In 1943 the national office of the National Conference of Christians and Jews asked me to help in the formation of a chapter in Charlotte.

I immediately enlisted the services of two very charming ladies— a Presbyterian, let's call her Mrs. G., who had also been president of a local Woman's Club, and Mrs. Minnie R., a Jewish woman of dedication and wisdom. I gave them the printed material and further briefed them on the work and the value of the organization and I furnished each with a list of fifty prospects, twenty-five Christians and twenty-five Jews.

At the end of the first week, Mrs. G. had nine applications and five-dollar checks, and Minnie had two. At the end of the second week Mrs. G. brought me fourteen and Mrs. R. three. I knew that Minnie was a very hard worker and I figured that it must be

in the method of approach. So I asked Mrs. G. to tell us how she achieved this success.

Mrs. G. told us, "I go to see my prospect. I say to him that we are trying to organize a local chapter of a famous national organization which had been founded by Chief Justice Charles Evans Hughes and that this National Conference of Christians would be a good thing for Charlotte and—"

At this point I interrupted my co-chairlady: "Mrs. G., the name of this organization is The National Conference of Christians *and Jews.*"

Mrs. G. looked at me very innocently and said, "I know that, Mr. Golden, but I can get more applications the way I do it."

Separate-but-equal cemetery

IN VIRGINIA there's a segregated cemetery for dogs— "white" dogs in one section, and toward the rear, with a fence around it, lie the "colored" puppies.

Out yonder

THEY found it necessary to change the pattern of anti-Semitism centuries ago. The anti-Semites realized that this association at the local level nearly always eliminated prejudice, and so they created a nasty trick which exists to this day—"These are all right, but watch out for *those* out yonder." And the "out yonder" always changes with the times—Vilna, Vienna, Prague, Berlin, Frankfort, Paris, London, New York, and now Miami. Without this highly effective trick, creating a fear of the unseen, there would hardly be a problem of any consequence. "The Jews in St. Louis—ah, we have fine Jews here, but it's them Jews in Miami, there're the ones you all have to watch out for."

The benefits of incorporation

WHEN I was a witness before the North Carolina General Assembly, I realized for the first time how much our corporate laws contribute to reason. One of the witnesses for the other side, informally announcing himself, said: "I am president of The White Men, Incorporated." This took the edge off the whole thing and hardly anyone was able to keep a straight face. Think how many millions of lives might have been saved in ages past if men like St. Bernard had announced, "I am President of Crusade Against the Saracens, Incorporated." The folks might not have followed so blindly.

This does not make for dignity for the new Klan. Even knuckle-heads hesitate giving their all for the Ku Klux Klan of Georgia, Incorporated. I receive a sheet called *National Crusader* and recently they had a photo of one of their leaders above the caption: "The Rev. Dr. Merle E. Parker, Supreme Grand Counsellor for Divine Meditation, INCORPORATED."

As long as they incorporate, there is a chance for reason.

The absence of logic

ALL of the logic that the white supremacists can muster against the Supreme Court decision outlawing segregation is based on the assumption that the Court acted on sociology instead of law. How is it that in this great South with its many world-renowned universities there hasn't been a single professor of psychology, sociology, anthropology, or philosophy who has written a single statement backing up the segregationists' claims?

Only in California

IN CALIFORNIA exists an organization known as the "Great Council of California Improved Order of Red Men." The object of this fraternity is "to emulate the noble traits of the Indian and their love of freedom and their devotion to their friends."

A pamphlet signed by the past Grand Pocahontas gives the set of rules for the Woman's Auxiliary of the Great Council of California Improved Order of Red Men. In order to join, you must be white.

The basilisk

IN THE South today there is a basilisk—definition: a legendary monster whose mere look was enough to cause complete paralysis.

Here is the South, with its strong heritage of freedom, which gave to America its concept of free government, the ballot, and the separation of church and state; where the ratio between production of raw material and manufacture is approaching the best balance in the world; which enjoys the best climate on the continent; the "most American" section of the nation; where people pioneered the idea of America's responsibility in world affairs; where legislators saved the Draft Act two weeks before Pearl Harbor; where congressmen saved the Lend-Lease Act which helped rescue Western civilization; and where we may find some of the kindest people in this world. And now this great civilization stands paralyzed—and what is it all about? It involves the possibility that no more than 8 per cent of Negro children would be eligible to go to predominantly white schools. That is all this paralysis involves.

PART 6

The Status Wanderer

Israeli short story

I TOOK a taxi in Jerusalem for Haifa, a drive of about two and a half hours. The taxi driver was a man in his mid-fifties. His name was Bazalel Katz, and we had a long, extended conversation.

Mr. Katz told me he was born in Germany. His parents were Orthodox. And because of his name, other boys made fun of him. He grew to hate the name "Bazalel." He begged his father to let him change it. He even had another name picked out—Heinz. But his father said, "Your grandfather was Bazalel, and you will remain Bazalel. You will not change your name while I am alive."

When Hitler became Chancellor, the Katz family moved to Vienna. The young man's name still caused him discomfort. "How do you spell it?" they'd ask. "What kind of name is that? What does it mean—Bazalel—and how do you pronounce it?" His name tortured him all over the continent of Europe.

Then he came to Israel in 1938. At the port of entry the immigration inspector asked his name. "Bazalel Katz," he replied.

My taxi driver said the immigration inspector kept right on writing. "Can you imagine that?" he said. "The inspector didn't even look up. He just wrote the name. I was home."

W. C. Handy

ALL those who were called upon to speak at the funeral of W. C. Handy ("St. Louis Blues") repeated his famous line: "I hate to see that evening sun go down."

The cynic may say, "Mr. Handy knew nothing of philosophy, why read meaning into a line that he probably did not understand himself?" But that is just the point. Poetry is probably the greatest of human expressions; the line comes to the poet and it looks good to him, and this is enough. Sandburg wrote about this very thing: "Poetry is the opening and closing of a door, leaving those who look through to guess what is seen during a moment."

And this great Negro, Mr. Handy, did indeed open the door with that wonderful line. He was telling us the story of his people, their zest for life, the line of life affirmation. Thus, "I hate to see that evening sun go down" may be related to one of the most sorrowful lines in literature, Macbeth's lament, "I 'gin to be aweary of the sun." His queen has just died, and Birnam Wood is beginning to come to Dunsinane. It is when you are dying that you want to see that sun go down.

"I hate to see that evening sun go down" was spoken of a people who have a burning desire to live because they are literally on the threshold of life itself. It is an immortal line in American literature.

The status wanderer—The story of my father

MY FATHER wore a Prince Albert coat and a high silk hat, and when he walked out of the house he automatically put his foot up on a chair, and my mother ran with a cloth to polish his shoes. As my mother polished, my father usually said the same thing: "Oy, de krizshes" (Oh, my aching back). She was polishing, and his back hurt.

This polishing of his shoes by my mother was not a matter of subservience. On the contrary, my mother made all the decisions. My father leaned on her for everything concerning day-to-day living—the raising of the children, the decision on whether to move from one apartment to another, and the handling of what money came into the house. My father never handled a dollar in his life. He refused to be annoyed with such trifles. My mother put handkerchiefs in his pocket and shined his shoes, and we

children took turns polishing the silk hat, which was a great thrill
and privilege. I remember that the silk hat had a band that read,
"Youman Bros.—Fifth Avenue, New York." How my father ever
got a high silk hat from Youman Bros., Fifth Avenue, to Eldridge
and Rivington Streets is still a mystery to me.

I should start the story of my father by saying that he was a
failure. But his type of failure has not yet been explored in
immigrant sociology. We have had stories of the "Horatio Alger"
immigrant who went from cloaks operator and peddler to manufacturer and retail merchant. We've also had the story of the
immigrant in terms of the class war, the fellow who worked all
his life in a sweatshop and got tuberculosis, or was killed on the
picket line. But we have not yet had the story of the immigrant
who failed because he refused to enter the American milieu on
its terms—to start earning status on the basis of money. My father
therefore went down with the ship, or I should say, he went down
with the silk hat.

The polishing of the shoes was a homage my mother paid to a
brilliant mind. She was no different from the young students and
the elderly men who hovered around my father. And the young
and old paid him the great respect of always addressing him as
"Reb," a title you confer only upon the very pious and the very
wise, and he was Reb Lebche to everyone except his immediate
family during all of his adult life.

When he made the complaint about his back, my mother, a
pious Orthodox woman, used to look up at him and quietly say,
"You'll outlive me twenty-five years." Her prediction fell short a
few years. My mother died of cancer in 1924 and my father died
of old age in 1941. (The date of his birth, 1859, was a source of
pride when I was in school. I thought of my father as a contemporary of Abraham Lincoln.)

My father Lebche (Lieb) Goldhirsch came to America in 1900
from the Galician town of Mikulince in the Austro-Hungarian
Empire.

The story of my father must be told in terms of the early
twentieth-century immigrant era in America when there were Jews
who, though poor, still had status. It was a vanishing civilization

but good while it lasted. This made my father something of a snob. He could never understand how it was that the son of a coal dealer or the son of a tailor could go to City College as an equal with me. The very idea!

"In America we don't need you with your yikhus (status)," the folks began to say. But my father held out. He felt that no matter how much money these other fellows made, they did not dare to wear a high silk hat. If the peddler made a million dollars he would still wear a cap, or at best he might toy with the idea of a fedora or a derby.

This yikhus (status) culture involved not only the learned man, as in the case of my father, but also the woman who was particularly handsome. "She's so stately." "She's such a beautiful woman." It was not beyond these handsome women and learned men to take advantage of their positions. In fact, some of them got to like it very much. My father, for instance, did not have to go to any shop, nor did he have to "dirty the hands." You can't ask a man like that to work with his hands! The entire status culture of eastern European Jewry was based on this very idea: not to "dirty the hands."

Because he was a man of great stature among his landsmenn, my father automatically became the president or the secretary of his burial society, his charity organization, and his fraternity. I remember a heated argument that concerned some policy of one of these societies regarding the budget, an insignificant matter, really. Yet a man rose and attacked my father. This man was an "unter-presser." An unter-presser was an apprentice to a pants presser in a garment factory. In European caste-conscious society this would have been low status, but it was an improvement over what he had been. He had been a "drikker," a fellow who worked in a dyeing plant and who pressed the cloth into the dyes with his great strength. He pointed a finger at my father and he said, "Reb Lebche, in Europe when you saw me walking down the street you walked on the other side; but in America, when I see you coming down the street I walk on the other side." If my father, Reb Lebche Goldhirsch, was wrong in spending his entire life in America basking in his yikhus, so too was the unter-presser wrong.

Because my father did have a giant brain. He had a brain that absorbed knowledge like a sponge takes water. The late Oscar H. Geiger, founder of the Henry George School of Social Science, once told me, "Harry, if your father had been born in Ohio he would have been the President of the United States or the man who makes the President." And yet when I write about my father, I know I speak for many thousands of these "status wanderers" who refused to enter into the American civilization on the terms demanded of them.

Reb Lebche hung on desperately to the fringe of the upper-echelon activities; a teacher now and then and a B'al Tiphelah (the scholar who chants the prayers in preparation for the cantor) every Rosh Hashanah and Yom Kippur. He chanted the prayers for Rov Seidele Rovner who was his closest friend. I can still remember the thrill of listening to these two elderly gents singing at our table and my father saying, "It's his, it's his own melody composed right here." My father also had a license to perform marriages, and he performed many hundreds. The couples came to our home, some of them with babies in their arms, others with grown children. They had been married at the proper time according to the Jewish ritual, but now they realized they also needed a civil marriage certificate to be recorded in the office of the clerk of the court. On these occasions my sister Mathilda would be summoned from school or from the street and she banged out the opening bars of "Here Comes the Bride," and my job was to complete the certificate and the stub for the county clerk.

All of these projects of my father's were free-lance: he was a free-lance writer, a free-lance music critic, a free-lance philosopher, a free-lance marriage clerk—everything was free-lance. He felt the need to earn some money. My mother sewed for the neighbors and for a great many customers. She was a genius with the needle. If I was ready to go to school and did not have a clean jumper, my mother took a piece of muslin and fitted me while I was having breakfast—which led to a miracle, repeated often, for she was stuffing the finished shirt into my pants as I went off.

My father became a citizen in 1910. He and a group of other Galitsianers studied the American Constitution, the Declaration of Independence, and the laws of New York State, and went down to a Manhattan courthouse where a sober, dignified, white-haired Irish judge questioned them about American history and American legal and political processes. They raised their right hands and. forswore allegiance to Emperor Franz Josef and pledged themselves to American destiny. After the oath, the judge said, "Now you are all American citizens." Lowering his voice, he continued, "And don't forget to vote the straight Democratic ticket." He told this story about Tammany for the rest of his life and he always laughed, "Amerika goniff."

My father agitated among other things for the rabbis to receive the same consideration on the railroads as the rest of the clergy— half fare—and then one day he himself received a notice granting him this privilege. It was addressed to "The Reverend Leib Goldhurst," and for the rest of his life my father loved President William Howard Taft. A wonderful decade, 1902-1912. The major project of the national administration was the inauguration of the parcel post system. For Taft there was sentiment, but for the real political conviction and affection it was all Roosevelt, Theodore Roosevelt. "Rawza-veldt" my father would say slowly to make it last as long as possible. And sometimes in a lighter mood, he would refer to Roosevelt matter-of-factly, as plain "Tudder" (Theodore).

One of my father's favorite expressions was "You're entitle" or "I'm entitle." I always corrected him. "Pop, the word has a *d* at the end. You're entitled. I am entitled." He would look at me in all seriousness. He understood but he would persist, "You're entitle (to your opinion)."

Reb Lebche never spent a day without the Orthodox *Jewish Morning Journal* which out-Republicaned *The New York Tribune*, but he had great respect and admiration for the Socialist *Jewish Daily Forward*. "Abe Cahan (editor of the *Forward*)," my father would say, "is conducting a university for the Jewish immigrants and it only costs a penny a day."

In his writings Reb Lebche performed a few interesting services.

Forty years before the interfaith movement began, my father wrote a lengthy letter for the *Jewish Morning Journal*:

> The Yiddish press does not write enough material about America itself—the freedom of America. In Europe I was scared every time I met a Gentile on the street; and I went far out of my way to avoid passing a church. Here in America I pass a church, stop and examine the architecture and suddenly the priest comes out, and he smiles and says "Good morning" to a bearded Jew. This is a development in the history of our people worth expanding into a whole series of articles. The priest smiles and says "Good morning" because he's in America, too. It's America that made it better—not only better for me, a Jew, but also better for him, a priest.

In all fairness to Reb Lebche and to my readers, I must also say that my father was a Darwinian rationalist. I once kidded him about his strict observance of the Sabbath and of every holiday and ritual and he replied, "A people cannot exist without *form* or without *ritual* or without *memory*. Furthermore these men are my brethren and the synagogue gives us fellowship and strength; my good brother, Dudja Silverberg (a very pious man) goes to the shul to sit with God—I go to the shul to sit with Dudja and my other beloved fellow Jews."

If Reb Lebche's "money-making" activities were all free-lance, his work in charity was a full-time job. In those days the various societies would hold benefits for some worthy charity—and my father was usually called upon to make the appeal from the pulpit of the synagogue or from the stage of a theater benefit. Luckily my brother Jacob and I were able to re-create for Reb Lebche his Big Status in relation to charity. He went back to Europe in 1929 and we gave him four thousand dollars in Romanian lei and Polish zlotys so he could marry off twenty or thirty Jewish girls in Mikulince and other Galician towns. It was a great moment for Reb Lebche to stand in the back of an automobile riding from Mikulince to Radowitz; the folks followed the car in gratitude and pride and threw addresses and messages into his auto for delivery to relatives in America.

In his declining years he came to identify himself completely
with those Jewish girls to whom he indiscriminately gave a dowry
during his moment of triumph. He made them the symbol of
the whole tragedy of Nazism, and while he died before we knew of
the massacre of six million Jews, Reb Lebche sensed it was coming.

About two years before his death, Reb Lebche asked me to
drive him out to the cemetery in Brooklyn. He was still the
president of all his societies, and members of the burial society
had filed complaints with the cemetery people that water was
seeping into the burial plots. My father went to investigate. As we
entered the cemetery gate I saw the empty plot of ground almost
hidden in a vast sea of gravestones, the plot which had been set
aside forty years before for the founder and president of the society,
my father, Reb Lebche. While my father was talking with the
cemetery fellow, I walked back to the gate and just kept looking
at that one small empty space; but soon my father was behind me,
and of course he knew exactly what I was thinking. Reb Lebche
smiled and said, "You know, my son, if this were to happen only
to me, I'd have you write a stiff letter of protest to Congressman
Perlman, but look who else has died—Der Rombom (Maimoni-
des), Jawr-ch (Henry George), Jeffer-sohn, and Rawza-veldt—
am I any better than they?"

When my father died the eulogy was spoken by Judge Herman
Hoffman, the grand master of the Brith Abraham Order, and
once judge of Special Sessions in New York. Said Judge
Hoffman: "This man, Reb Lebche, whose body lies before us,
could never borrow three hundred dollars on his signature at any
time in his life, but he distributed hundreds of thousands of
dollars entrusted to him by others for charity; there were factory
workers and peddlers who stopped off in Reb Lebche's apartment
on their way home and handed him two and three dollars in an
envelope without their name or their address but with one oral
message—'Reb Lebche, this is for someone who may need bread
tomorrow.' "

The death of Mario Lanza

I DID not know Mario Lanza, but I saw him about three weeks before his tragic death.

It was at a performance of Aïda in the amphitheater of the Baths of Caracalla erected by the Roman Senate between 215-217 A.D. in honor of the Emperor Caracalla and his two sons. It was the most impressive performance of an opera I have ever seen. It was a beautiful night and the stage held nearly one thousand performers. The amphitheater is so large that Rhadames galloped across it in a four-horse chariot when he came home from the war. And his troops were no mere Metropolitan Opera supers. They were whole regiments of armored men with weapons and camels. The singing was magnificent. It was all glorious and unforgettable.

During the first intermission there appeared to be a considerable disturbance two or three rows behind me. A large crowd had gathered and upon further investigation I found that Mario Lanza had been recognized and that now hundreds of Italians and American tourists were crowding around him to get him to autograph the program. After the second act the word about Lanza had spread. An even bigger crowd collected. They kept Lanza busy signing books and answering greetings, but it appeared that he was terribly tired. I was close to him when he left the arena before the beginning of Act 3. As he left his little son said, "Papa, why did you take off your dark glasses?"

Mr. Daniels' decision

WHENEVER I visited Raleigh I called the office of Josephus Daniels, the late editor of The News and Observer and Secretary of the Navy in the Wilson Administration. He was an old man and did not sit at his desk for long periods of time. He was usually "out." So I left my name, and that's all. I never waited more than a half-hour. The call always came. Mr. Daniels wanted me to come right on over to his home. On one of these occasions Mr. Daniels showed me a beautiful bronze plaque on which was mounted the Ten Commandments in gold leaf. It had been presented to him by a Jewish fraternity in Brooklyn, New York. Mr. Daniels prized it highly. Then he told me the story behind the bronze plaque with the gold Ten Commandments. He had it all in a single file marked HERMAN BERNSTEIN, the same Herman Bernstein whose name I had heard in my home on the Lower East Side of New York. He was the founder of the Yiddish language daily newspaper, *The Jewish Day*. Early in 1915 Mr. Daniels, Secretary of the Navy of the United States, received a letter from Mr. Bernstein. Mr. Bernstein told of the desperate condition of thousands of starving Jews in the Near East. He said that the necessary relief funds had been collected, that the medical supplies and food had been purchased, but that the committee could not get a ship for love or money. Mr. Daniels knew that there were regulations against the use of Navy vessels for a private mission even if the mission were one of mercy. But then this wonderful Josephus Daniels thought of an idea. The Navy was sending colliers into that zone to supply coal to the American ships in the Mediterranean, and he thought he could reduce the amount of coal in the next two colliers and give the space to the supplies for the Jewish refugees. Mr. Daniels went to President Wilson who suggested that he, Daniels, mention it as a matter of record to both the majority and minority leaders of the Congressional Committees on Naval Affairs. Everybody said, "Go Ahead." The ships *Vulcan* and *Starling* carried this food to Palestine. With a twinkle in his eye Mr. Daniels told me that he put one fifty-pound bag of coal on each ship and filled the rest of the space with matzohs for Passover.

Did Theodora write our laws?

THEODORA was not only one of the great courtesans in Rome, but also an accomplished actress. The fact that she was a lady of joy almost denied her the right to marry Justinian, Emperor of the Eastern Roman Empire. Roman law forbade the marriage of senators and whores. Justinian got around this by repealing the law long enough for him to marry Theodora.

Theodora was a gem. She was a woman who had worked in every brothel in Rome and had slept with Persians, Jews, Greeks, pirates, and Turks. She may have been overly sensual but she knew what was going on all over the world. She took her own mass-media polls and her store of information was invaluable. When Justinian ascended the throne she ruled with him. Whatever her previous life had been, as empress she was beyond reproach.

She knew how to exploit power, was jealous of anyone with influence, and absolutely unforgiving to her enemies. And unlike most ladies who played with Roman politics, she died in familiar surroundings—in bed. When anarchy threatened to take over Byzantium in 532 A.D. she rallied Justinian and the court and set out on a large-scale bribery scheme to achieve peace. It worked. And for the first and only time in history.

While Justinian was Emperor he codified all the Roman law in the Corpus Juris Civilis. It was the first great collection of juristic literature all over the Eastern Empire. Justinian urged building and Roman architecture flourished. He was the first Roman emperor to advance his own theological views and make them stick and he encouraged the missionary movement which converted to the Christian Gospel the peoples of southern Russia, the Caucasus, Arabia, the Sudan, and even those in the Sahara oasis.

Thousands of our American lawyers will argue cases tomorrow morning based on laws written by Justinian. But it is easy to figure out who Theodora was. She was Justinian's ghost writer.

Bishop (Sweet, Sweet Daddy) Grace

MOURNERS' wails drowned out the brass bands of many a Southern "House of Prayer for All People" when death took Bishop C. M. (Sweet, Sweet Daddy) Grace last January.

On one of his visits to Charlotte, which the wealthy Bishop called "the center of my circumference," he estimated that his organization had at least three million members, with many expensive churches and dozens of apartment houses in the South, as well as in the Negro sections of New York, Philadelphia, Detroit, and Chicago. (In 1958, he bought out the Harlem kingdom of a competitor, Father Divine.)

Worship was interrupted in his domain for sales talks and demonstrations of Daddy Grace Toothpaste and Daddy Grace Cold Cream. Bishop Grace also had an interest in a chain of restaurants, a coffee importing business, and many other side interests and investments. In addition, he owned a private estate fronting the ocean, twelve miles outside Havana, Cuba.

On his semiannual visits to each of the churches, his flock welcomed him with a parade, in which his chauffeur-driven limousine proceeded slowly between two rows of cheering, singing, rejoicing, and stomping worshipers, shouting, "Sweet, Sweet Daddy!" Some of the more devout followed in the wake of the Bishop's car, scooping up the loam with his tire tracks, and tucking the bits of earth into handkerchiefs and pocketbooks. On these occasions his assistants sold Daddy Grace Coffee, which the Bishop imported from Brazil and prepared for sale in a refinery in Philadelphia. Others offered Daddy Grace Handkerchiefs, moistened with "a tear of the Lord," while a big white truck took up its place in the crowd with Daddy Grace Ice Cream Cones.

Bishop Charles Manuel Grace started his career more than thirty years ago. His origin was shrouded in mystery, although it is generally believed that he was a Caucasian of Portuguese origin. He died at eighty or thereabouts, a two-hundred-pound six-footer with a large, handsome face. His thick gray hair rested gracefully on his shoulders.

Unlike Father Divine, Bishop Grace did not believe himself to be God but, rather, that his status was that of "messenger" with vast healing powers.

When I interviewed him in Charlotte, Bishop Grace had just returned from a vacation on his estate in Cuba, a trip which he said had been suggested by the angels, who later ordered him to cut the trip short and return to work. "Wherever I go, the angels prepare everything for me," said the Bishop. He told of an incident in 1949, when he left on the *Queen Elizabeth* for Europe. His bags were not examined by customs officials when he arrived in Cherbourg. He and his chauffeur went to Paris with no delay. Europe had had no rain for a long time. "I brought it rain," he said. He went to Rome where again he was not required to have luggage examined, nor to go through other red tape which harasses the ordinary traveler, and the chief of police escorted him to the best hotel. They had had no lights in the hotel there because of the lack of rain—but the rain fell and there was no lack of light while he was there. When he came back to New York there was a band playing "Three Cheers for Daddy Grace"; and more than five thousand people met the boat to welcome him. There was again no delay, and a parade of seventy-one cars escorted him to Fifth Avenue and out to Harlem, with horns blowing and other happy sounds. In New York, just as in Europe, there was dire need of rain, but as soon as he got there, the rains fell.

The services conducted by Bishop Grace were similar to those of the Holy Rollers, but with far more rhythm. First, the worshipers awaited the Bishop's entry. To the accompaniment of "ruffles and flourishes," furnished by a Bishop Grace Concert Band, he was escorted to a throne by a group of uniformed Bishop Grace Soldiers and evening-frocked Bishop Grace Queens. His sermons lay heavy stress on morality and the sanctity of marriage. He opened the service with, "I hope none of you has been up to your old tricks again," to which the worshipers responded, "No, Sweet Daddy Grace, no, Sweet Daddy." Then followed the most im-

portant part of the ritual, which was the baptismal ceremony
(Daddy Grace believed in total immersion). In certain areas where
there were no pools, Daddy Grace turned a fire hose on his converts. Another part of the service of The United House of Prayer
for All People was the laying on of hands, which left some members in a state of ecstasy. This was followed by "speaking in un-
known tongues," and in this department, Bishop Grace excelled.
It was during the hollering, shouting, and speaking in tongues—
"smeeg tar grishmum smeegy, smeegy"—that most of his people
really began to feel the spirit; the children danced a sort of
hopscotch, while their elders, women particularly, cavorted sensu-
ously. At a given signal the Bishop's seneschal demanded complete
silence. You could hear a pin drop, as Daddy Grace cupped his ear
and went into a trance. He nodded understandingly between stage
whispers: "Yes, Lord . . . I understand, Lord . . . All right, Lord . . .
I'll tell them, Lord." The blare of the trumpet broke the spell, and
Daddy delivered the thunderous message: "I WANT MY
PEOPLE TO DO RIGHT!" Above the deafening rhythmic fervor
of the response, the clarion-voiced seneschal was heard again,
"Sweet, Sweet Daddy Grace" and "Thank God through Daddy
Grace." The time had now come for the "love offerings" to begin,
and these went on continuously.

During the taking of the love offerings, the seneschal again took
over, barking out commands and phrases to the blare of the
trumpet: "We all love our savior!"

"Amen!" shouted the worshipers. Occasionally, Daddy Grace
left the throne and did a little sashay step with hands on hips,
between the rows of ecstatic worshipers. "Blessed be our world
savior, Daddy Grace!" shouted the seneschal over a public-
address system, which carried his voice to every corner.

At the end of a Charlotte meeting some years ago, Bishop
Grace reported the theft of a valise containing over twenty-five
thousand dollars. The Charlotte Police Department apprehended
the thieves and recovered most of the loot for "Daddy."

Back in 1934 an indictment for income tax evasion was dropped
when the gifts of his parishioners were ruled tax-free.

(Grace was once convicted of a violation of the Mann Act involving a twenty-year-old, piano-playing assistant, but his sentence was set aside on appeal.)

Bishop Grace said that whenever he spoke the angels took it all down in shorthand.

To criticism of his one-man rule, he pointed to the Scriptures: "Have not God's 'Appointed' throughout the years been single individuals? Take Noah, for example—one man—one man on whom depended the rebuilding of the world. Another example, Moses—one man—one man to lead the children of Israel out of bondage."

It is always one man, and to multitudes of Negroes in the Southland of milk and honey, that one man was Sweet, Sweet Daddy Grace.

Biography of an upstart

A LITTLE over a hundred years ago Ignaz Semmelweis was a young doctor working in a charity ward of a clinic in Budapest. Ignaz spent all his spare time worrying about the fact that four of every ten women died in childbirth. He brooded over this so long that finally an inspiration came to him, and he made some experiments. To his tremendous good fortune, he not only found an answer, but tested his findings to his complete satisfaction. Ignaz Semmelweis was timid about disclosing his findings to his superiors; he realized it would take from two to three months to get an interview with the authorities. He decided that it would be best to put his findings into practice, so that when he did finally come before his superiors, he could confront them with a newly discovered scientific fact. Finally the big day came and Semmelweis appeared before the directors of the clinic. He told them that he had discovered a method which would greatly reduce the number of deaths in childbirth. He produced his clinical records, which showed that out of his most recent fifty charity patients none had died, whereas the records of the other wards continued to show the devastating toll of death.

With this impressive evidence, Ignaz Semmelweis then made a historic announcement: "Sirs, I have discovered that if the doctor washes his hands in solution, before delivering the child, the danger of death will be greatly reduced. Please tell the doctors to wash their hands."

The "status quo" boys turned purple with rage. "Is this all you have to say? You dare to expose the medical profession to scorn and ridicule?" The head of the clinic (the one with the beard) told Semmelweis that he was a disgrace to his profession and that his impertinence could easily result in his discharge. With tears in his eyes, Ignaz kept pointing to his records, "None of them died!" His persistence only added to the rage of his superiors, and he was fired. He spent what little money he had saved, traveling over the country, pleading with physicians, writing letters to editors, and to medical societies. Every door was closed to him, and he could no longer find a job. Finally, Ignaz decided to go to the common people—those whose wives and mothers were dying at the rate of four out of every ten. He printed little circulars, which he distributed to workers outside the large factories. These circulars read: "Don't allow a doctor to deliver your wife of a baby, unless he washes his hands first." The working men laughed at him and tore up his circulars. And Ignaz Semmelweis went his way, a bewildered man, pleading with humanity.

Winston Churchill's accident

In 1931 Winston Churchill was in America on a lecture tour. He had finished dinner one night and was on his way to visit his friend Bernard Baruch. But he had forgotten Baruch's address. He knew it was in the 1000's on Fifth Avenue so when his cab started to pass the 900's, he asked the driver to stop and he got out to ask directions. A Londoner, Churchill disembarked and instinctively looked to the left, forgetting that in America traffic flows exactly opposite to traffic in Britain. He stepped across the street directly into the path of a car coming from the right. He was suddenly aware of a vast glare and of a man aghast.

Mr. Churchill has preserved his impression of the accident in an article he wrote at the time for the North American Newspaper Alliance. He says that he thought at this moment, "I am going to be run down and probably killed." He was hurled forward with a violent impact. He was fifty-seven years old and he had come to America to become a traffic casualty. But he, and the world, were fortunate. Ten years later, of course, he was Prime Minister of England during England's gravest hour. He had been spared to lead the free world to victory over Nazism and Fascism. How more desperate this world would have been if Churchill had died that night on Fifth Avenue!

By the time he reached the hospital on the night of his accident, he was in complete control of his faculties, although he suspected he had broken several bones. A few hours later the distressed Mr. Baruch rushed to the hospital and the first thing Mr. Churchill asked was, "Tell me, Baruch, were *do* you live?"

Dr. Graham's victories

DR. FRANK PORTER GRAHAM, for twenty years the president of the Consolidated University of North Carolina, returned to North Carolina recently, to Durham, where he attended a committee meeting of a few embattled social workers. He passed up his dinner, happy as a lark. He was busy, busy preparing a resolution to help migratory workers of America. I don't know into what cubbyhole one of the President's sixteen corresponding secretaries will stuff this resolution—but this is irrelevant. Frank Graham, however, is not irrelevant.

Senator Wayne Morse once said, "Dr. Graham is the most Christlike man I have ever met."

In his own quiet way, Dr. Graham won for the United Nations its first great victory, by the successful mediation of the dispute between the Netherlands and Indonesia. This victory, as great as it was, is dwarfed by the untold number of victories he achieved as an educator and university president.

Who knows how many men and women changed the entire course of their thinking because of their contact with Dr. Graham? One time the person may be a country editor, or a surgeon, or a proprietor of a textile mill, or a clerk in some establishment, and you hear some views on politics and life which cause you to raise your eyebrows, and you wonder, how did this happen, way out here in the country, and the answer comes quickly enough when the man says, "Dr. Graham always said . . ."

Students at the University of North Carolina during the early years of the Depression formed a line to give notice that affairs at home made it necessary for them to quit college. Dr. Graham nipped those tragedies in the bud. He handed each of these boys a blank promissory note. He told them to fill it out in the amount required to finish the year. "Sign it; somehow you'll pay for it; but stay." Dr. Graham then went out knocking on the office doors of the rich men in North Carolina, and in those years he was able to gather a fund of close to a hundred thousand dollars to back up the promissory notes of those students. These students are the leaders of this State today. Each of them is a victory of Dr. Frank Porter Graham.

David Dubinsky

> Chicken in the bread pan
> Pickin' at the dough.
> Swing your partner,
> Dosi-do.

I watched one hundred Southern girls and women in evening gowns form a circle and dance to the calls of the band leader in the air-conditioned ballroom of the Hotel de Soto in Savannah, Georgia. They were seamstresses attending an annual conference of shop foremen of the International Ladies' Garment Workers' Union. I said to my host, David Dubinsky, "Turn the clock back twenty years and these girls are in the swamp country somewhere with maybe one pair of blue jeans."

Mr. Dubinsky laughed. He is a short man with a huge head, but after you are with him a while, you realize he is actually quite a handsome man. His rich laugh reveals the quality which I am sure has helped him reach and keep the position he has held for the last quarter of a century in American labor—the head of the ILGWU. That quality of humor, rich and subtle.

At the opening of this Savannah conference, he read an editorial which said, "The South does not need the likes of David Dubinsky." He thereupon made a public offer of an organizing moratorium for the South: "We do not need members," he said. "We have plenty of members. We do not need money. We have so much money I am begging the national and State legislatures to enact laws for the control of union welfare funds. Since we need neither members nor money, I will therefore sign an agreement not to organize any establishment in the South for a period of five years if the said establishment agrees to raise its minimum wage (in intrastate commerce) to $1.25 an hour."

At victory's doorstep

THERE is a sad irony in the history of a man who one day watches everything he has built up collapse. There is an even sadder tragedy when he realizes his life has been fruitless. Napoleon on St. Helena saw the restoration of the Bourbon monarchy before he died. D. W. Griffith, the first great movie director, spent fifteen years drifting around Hollywood unemployed. Not as sad, perhaps, but more ironic is the story of the man who does not get to see the results of his daring and ingenuity and hard work—the man who dies on the threshold of fame or final victory. Sam Warner, of the famous movie corporation Warner Brothers, was such a man. There were four Warner brothers, Harry, Jack, Sam, and

Alfred, and they had become movie producers by renting nickelodeons. But in the 1920's their corporation was in a tight fix. All of their money was invested in the studio, and the corporation did not own any movie theaters. The bigger movie companies would not rent them theaters and the banks would not lend them the money to build their own. Sam Warner and his brothers took a huge gamble. They bought the patent rights to Vitaphone and planned to produce the first talking picture. The movie industry thought these minor producers, sunk in debt, were crazy. They were investing in a crackpot invention, which all of the major studios had turned down. The people didn't want talking motion pictures, everyone said. Sam Warner believed in talking pictures; moreover talking pictures were his only out. The picture the Warner Brothers produced, of course, was *The Jazz Singer* with Al Jolson (who took cash for his salary instead of stock and easily lost several million dollars in this transaction). The movie opened on October 6, 1927. The lines of people were several blocks long, waiting to hear the great Jolson sing. The Warner brothers had brought about a revolution in the film industry but Sam Warner did not see it. He died just before *The Jazz Singer* opened.

President Franklin D. Roosevelt, who died on April 12, 1945, just missed knowing that the Allies had won the unconditional surrender of Germany. In the early 1930's Roosevelt knew that World War II was going to be "our" war and he struggled with this realization against bitterness and acrimony and invective. On that April day in 1945, one of Roosevelt's last official acts had been to approve a postage stamp commemorating the founding of the United Nations, a dream which had not yet materialized. He was stricken while posing for Madame Elizabeth Shoumatoff. Just three weeks later, on May 7, the German government of Admiral Doenitz said it had had enough.

Another man not able to hear civilization's applause was John A. Roebling, who had built suspension bridges in Cincinnati and throughout the country and who had engineered the railroad suspension bridge over Niagara Falls. He conceived the largest suspension bridge in the world—he wanted to join Manhattan island and Brooklyn. This was considered folly at the time; but

Roebling worked unceasingly and in 1867 the New York State Legislature granted a charter to a group of private citizens to raise the money for this improbable venture.

Roebling's initial plans and estimates had been so thoroughly worked out that he was hired as the engineer without any change in his proposals. Brooklyn Bridge began to become a reality. But work had no sooner started when Roebling, on June 28, 1869, caught his foot in a shifting pier plant and lost two toes, and the infection brought him down with tetanus. He died in his son's house where he could look out at the men working. Even on his deathbed his inventive mind was at work. The day before he died he had made a drawing of an apparatus designed for lifting him up in bed.

The bridge took the health of his son, Washington Roebling, too. Washington Roebling spent too much time in the underwater caissons and collapsed one afternoon in the spring of 1872. He, too, supervised the work from his bedroom for the next ten years until 1883, when the Brooklyn Bridge was formally opened and President Chester A. Arthur, two State Governors, the Cabinet, and the Seventh Regiment crossed over from New York to Brooklyn. To this day, the Brooklyn Bridge remains one of the architectural and functional marvels of the world. More than that, the bridge brought Brooklyn into the city in 1898 as one of the five boroughs, creating the fantastic phenomenon of eight million people, the City of New York.

Mrs. Frances Perkins

MRS. FRANCES PERKINS' book on F.D.R., *As I Knew Him,* is still the best one written so far; but an even greater book would be her own story. This wonderful woman entered public service way back after the tragic Triangle factory fire which pointed up the terrible conditions in the sweatshops; and the struggle for better economic conditions received a tremendous boost when Mrs. Perkins (whose ancestors had come to America on the *May-*

flower) joined the liberal movement. To how many people is it given to lead so consistently useful a life over a period of two generations? She has earned the gratitude of every man, woman, and child in this land who receives a pay check.

Mike Jacobs' prediction

WHAT a wonderful country! A man like Mike Jacobs can make six or seven million dollars out of the prize-fight business. The late Mike Jacobs really dominated the fight racket, even in the days of Tex Rickard. Rickard didn't budge without Mike— Michael Strauss Jacobs. I first saw Mike Jacobs maybe forty-three years ago, in the Hotel Normandie on Broadway and Thirty-eighth Street. Jacobs had about ten feet of space in the lobby of the hotel where he sold opera tickets. I knew his brother Jake much better, and I remember that when Mike was on top of the world, Jake was selling flowers from the sidewalk on Eighth Avenue.

The last time I spoke with Mike was on the corner of Broadway and Forty-ninth Street. He was promoting one of the Joe Louis fights and he and I were watching the line of buyers in front of a special window. I said, "Mike, it doesn't look like a big enough line, does it?"

Jacobs replied, "Listen, wait till Friday. They all get their WPA checks on Friday—then you'll see something."

I made it my business to examine the ticket line on Friday. The line was two blocks long.

Mike the Horse

I KNEW some of the characters in the great Damon Runyon stories: Black Hat Gallagher, Sad Sam, No Nose Cohen, and Harry the Horse. Actually, Harry the Horse's "real" name was Mike the

Horse; his "official" name, the one that went on police blotters, was Al Leroy; but only a very few people knew that his name at birth was Joe Abrams, and that he had originally come from Coney Island. When someone asked, "Have you seen the Horse today?" there was no doubt that the party referred to was Mike the Horse. He earned that nickname because he was always "on the go." He rarely smiled and never uttered an unnecessary word. He was a "horse" for work. If a gambler about town wanted a diamond ring for his sweetheart, Mike the Horse would bring it to him in a matter of minutes. He could get you anything from a pair of silk pajamas to a hundred shares of New York Central Pfd.

One interesting phase of Mike the Horse's activities escaped the pen of Damon Runyon. This "job" came during a slack season for the Horse, and showed what a resourceful man he was. He created the profession himself. He became a "bender" at floating dice games. At these games were some of the rich industrialists and playboys who did not like to bend down to pick up dice or money, so Mike the Horse performed this chore for these fancy dans, at the rate of fifty dollars a night, and it certainly helped to tide him over a couple of depression years.

Lasky understood

I WAS saddened by the death of the motion-picture tycoon, Jesse Lasky. I had never met him. But of all the Hollywood producers and proprietors, Mr. Lasky had a warm spot in my heart —always.

In P. S. No. 20 on Rivington Street we saw the very earliest movies, and it was Mr. Lasky who had sent them. Some years later there was a big "preview," the forerunner of all those monster publicity stunts which were to come later. Mr. Lasky had sent down to us a new motion-picture starring Geraldine Farrar in *Joan of Arc.*

Why did Mr. Lasky do all of this? There was no publicity and —there was no charge. Fortunately, we meet many more Jesse

Laskys in life than we expect—the men who *understand,* the men who "get the point."

Mr. Lasky was never more than a name to me, but I mourn his loss.

Lorena and Uncle Tommy

AMONG my friends on the West Coast is Lorena Willis, a girl who once sang in the beer saloons of the Gold Coast and was a Wobbly. Now she runs a rooming house.

Lorena always cared for people. To this day she says the old-time Socialist conscience has her in its grip. She started caring for people when she was five, and she remembers her Uncle Tommy's very delicate throat. Only five, she says, but she worried all the time about Uncle Tommy. Sometimes he would wake up after a night on the town and his throat was in bad shape and the only thing that could help him was to gargle. He'd send little Lorena next door for a quart of cold beer and Uncle Tommy would gargle that beer, managing to swallow most of it. By the time he'd gargled a second quart of beer, Lorena says, old Uncle Tommy and that delicate throat were as good as new.

Walter Damrosch

How we miss Walter Damrosch! Mr. Damrosch spent his entire life trying to drag America into the symphony hall. Mr. Damrosch did more to teach America good music than any other human being living or dead. For years he conducted those wonderful Saturday broadcasts for children, and who can ever forget the delightful accented voice in a background of Mozart— "And now, the young officer is bowing low to the mother and asking permission to dahnce with the beautiful girl . . ." Oh, where are the Damrosches of yesteryear?

The diet addict

My brother Jacob is a diet addict. Not only does he carefully regulate his own diet, but he wants to regulate everybody's diet. It's worth your life to order a good meal when you go to a restaurant with him. You feel like a criminal ordering a steak and potatoes after he's asked the waitress for the vegetable plate and prunes.

But he has been hoist with his own petard.

I found him in the nearly deserted dining room of a hotel late one afternoon. I sat at his table and noticed he was eating a monumental slab of pie. I said nothing. After all, it was his business. But he was clearly annoyed. He fussed with his fork a minute before he dogmatically declared, "Apples are very good for you."

PART 7

Nursing the Votes Along

Culture invades Tammany

IN THE old days of Tammany, if someone ran into an executive board meeting and yelled, "Your saloon is on fire!" all the delegates would run out to see the extent of damage to their businesses. Once upon a time, a Tammany district was considered lucky if its leader could read. Nowadays there are Tammany leaders who can read music.

Recently the West Side Democratic Club in New York City sponsored a month-long art exhibit. The old card-playing clubs have gone and in their place have come the political clubs that put the emphasis on culture.

I used to go to the old Joe McCormick Club. McCormick's clubhouse had thirty chairs and sixty spittoons. You never used the spittoon by your chair, you used the spittoon two chairs away.

Joe McCormick was the marriage clerk at City Hall and he got into trouble over his income tax. He apparently neglected to report the fees he wasn't entitled to collect. A license cost two dollars— that was it, all the city asked. But Joe McCormick had an additional system of fees. I know. Joe McCormick married me thirty-four years ago. It was the first time I had seen old Joe McCormick without his hat.

After the ceremony, he said, "Kiss the bride," and casually opened the middle drawer of a large desk in the center of the room. The inside of the drawer looked like the inside of a cash register. There were slots for fifty-, twenty-, and ten-dollar bills. Money was piled high in each slot and there was no chance of anyone missing either the drawer or its meaning. Joe McCormick didn't say a word. While everyone shook hands, the bridegroom was overcome by the feeling that if he didn't put a bill into one of those slots his marriage wasn't legal. Some of the less sophisticated bridegrooms handed Joe a bill. Joe never took it. Joe never uttered a word except, "Kiss the bride." He merely inclined his head toward the open drawer.

But the old Tammany Club is gone, and with it, the old district leader. In their place is the new club with an artistic skylight, Swedish furniture, Picassos on the wall, and connoisseurs to explicate them.

Tantamount

IN NORTH CAROLINA, as in the rest of the South, the Democratic primary is you-know-what to election. (With the possible exceptions of "victuals" and "titmouse," the word "tantamount" is probably the ugliest in the English language. It sounds like a disease or the name of a cemetery—"Last stop, all off for Tantamount." Except for "tantamount" I believe the South would even now have a two-party system.)

During the next Democratic primary season let us count how often *The New York Times*, *New York Herald Tribune*, and *Time* magazine use the word "tantamount" in their political stories out of the South. But "tantamount" is not the only thing that will be stirring. Primary time is a headache for the regional sales managers. Hundreds of their sales-women stop selling greeting cards and vanilla extract and take to the political hustings: "How much is he paying this year?" "Mary, what's Mr. Shmendrick running for? I'm working for him."

But Democratic primary time always sends me to my own archives to read a true collector's item. The letter was from a politician, one of the many for whom I have done a bit of work now and again during primary campaigns.

I had sent the politician copy for a proposed campaign broadside. He returned it with these instructions: "Dear Golden, get me about 20,000 of the circulars. I want 10,000 with the union label and 10,000 without the union label."

What is a liberal?

IN THE 1912 campaign, speaking from the Manhattan Opera House on October 19, President William Howard Taft said, ". . . the continuation of *liberal* government depends on the reelection of my administration." Mr. Taft was running against Theodore Roosevelt, the Progressive Party's candidate, and Woodrow Wilson, the Democrats. Yet this conservative Republican wanted to call himself a "liberal."

Liberalism is the one theme every candidate for public office stresses more often than any other. Despite the fakers who try to make the word "liberal" synonymous with "Red," the people rush to rehabilitate the liberal tradition whenever it is shaky. The pattern is the same whether it is America of the McCarthy era or France of the Reign of Terror.

As a consequence, sometimes no term can be as misleading as the label "liberal." Take the example of Hamilton and Jefferson, who were on opposite sides of the political fence. Hamilton believed in a strong central government, a national government so strong there was no possibility of placing any checks upon its power. Jefferson hated and feared a centralized government. Hamilton's ideas and decisions were nearly always correct with respect to the future of this country. Jefferson imagined the America of the future as a great agricultural nation. He not only closed his eyes to industrialization but determined to fight it tooth and nail. Hamilton stood on the banks of the Hudson River and said, "Someday a great empire city will stand here." Jefferson spoke of an agrarian society composed of small county seats and farmers.

Then why is it a liberal thinks of himself as a Jeffersonian when modern American liberalism has always espoused a strong Federal government and a highly industrialized society? The reason is Jefferson's humanism—his concern for people. States' rights or not, when you think of anything political in terms of people you are on the right side. Hamilton was nearly always right, but he also said, "The people is a beast." Jefferson fought for the Virginia statute of religious freedom. When he wrote his will he made certain that that would be written on his tombstone.

Thus the liberals (Jefferson), who were in control of a strong Federal government (Hamilton), gave us social security, a minimum wage and hours law, unemployment insurance, and collective bargaining. It has been said that a liberal is a man who does not desire to detach himself from those elements in society he wishes to reform.

The ladies' committee

THERE is a world of difference in the emotional make-up of a men's committee and a women's committee. A men's committee that wants to do good will do good. An orphan will go to college, the mayor will hire a city planner, a funeral will be well-attended. A women's committee that wants to do good will kidnap children for a trip through the museum or inflict a dance recital on some tired husbands.

A ladies' committee will not function unless it is anxiety-ridden. The whole point of a ladies' committee is to absorb as much anxiety as possible.

When the cultural committee proposes to import a speaker from Chicago with expenses and fee, the executive committee will never hand down a unanimous decision. The decision to invite the novelist will be 103-1, the one negative vote coming because the novelist is divorced. How will a divorced man affect the community? This is Anxiety No. 1. Anxiety No. 2 will be when the executive and cultural committees get into a hassle over who will entertain the novelist at the tea. Anxiety No. 3 is the tea itself. It is held at 2:30. After the several chairmen, the president of the board, and the hostess have welcomed everyone, it is almost 2 o'clock, and those little tummies start grumbling in simultaneous cannonade.

Anxiety No. 4 occurs with the arrival of the novelist. The chairman of the cultural committee will trap the novelist for a long discussion about an article which oppeared in *Commentary*, which the novelist will immediately confess he has never read. Promptly, he gets a description in infinite detail about the article. While this discussion is going on, however, the cultural committee chairman is effectively excluding from any introduction the executive committee chairman and her cohorts. This brings on Anxiety No. 5. The executive committee will have to ride through a proposal that next year the public relations and publicity committee must make arrangements for the executive committee and each subcommittee chairman to meet *all* guests.

A visit of state

No PUBLIC official ever enjoyed the affection and the blind devotion of the Jews on the Lower East Side of New York as did Theodore Roosevelt. There are several reasons for this, the most important being that Theodore Roosevelt had been the police commissioner of New York City, and thus had come in contact with thousands of Jews at the level of storekeeper, student, pushcart peddler, housewife, factory worker, and intellectual. No other non-Jewish government official ever knew Jewish life and problems as did Mr. Roosevelt. He was the first President to appoint a Jew to the Cabinet—Mr. Oscar Straus; and you haven't any idea what that meant at the time. There were special buttons made to commemorate the event, with two names imprinted on a background of red, white, and blue—Roosevelt and Straus.

It was at the height of the great immigration of Jews from eastern Europe. Close to a million had just come from the ghettos in Russia, Poland, Romania, Hungary, and Austria. They had come from a civilization which did not even allow them to go to a public school; and here they saw one of their coreligionists sitting in the Cabinet of the President.

Mr. Roosevelt had promised that when he became President he would make a "visit of state" to the Lower East Side. He was as good as his word. It was the gala day of all gala days. President

Roosevelt went to the Little Hungary, a world-famous restaurant owned by Mr. Max Schwartz. The Little Hungary was a fabulous eating place, where food was considered one of the higher arts, and where the rich and the great came to dine and drink the excellent wine which flowed from a spigot at the bottom of each bottle. Theodore Roosevelt was escorted to the Little Hungary by rabbis and other dignitaries of the section. A highly dramatic incident occurred on the line of march. A week or so before, President Roosevelt had expressed himself, in his usual outspoken manner, on the birth-control movement sponsored by Margaret Sanger. It was a new social philosophy at the time and we can forgive Mr. Roosevelt, if he felt that, as the head of the nation, he was expressing the opinion of the majority. Anyway he said birth control was immoral and that he was a great believer in large families, which he was, indeed. There was no connection between the President's statement and his visit to the Lower East Side. But the controversy was fresh in the minds of the people, and as President Roosevelt walked down the street, Jewish mothers began to breast-feed their babies in full view. It was their way of showing the president that they were "for him."

Unequal spheres of influence

It is incorrect to say that the world has two equal spheres of influence. The spheres are not at all equal. One of the most significant sociological developments of all time is that if most of the people of the world desire to be anything, they desire to be Americans. Outside of the geographical area of Russia, no one desires to be a Russian.

Both countries in the past have had extensive immigration. People once became Russians, but when Stalin ascended to power, Russian immigration stopped as effectively as if the Soviet had passed a McCarran-Walters Bill.

The urge to become an American has never abated. There are people waiting hopefully for a quota assignment. This is an advantage we have over the Soviets which is worth more than the H-bomb, but we have not yet learned to exploit ideas.

Eisenhower and Truman

I WATCHED President Eisenhower's birthday party on TV back in 1956, and my partisanship gave way to deep admiration and respect for both the actor Robert Montgomery and the advertising agency of Batten, Barton, Durstine, and Osborne.

This was wonderful. The President and Mrs. Eisenhower were seated in the center of a group which included son, daughter-in-law, and grandchildren. From off-screen came the voice of actor Jimmy Stewart: "Mr. President, we will now hear Howard Keel and Kathryn Grayson sing your favorite song, " 'Down Among the Sheltering Palms.' "

And millions of people felt themselves "safe and secure from all alarm," nestling in the shelter of the everlasting arms.

> What a fellowship,
> What a joy divine,
> Leaning on the
> Everlasting Arm.

That is why the City of Washington once found it necessary to pass an ordinance prohibiting adults from climbing up on Lincoln's statue and sitting in his lap.

President Eisenhower's popularity has always rested on the human instinct to follow the "Great White Father." The fact that Roosevelt's elections suited me does not alter the fact that his political success also was due to this urge to transfer the burdens and worries of society to the shoulders of the "strong man." The advances we have made from time to time were because once in a while the great White Father turned out to be a Lincoln, a Gandhi, or a Roosevelt.

President Truman could never achieve this status in the minds of the people. This was due partly to the fact that he wore a colored sport shirt and interrupted the pinochle game to ask,

"Do you boys think I did the right thing today?" He was the man who told a civic club some time ago, "There are a million men in the country who could handle the job of President." That is just the thing *not* to tell the people. They want a man in a cape or with a riding crop, someone aloof from the crowd, who looks and acts like he can fix everything. The people have too much on their minds to worry with fellows like Truman who sits around the cracker barrel annoying them asking for advice. First of all, there's a World Series, with football right around the corner. In addition there are Ernie Ford, *Wagon Train*, Perry Como, Gene Autry, Superman, automobiles, and a little over three hundred million comic books to be read every year.

Nursing the votes along

I REMEMBER the immigrants coming from Ellis Island once or twice a week. Many of them used to walk down the middle of the streets of the Lower East Side with large tags around their necks. Usually they were shepherded by an assistant to the Tammany leader of the district. Of course, Tammany Hall was interested in getting their votes eventually, but that was to take a long time; in the meantime, "The Hall" had to nurse them along; and they did a pretty good job, even if it wasn't motivated by altruism. When the Irish immigrants came off the boat, the Tammany flunky had job applications ready for each young Irishman—fireman, policeman, and motorman.

The Italian immigrants used to go across the Bowery into Kenmore, Mott, and the other streets of what is known as Little Italy. The Jews stayed east of the Bowery, settling in the tenements of Delancey, Forsythe, Allen, Orchard, Ridge, Pitt, and other streets right up to the East River; and then, of course, later, across the East River into Williamsburg (Brooklyn). At Ninth Street, or Tompkins Square Park, you began to meet the Poles, and here you could see the Roman Catholic churches with the rounded domes and double spires of the old country. The Germans went to the Upper East Side, known as Yorkville; and the entire West Side, from Sixth Avenue to the Hudson River and from Fourteenth Street up to the Sixties, belonged to the Irish.

A familiar sight in all the sections of the city was the roaming three-piece German band. It played two tunes—"Ach du Leiber, Augustine, Augustine" and "My Hat It Has Three Corners"— and the folks in the tenements responded with coins wrapped in bits of newspaper. Beer was ten cents a pitcher (about four large glasses), and with a five-cent schooner of Pilsener you could get a large platter of corned beef and cabbage and other cooked dishes free. On many Sunday mornings kids would compete with one another for the privilege of sweeping one of the corner saloons. The pay for this chore was the money you'd find in the sawdust. And over all of this the big Tammany district bosses—men like "Big Tim" Sullivan, Christopher D. Sullivan, Solomon Goldenkrantz, and the Ahearns—ruled like benevolent feudal barons of old; a half-dozen mother hens waiting for a million votes to hatch. On alternate nights their clubhouses were turned into confessionals, relief societies, and employment agencies—all, all for the day when the immigrant would become naturalized and the boy reached the age of twenty-one. Sometimes you could vote even before you were that old.

Are ghost writers necessary?

Of course.

Approximately 90 per cent of political candidates are lawyers, and that fact alone makes ghost writers necessary. Lawyers spend their entire lives exploring the past, and thus lack the imagination necessary for a good political speech, which must always hold out a promise for the future. By education, training, and practice, lawyers are concerned entirely with what has already happened. "This is what *has happened* to me," says the client—always in the past tense.

If Columbus had consulted a lawyer before embarking on his

voyage of discovery, the lawyer would have advised him against making the trip.

He would have pulled a couple of volumes off his shelf: "Oh, I have it right here. We need go no further. It's all right here. The statute of the year 1178, annotated in the year 1261, Part 2, amended in the year 1481, Shmendrick versus Pippick—the earth is flat."

And that's that, until a new decision gets in the book. Fortunately Christopher did not go to a lawyer. Instead he hired himself a good ghost writer who helped fire the imagination of Queen Isabella and two financial backers.

If there were no ghost writers, most candidates for public office would have to play the guitar and sing, "I'm back in the saddle again."

Ben-Nit, Mitch-Hell, Hill-Quit: Hyl-In!

THE country was at war, but World War I did not have universal consent and there was much political dissension about our entry. This dissension was reflected in the passage of the Espionage Act, in mass arrests, and in the imprisonment of Eugene V. Debs. In the mayoralty race of 1917, New York City had four candidates, two of them considered great men of American politics. The four were: John Purroy Mitchel, Fusion candidate for re-election; Morris Hillquit, the Socialist candidate; John Francis Hylan, the Tammany nominee; and William F. Bennett, the Republican. One of the Tammany slogans pasted up around town read: "Ben-Nit, Mitch-Hell, Hill-Quit, and Hyl-In!"

Mitchel and Hillquit, of course, are the two men who live on in political history. Next to Gaynor, John Purroy Mitchel was possibly the best mayor New York ever had; and very possibly Morris Hillquit would have been, too.

Morris Hillquit was a Latvian Jew who came to America in 1886. He became active in the Socialist Labor Party which was led by

Daniel De Leon. After a while, however, Hillquit formed a splinter group and eventually wrested control from De Leon. This was no mean achievement. De Leon was the first Marxist able to write prose a workingman could comprehend. De Leon had a witty, facile style and the European Communists used to call him the "Yankee Socialist." But Hillquit spotted De Leon's essential weakness. De Leon thought political action had for its end only agitation. It was Hillquit who transformed American socialism into a parliamentary and constitutional procedure toward equity. He formed a party called the Social Democrats and under its banner was five times a candidate for Congress. He was never elected to public office but he made political history in 1924 when he led the Socialists into the camp of La Follette's Progressive Party.

Yet running on the Socialist ticket in 1917 and running as a pacifist, Hillquit received the largest vote of any Socialist before or since. It was a three-cornered race between Hylan, Mitchel, and Hillquit. Hillquit received nearly 100,000 more votes than Bennett, the Republican. And this vote was achieved against some of the most powerful men in American politics. Theodore Roosevelt campaigned against Hillquit and, because of his pacifist leanings, accused him as "the Hun within our gates." Charles Evans Hughes called Hillquit a traitor and Clarence Darrow (whom the Jews worshiped), after a long persuasive talk with Woodrow Wilson, campaigned against Hillquit along the Lower East Side. What really hurt Hillquit's campaigning, however, was the presence at all his rallies of official stenographers from the U. S. Attorney General's office. They recorded everything he said with a view toward prosecuting him under the statutes of the Espionage Act. Hillquit was a lawyer and he took care in his speeches not to offer the Attorney General grounds for indictment.

Although socialism was supposed to have died at Sarajevo, Hillquit still scored heavily. What made him popular was that he was running on a platform, "The City for the People," which demanded a vast program of public housing. Public housing was an idea Hillquit had borrowed from John Purroy Mitchel. But neither Hillquit nor Mitchel were as radical about public housing as the late Mr. Republican, Senator Robert A. Taft; and this could happen only in America.

It was during this campaign, too, that Joseph V. McKee, who later became mayor upon the resignation of Jimmy Walker, entered politics. McKee ran for the Assembly against a female Socialist who was drawing big crowds. Finally McKee made a speech in which he said that he knew very little about this socialism, but if it were any good at all, the Democrats would have it. McKee did not realize what a prophet he was.

John Purroy Mitchel was an Irish Catholic. He was a self-made man in the Horatio Alger tradition, even to the mortgage on the family homestead. He first won election as mayor in 1913 by campaigning against Tammany graft. But this man was no humbug. Under his rule everyone got to talk in New York City—the "I Won't Works" and the Wobblies and the unionists and the bitterly anti-British Irish Nationalists. Where Tammany would have jailed all these speakers, Mitchel only policed them. All of them got a street corner, although Mitchel was quoted once as saying, "The street corner they can have, but I'm not giving them the soapbox." Mitchel made free speech a continuous, usable right in public places. He was also the first to introduce "scientific" government. He hired insurance experts and put them in the Fire Department and the fire rate went down. He reorganized the corrupted Police Department, prepared New York City's first corporate stock budget so that everyone knew where the city stood financially. He introduced a "pay-as-you-go" tax plan, the first of its kind, to help relieve the depleted treasury and eventually this plan was adopted by the Federal Government in World War II. Mitchel also bought up sections in New Rockaway to be reserved for public use and in tandem with Jacob Riis, who wrote *How the Other Half Lives*, started one of the first city housing developments. Mitchel ran afoul of the Catholic Church, curiously enough, although he himself was admirably Catholic. He challenged the advisability of city support for Catholic orphanages and this in the long run helped defeat him. Like Parnell, when Catholics turned against him, Mitchel was cruelly treated. And this brought down upon his head the wrath of William Randolph Hearst; and when that happened to you during those big Hearst days, all you could say was, "And may the good Lord have mercy on my soul."

The Hearst papers came out one day with a screaming headline, VANDERBILT CALLS ME JOHN. Hearst claimed that one of his reporters had overheard the mayor boast, "Vanderbilt calls me John," and from that moment on Mr. Mitchel went down in influence and prestige.

Immediately after failing to win re-election, Mitchel volunteered for the armed services. He undertook pilot training and was commissioned a major. But on July 6, 1918, on a training flight over Gerstner Field in Louisiana, Mitchel fell from the cockpit. Theodore Roosevelt led the funeral parade down Fifth Avenue. John Purroy Mitchel was not yet forty years old. A man who had the mind and the integrity to become President of the United States was another victim of the political phenomenon that Wagner will learn about—that to be mayor of New York is to enter a political graveyard.

Judge John F. Hylan, the third of this political trinity, won by a narrow margin over Mitchel. Hylan had been politically active for only eleven years before his election. While he might have been only a minor Brooklyn judge, he was admirably shrewd. He got into politics by organizing the fictional Allied Boards of Trade and Taxpayers Association of Brooklyn. Total membership consisted of Hylan, two other lawyers, and a vaudevillian. This alliance used to send out daily publicity releases criticizing Mitchel, taxes, the Socialists, and constantly endorsing Judge Hylan. The Allied Boards of Trade and Taxpayers Association brought Hylan to the attention of Charley Murphy, the Tammany boss, and Murphy bit. Four days before the election in 1917, Murphy found out the Association's office was only a battered postal box. But it was too late. Hylan was mayor.

Hylan was unflinchingly honest, yet not too bright, and despite his 420,000 plurality in 1921, Tammany ditched him for James J. Walker.

Mayor Hylan was nicknamed "Red Mike," and like his colleague in Chicago, Big Bill Thompson, he went all out in attacking the British Empire during his two campaigns for mayor of New York. In his memoirs, the Duke of Windsor writes how Hylan received him when he visited the country as the Prince of Wales. To the Prince's invitation to lunch with him aboard his yacht *Renown*, the mayor, extremely nervous about his Irish following, replied, "Sorry, Prince, can't do. Everyone here knows I don't eat lunch." His speeches, of course, were prepared for him by the Hearst staff and on one occasion, while in the course of delivering an address, he came suddenly upon a joke which he had never heard before. He put the manuscript down, held his big stomach, and laughed like hell.

Hylan spent much of his time as mayor trying to help Staten Island, which was a noble cause that suffered from a crushing geographical fact. Staten Island just isn't near anything. The Stapleton piers in Staten Island, built at a cost of thirty million, never had a ship berth there, and to this day, the empty, rotting piers are called "Hylan's Folly." He was a sort of benign demagogue who insisted upon keeping the five-cent subway fare "against the interests," for which bit of chicanery the city has been paying ever since.

William F. Bennett, I understand, went back to his law practice. In New York City politics the Republicans were always going back to their law practice.

From the Hylan election in 1917 until La Guardia took office in January of 1934, Tammany ruled New York.

The Republicans and the post office

PRESIDENT Rutherford B. Hayes expanded the service to two deliveries a day to business establishments. President William Howard Taft inaugurated the parcel post system, and President Eisenhower has gone all-out. First he replaced those awful post-office pens with a ball point job, then he had the mailboxes painted

red, white, and blue; and now we have the advances in postal
rates.

The mother of the Republican Party must have been frightened
by a postmaster.

Whither the pamphleteer?

THE pamphlet was an intellectual stimulant. The late
Bernard De Voto was really a pamphleteer in the best tradition
of the Western world, and so is Gerald Johnson of North Carolina and the *New Republic*. Actually Emanuel Haldeman-Julius
was the last pamphleteer of the old school—getting an idea hot
off the press, distributing a couple of thousand copies, and starting
a hundred debates around the country. The tradition of pam-
phleteering, with all its controversy and theorizing, may be a thing
of the past. Because of the vastness of the radio and TV audience,
such intellectual stimulation is not possible. Today at the TV set
you see an eight-year-old boy, and his forty-year-old father, and his
seventy-year-old grandfather, all laughing at the same thing at the
same time and biting their nails at the same mystery story. If
their ages were added up and divided by three, it would not be
so bad, but in order to hold the audience television must make
sure that the eight-year-old gets the point.

The only true interfaith work

SOME years ago I made a speech in a fairly large city, and
beside me on the dais was a leading citizen who is also the most
noble of philanthropists. During the preliminaries a handsome
young lawyer was delivering a talk, and his language was brilliant.
I leaned over to my philanthropist neighbor and said, "What a
fine service that man would perform for the city and the State if
he entered politics."

The philanthropist, with a big smile, whispered to me, "He wanted to run last year but I stopped him. I don't think we should stick our necks out." But of course our philanthropist friend told this to the wrong man. For me all his "good works" were reduced to nothing.

In the search for self-esteem and in the attempt to prove individual worth we often start at the wrong end. We try to join the country club or the garden club, and if we are rebuffed, we give up, frustrated, chagrined, and disappointed.

But *politics* is the only true level of both participation and acceptance. Politics is synonymous with America; the only true "interfaith" work. The statement I often hear, "A Jew must not lose, it would look bad," is the worst kind of nonsense. I urge every audience to see to it that a Jew runs for public office in every primary, and if he loses, he should run again, and again; and if he gets tired of running, you must groom some other young fellow to run in his place. The only bit of restraint that I believe may be involved in this situation is the necessity of picking an outstanding man, a man of education and culture.

We once had a tough Congressional race here, and Speaker Sam Rayburn came to Charlotte to make a speech, and the committee was confronted with a serious problem. How about the four or five Negro leaders, the men who work among the ten thousand registered voters of their race? It was a bit humorous to watch five old-time Southerners pleading with the hotel manager to serve those Negroes in the main ballroom of the fancy hotel.

The only effective intergroup work is political action. All the good-will pamphlets, Brotherhood programs, and pleas for tolerance are good, but after you throw them all into the river, go out and vote and run for public office. There is no other way.

The age of metaphor

THE next Democrat who comes up to me and says, "Oh, my, what will happen if Nixon becomes President?" I promise to hit the fellow over the head with a rolled-up newspaper.

Nothing would "happen." As a matter of fact, Mr. Nixon might be so overburdened with discomfort over his earlier days as a politician, that he might very well become a more Socialist President than Ike, and spend most of his time receiving plaques from "liberal" and "civil rights" organizations.

There *is* one disturbing element. If Nixon succeeds President Eisenhower, this entire era may become known in history as the "Eisenhower-Nixon Age of the Metaphor."

"I haven't studied the problem yet, but *I think it's our ball.*"

"*Let us put our shoulders to the wheel.*"

"Well, I have not seen the statement to which you refer, but I will say this, that we've got the *ball on the five-yard line.*"

"If you look at the over-all picture, you will see that *we have dignity and human freedom on our side.*"

"You are telling me something about my administration I had not heard before, but I will say this, *we will raise our standard for dignity and the liberty of man.*"

"We must remember that *this is only the first down on the forty-yard line.*"

Can we really take this for four or eight years more? And what in the world happened to the rolling stone that gathered no moss?

Summing it up

ONE of the best political speeches I've ever heard came from a Southerner running for a county office. He said, "Remember the symbol of the Republican Party. It is the elephant, the

giant that stomps through the jungle clumping little animals un-
derfoot and swinging its weight around. But the symbol of the
Democrats is the little mule, the same blessed animal our Saviour
rode in Jerusalem two thousand years ago."

New Chinese custom

IN AN ARTICLE the reliable *Manchester Guardian,* their
correspondent, Robert Guillain, from Hong Kong, after studying
Communist China for one year, stated:

"Chinese fathers told me that the master of the house is now
the youngster. 'When we hear the noise of his slippers we all stop
talking.' "

Even six thousand miles away it is frightening.

PART 8

God Bless the Irish

God bless the Irish

Gᴏᴅ bless the Irish. Another St. Patrick's Day has come and gone and it always leaves me—a Galitsianer—limp with admiration and wonder. Of the immigrant groups that came to our shores it is the Irish who have achieved the highest prestige and security. The story is one of the most remarkable in all history. Within one hundred years the Irish have conquered America.

One hundred years ago the Irish were hounded by the bigots. The Know-Nothings (strictly an anti-Irish party) even came close to electing a President of the United States. Former President Millard Fillmore ran on the Know-Nothing Party ticket and lost in a close race to Buchanan. In those days Irish laborers were found dead beside the railroad track they had laid the day before.

What is the basis of the Irish success story? First, let us not overlook the personality of the Irishman himself. He is handsome, happy, sentimental, and given to song and humor; he is also brave and a fighter—all the attributes of the American ideal.

Then, all immigrant groups had one goal in common. They wanted to become Americans as swiftly as possible. And the Irishman had these advantages from the start: he not only "looked" like an American on the day he arrived, he spoke the language.

But there was more to it than his personality and his historical "advantages."

It was *politics*, the greatest of all American expressions. The Irish Catholic was a born politician.

For the first twenty-five years of the twentieth century, Tammany Hall was under the control of the Irish and the Jews. The Irish were the top leaders; the Jews were in the second echelon.

In the days when men like Charles F. Murphy, James A. Foley, Alfred E. Smith, Max D. Steuer, and Nathan D. Burkan were making policy, there was a song around town called, "If It Weren't for the Irish and the Jews."

There was the loud refrain:

> If Tammany Hall should ever fall,
> There wouldn't be a hall at all,
> If it weren't for the Irish and the Jews!

But there were significant differences between these two groups.

The differences between the Irishman and the Jew in American terms can be summed up in two letters of the alphabet—two letters repeated twice—*sh sh*. The Irishman did not know from *sh sh*, whereas the Jew was taught from the day he got off the boat that *sh sh* will make him a better American. The Irishman played everything by ear and he made sure that the leprechauns haunted the American way of life. The Irishman became a good American by being a good Irishman.

Who can ever forget what the American Irish contributed to the establishment of the Irish Free State? England had to bow to the will of the American Irish in Boston and New York who, as American citizens, exerted every possible political pressure on the State Department and on the Congress. And whenever a voice was raised about "voting blocs" and "political pressure," the Irishman shouted, "Up Sligo—let's invade Canada!" I remember when an Irish hero came to visit New York. He had led a group of patriots in blowing up a Black and Tan police headquarters during what the Irishman always called "the trouble," and they introduced this fellow from the prize-fight ring in old Madison Square Garden, and the fans set up such a howl that they had to delay the main bout for a full hour.

Years later came the crew of an airplane which had made one of the first east-to-west Atlantic crossings. It was a German flight captained by a fellow named Kohl, and one of the crew of five happened to be an Irishman by the name of Fitzpatrick. When they introduced the flyers from the ring, Joe Humphries shouted, "The great hero-flyer Fitzpatrick and his four assistants!" and the crowd went wild of course.

But *politics* did it for the Irish. They practically invented the word. They knew from the start the essence of America and what makes it tick. (No one has ever questioned the loyalty of those millions of American Irishmen who helped establish the free state of Ireland, and of course it is a perversion of the American spirit of freedom to impugn the loyalty of Jews who wish to aid their brothers in Israel to achieve a similar end.)

In assessing the prestige of the American Irish, let us not overlook the power and strength of their Church.

In 1873 Prince Otto von Bismarck initiated a series of laws aimed at crippling the Roman Catholic Church. Prince Otto laughingly proclaimed a new policy of "Non Canossamus," meaning that his laws would never again make it necessary for a European head of state to bow before the Pope as Henry IV had bowed before Pope Gregory at Canossa in the year 1077.

We go from the year 1077 to 1873 and to 1958. The Protestant Anglo-American world reported every single detail about the death of Pope Pius XII and cheered the election of the new Pope John XXIII. Despite Bismarck, or perhaps because of him, the Catholic Church has more adherents and greater influence today than at any time in its history.

The Roman Catholic Church has many sources of strength, but chief among these is its tie with history. The Roman Catholic Church won over its competitors, the Greek and Orphic mysteries of Mithraism and Isisism, says Edward Gibbon, because it had the historical figure of Christ. And Pope John XXIII is in direct descent from Saint Peter, the first Bishop of Rome. For hundreds of millions the Church satisfies man's everlasting search for the Absolute.

The Church, however, has never been content to provide only continuity and unendingness. It has never remained static. It has not only produced its own heretics, but absorbed them. It has produced both the yes and no on every question. Once Dante's works were publicly burned by the Inquisition, but today he is the chief poet of the Catholic world. The *Summa Theologica* by Saint Thomas Aquinas was near-heretical in the twelfth century. Though the Church has never designated an official philosopher, Saint Thomas's philosophy is the base on which all consequent Church philosophy has been built. The Church's leaders often fought a new idea tooth and nail, but only to a certain point. It may come as a surprise to some to find students in a Catholic college using a text which describes the theories of Charles Darwin. This story of the absorption powers of the Church may be summed up in the dramatic story of Galileo, whom the Church forced to recant, down to the present day when the priests at Georgetown University record every earthquake and tremor on this planet. They take everything in stride.

The Church has other strengths, not the least of which is the fact that the Vatican has established an identity of complete and unrelieved opposition to Soviet Russia and world communism. The consistently adamant policy with which the Church condemns communism derives from the fact that the problem of communism concerns the Church very deeply. It involves the Church more than any other institution. Except for the great Catholic philosopher, Jacques Maritain, Catholic authorities have placed no emphasis on the fact that communism is a Christian heresy. Outside of Asia, 90 per cent of all communists in Russia, Italy, France, Hungary, Romania, Bulgaria, Yugoslavia, and Poland are communist converts born originally into the Roman Catholic or Orthodox Eastern fellowships, or children of Roman Catholic or Orthodox Eastern homes. It is the Catholic countries in Europe, France, and Italy that have the largest communist populations, not Sweden or Denmark. The roots of communism can be traced to political and economic forces. But communism threatens the Church just as it threatens democracy.

The irony of this is that demagogues since Hitler have tried to identify Jews with communism. The Jews, perhaps more than any other single group in the Western world, live and thrive *only* because of capitalism, middle-class competitive capitalism, while the success of the Irish Catholics in America has been partly based on the fact that they actually avoided the turbulence of this same competition.

The Irish Catholic quickly found his niche in a sort of state security which comes with public service. He grabbed all the state jobs: policemen, firemen, sanitation department, inspectors of every description, prison-keepers, prosecutors, bailiffs, sheriffs, court clerks, postal clerks, letter carriers, etc.

If, God forbid, the communists did come, it is the Jews who as a class (capitalists) would be utterly destroyed, and the Irish would survive since the public services must go on. Anatole France would have done a wonderful story about this.

The American Irishman enjoys an immunity from all suspicion in these days of hysteria. He has his cake and he eats it too. And that is only the beginning of the "luck of the Irish." He produced a vast intelligentsia, too, which makes his immunity all the more remarkable. He was in there at the earliest beginnings of the labor movement, his priests were on a hundred picket lines and Father McGlynn in New York was a pioneer in the fight for the social and economic reforms which came fifty years later. There would be more reason to call the C.I.O. an Irish Catholic movement than to give it any other ethnic or religious designation. Yet the Irish Catholic in our American society is not identified at all with what Senator Mundt calls "controversial characters."

I have not mentioned it yet, but there is still another major factor in the rapid emergence of the Irish into the American middle class: The Irish forgeen each other like no other people in the world.

The word "forgeen" is one of those wonderful Yiddish words which loses some of its flavor in translation. Loosely, to forgeen means, "to rejoice in the good fortune of a fellow member of your clan or race."

The Jews do not forgeen each other. Not by a long shot. ("Look at him—who needs *him* to be an alderman?")

And the reason for this is not jealousy. It is history which has conditioned the Jew to look with suspicion upon good fortune. The Jew does not even forgeen himself. Many of my readers will recall how we always minimized the extent of any sudden stroke of luck. If a kid came out to the street with a brand-new dress, her mother had paved the way beforehand by telling everybody that an aunt in Boston had sent it as a hand-me-down.

The most important thing the Jew fears is that a public figure may set up a convenient target to be used—to shoot at all of them.

But the Irish—the forgeening Irish—have no such fears.

At the height of Tammany Hall's political power, Big Tim Sullivan was momentarily caught in one of those periodic newspaper exposés which are the calculated risks of all men in political life. It was revealed that Mr. Sullivan had accumulated a nest egg of one and a half million dollars during a ten-year period when his only visible means of support was a salary of fifteen hundred dollars a year as a New York State Senator. Boss Charles Francis Murphy of "The Hall" blurted out in amazement, "My God, do they really expect a man to get along on fifteen hundred dollars a year?"; and the voters seemed to share the indignation of Mr. Murphy and Big Tim.

Mr. Sullivan appeared before his constituents on the platform of Miner's Theatre on the Bowery and said, "Of course I'm worth money. I'm just an average Irish boy with a good clear head, for I don't drink or smoke and I haven't changed my residence since I got my money, and I ain't going to. I was born among you and I'm going to die among you."

With tears streaming down their cheeks the Irishmen cheered him to the echo, and their wives tightened the black shawls over their shoulders and muttered, "God love you for a good man, Big Tim."

Where a Big Tim Sullivan or a James Michael Curley could shrug it all off as something between himself and his constituents, a Jew in their position would have a tougher time. It would not be "Big Sam Goldberg" who got away with money but "the Jews."

The Negroes, who have had a similar history, also do not forgeen each other. Gunnar Myrdal in *An American Dilemma* tells of the light-colored Negro who went into the white section of a railroad station in a Southern town. A friend of his, a black-faced Negro, shouted, "Hey, Jim, get over here, you belong over on *this* side."

Not so the Irish and "the back o' me hand to ye." And they have no inhibitions at all about supporting their people when they are in trouble. The Irish simply feel that no Irishman can ever bring disgrace upon them. If he gets in trouble it's a frame-up and a libel.

This noble trait in the Irish struck me most forcibly when I witnessed the funeral of Bill Fallon, the "Great Mouthpiece." Bill had been convicted of subornation of perjury, bribing a juror, a very serious offense. The Jews and Italians would have buried such a guy in the middle of the night with the family holding their hats over their faces.

But there was Bill, "God love him," carried out of the Cathedral after a High Mass, with ten or twelve acolytes walking ahead of the casket, and the Irish lined up and weeping on both sides of the street.

The advertising agencies know that secretly millions of Americans would like to be Irishmen.

That is why forty million Protestants and two million Jews wear green neckties on the Seventeenth of March.

The Yemenites in Disneyland

WHILE I was walking through the charming streets of Disneyland, on my way to a speech in Palm Springs, whom should I meet but the INBAL Dancers of Israel! It was an amazing coincidence. When I was in Israel several months before, I was invited to a farewell party for the Dancers on the eve of their American tour. It was a joyous occasion in the home of Margalith Ovid in Ramat-Gan, a town a few miles outside of Tel Aviv. Everybody joins in at a Yemenite Party, children from the age of three and grandmothers of eighty-three.

Now, on the other side of the planet, came Margalith Ovid and Dahlia Kubani, the two prima ballerinas of the company, with an enthusiasm only Yemenites know.

The Yemenites are fascinating people. They are very dark, and their features are extraordinarily delicate. Some of the scholars say the Yemenites most closely resemble the Jews of ancient times. Whether or not this is true, one thing is certain: Jesus looked more like a Yemenite Jew than did the Italian student da Vinci posed for the *Last Supper*.

An interesting sociological story could be written about the Yemenites. They hardly ever make appearances in the criminal courts in Israel and are never litigants in civil actions. One might attribute this to their sense of responsibility. They deem a disgrace to one a disgrace to all.

They are intensely religious. But it takes no effort for them. It is a genuine part of their life, if not their life itself. It is strange to them if someone is not religious. (The mother of Margalith Ovid told me that she fasts every Monday and Thursday in accordance with strict Orthodox law, as a prayer for the welfare of her daughter in her travels. The tour lasts about eight months.)

In bringing the Oriental Jews from the Atlas Mountains and Morocco, the Government of Israel experienced great difficulty. Not so with the Yemenites. Although many of them had never seen an airplane before, they knew the Bible spoke of a return to Zion "on the wings of the eagle," and they boarded the planes with the aplomb of world travelers. In fact, they resent the designation "Magic Carpet" that describes their heroic migration into Israel. There was no magic about it to the Yemenites. It was simply a fulfillment of Biblical prophecy. The pilots tell the story of the Yemenites on a plane who, when it became very cold, built a fire in the middle of the fuselage floor to warm their hands.

And in Disneyland here came these wonderful people to greet me again.

Did H*Y*M*A*N K*A*P*L*A*N return?

If HYMAN KAPLAN and his friends, Miss Mitnick, Miss Valuskas, Mr. Schmitt, and Mr. Feigenbaum, were to matriculate suddenly into Mr. Parkhill's class, our present troubles with education would be much less than they are.

When the Hyman Kaplans went to school at the beginning of this century our educational system burgeoned and became one of the greatest school systems of all time. It had a purpose. Mr. Parkhill and his assistants, and all the grammar and high-school teachers, were devoting their efforts to make an immigrant population into a citizen population. This, these wonderful teachers did. But the American educational system has never been able to formulate successive goals. Education founders when it is wracked by the Scylla and Charybdis of P.T.A.'s and education courses.

There are no more Hyman Kaplans. The anti-immigration laws of 1921 and 1924, the laws of the 1950's with their ethnic and racial provisions, ended the stream of voluble, vital, ambitious immigrants.

The few Hyman Kaplans who are left bathe in the sun on Miami verandas, with the caps pulled low to shield their eyes. Occasionally they meet a few of their older contemporaries to play pinochle.

We no longer hear, "Julius Scissor had his Brutis, Cholly de Foist had his Cornvall, an' if Kink Judge got a bren in his had he vil make a profit from soch a semple!—Dat also epplies to Moscovitz."

Today this fellow is introducing Eleanor Roosevelt at a Bonds for Israel Dinner and getting minute-by-minute reports about the local motorboat regatta. His daughter attends Radcliffe and his son is at Dartmouth, sporting an Ivy League yarmulka.

Mark Twain's humor was about the agrarian society and it struck a responsive chord all over America. Then ethnic humor ruled. There was the Irishman with the big red nose and a can of beer, the Jew with the whining accent, and the Italian with his funny speech and a "hero" sandwich. But that humor, too, has gone. It isn't funny. It is an anachronism, just as Hyman Kaplan is an anachronism. Hyman Kaplan isn't going to return. Senator McCarran and Congressman Walter have made his return impossible, and so much the worse for America.

Religion's friends

THE greatest friends of religion are the rationalists, or, as the American Founding Fathers called themselves, Deists. Both the religious fanatic and the atheist are "brothers under the skin." One is intent upon persuading his neighbors that his faith is the one true religion; the other is intent upon persuading his neighbors not to believe in any faith.

When it came to the establishment of the United States of America, the Lord, in His infinite wisdom, planted twenty or twenty-five rationalists down here at precisely the right time. He knew that the greatest defenders of freedom were the fellows who did not believe in their own infallibility, who would not defend freedom by forcing everyone to believe as they did, and who would not defend freedom by fighting those who did believe in something.

This is the one miracle I believe in with all my heart and soul. It had to be a miracle because these few men embraced all creeds with a single glance, and harmonized them into a fabric of freedom.

Sabbath observance

In NEW YORK they used to arrest Jewish merchants for keeping their stores open on Sunday; but down here in Charlotte they recently arrested nineteen Gentile grocerymen for the same offence.

There is a terrible ambivalence surrounding Sabbath observance. The greatest inconsistencies exist in the Gentile community. It is not easy for a Jew to close his establishment on his Sabbath, Saturday. In our society it is on Saturday that the farmers and the industrial workers come into the business section to do their shopping. There is less excuse, of course, for this inconsistency among the Christians, because they have the law to support their religious holiday. But even with the civil authority behind the Sunday Sabbath, the degree of the observance appears to be without rhyme or reason. You can buy chop suey, but you cannot buy uncooked pork, you can buy apple pie, but you cannot buy an apple; you can go to the stock-car races and watch someone get killed, but you cannot get a haircut, and the most serious of all inequalities concerns the "drug" stores.

This started in New England where the laws of the "Still Sabbath," copied from Orthodox Judaism, were very strict, but they permitted the apothecary to fill prescriptions for the sick and bedridden. But of course today the apothecary sells everything under the sun, and filling prescriptions is a very small part of his business. Thus the drugstore operator has an unfair advantage over the fellows who must keep closed on Sunday, because he is indeed competing with the hardware stores, the appliance dealers, and the groceries.

And closing the doors of the barbershops, groceries, and all the other stores still does not make a real Still Sabbath. It is interesting to note that the completely Still Sabbath was known only to the Jews and to the Protestant sects of the British Isles and their descendents in America, with the Presbyterians following the Orthodox Jewish observance almost to the letter.

In all our sociological studies and surveys, I am surprised that no one has put his finger on a most important consideration in the Jews' intense desire to be self-employed. These fellows from Europe did not really care a hang about the economic structure or whether they were "employable" or not. They became peddlers and junk dealers so they could observe the Sabbath to the fullest extent.

On the Sabbath, from sundown Friday to sundown Saturday, no pious Jew or member of his family may blow out the candles or have any contact with fire or anything related to it. Therefore most of us had a Shabbos goy (a non-Jew) who performed these services, including the banking of the fire in the cookstove.

The Shabbos goy in our tenement house was an elderly Italian who performed these duties for ten or twelve families every Friday evening, coming back Saturday morning for whatever other duties may have been required of him. Some of the folks wouldn't rip open the laundry package, open a letter, or untie the string on a package. This close association resulted in an interesting human experience.

Often the Shabbos goy learned to speak Yiddish and looked on with chagrin when a child of the household violated one of the Sabbath rules. And of course the Shabbos goy would become enamored not only with the holiday spirit of the household, but with the food, and looked forward to that huge platter of mandel soup which many of the Jewish mothers saved for him. This mandel soup was a rich, golden chicken soup, into which were dropped crisp, brown mandeln (croutons of a sort), each one as light as a feather.

In Israel today there are hundreds of agricultural communities where on the Sabbath they milk the cows and sheep, only as a health measure, and immediately spill the precious milk on the ground—as a further symbol of the strict Sabbath observance. There must be no earnings or gain of any kind. Right here in the South, up to a few years ago, we had a few merchants who went through the legal ritual of "selling" their stores to a Gentile manager every Friday afternoon, and "buying" them back on Sunday afternoon.

The Sabbath observance of course is one of the truly great contributions to civilization. It raised the individual to the fullest dignity. "I am important" he was able to say, for the first time; and toward this new dignity the Jewish code significantly called for a complete change of clothing on the Sabbath, as well as special food and special religious rituals. This was a day of rest, joy, and devotion to God. It was against the Sabbath law to mourn or to weep on the Sabbath and it was even forbidden to carry anything, although a very young boy was permitted to carry his father's talis (prayer cloth) to the synagogue. In the small European towns, the bakery may have been at a considerable distance away, and yet it was forbidden to carry even the loaves prepared for the Sabbath. You should only carry within your home, a "single domain," but not from one outside place to another. The community therefore built an eyruv (a temporary fence) around the whole town. Usually the fence was either a heavy rope or wire, and thus the town became a "single domain," and the folks could "carry" from home to home. There was always the danger that there would be a break in this fence and the town would no longer be a single domain. Often Christian neighbors would volunteer to guard the eyruv and make any necessary repairs on the spot.

So now here is the Golden Plan to Promote Strict Sabbath Observance for my neighbors. Every Saturday night let us build an eyruv, this temporary fence, all around the City of Charlotte, including even the recently annexed suburban areas. Then anyone who desires may keep his establishment open, and the folks can "carry" to their heart's content and still be within the strict meaning of the Sabbath law. I am certain I can enlist the help of about fifty or sixty young Jewish fellows in town to man the barricades and guard the Charlotte eyruv to see that there is no break or disturbance to a day of rest, joy, peace, and devotion. I offer this Plan to the Charlotte City Council as a possible way out of their dilemma.

A true short, short story

MY SALESMAN friend always looks for a synagogue or temple in whatever city he finds himself on a Friday night. This time it was a small town in the deep, deep South.

He arrived a moment before the services began, and almost immediately all the lights went off. There was complete darkness except for the two red exit lights. Then came the flicker of a match and the outline of a handsome young woman up on the altar lighting the candles and saying the blessing. Now the lights went on again, one by one, and an equally handsome young man stepped forward:

"Ah would lakk for yo-all to open yo books to page one-fohty-foh, and read with me. . ."

At the end of this most fascinating service, the young man introduced himself to my salesman friend: "Are you a newcomeh?" My friend said that he was just passing through. The young man explained: "We have no Rabbah and we do the best we can by ahsevs." The young man continued: "Come on down to the social hall, the ladies always bring kiklik and stuff, and we have a few tables set up for bridge and rummy."

"Card playing on the Sabbath?" asked my friend.

Replied the young man: "That's mah doin . . . ah was the one who figured out how to get 'em heah."

The Jews are catching up

THIRTY years ago when the Jewish boys were studying law at the Catholic Fordham and St. John law school, the Irish boys were trying to get into Yale, Harvard, and Princeton. The Jews wanted to be Irishmen and the Irishmen wanted to be Episcopalians. In those days an Irishman would say, "I am Irish and what will you do about it?"—an aggression and an apology.

At this stage of our development the Jews did not yet say, "I am a Jew and I am proud of it." This bit of apologetics was still thirty years off.

But time's have indeed changed, and the Irish have it made. They no longer worry about going to Princeton. They will even elect a President of the United States within the next twelve years. Today the Irish get belligerent only about that short left-field fence in the Dodgers' Coliseum, and now they say, "I am Irish."

In 1960 the Jews are where the Irish were in 1920. Now it is the Jews who want to go to Princeton and it is they who want to be Episcopalians. They say, "I am Jewish and I am proud of it." The Puerto Ricans want to be Spanish, the Negroes want to be light-brown, and the D.A.R.'s want to be Cherokee Indians, but the Irish simply say, "I am Irish!" Ah, they've done done it, as we say in the Carolinas.

But the Jews are catching up. In another thirty years they will be as happy when their sons go to the Yeshiva College and to Brandeis University as the Irishman is now when his son goes to Boston College. The Jews will merely repeat after Jonah, "I am a Jew," and let it go at that. Yom Kipper will be practically a national holiday, and the Anti-Dafamation League will concern itself entirely with petitioning Walter O'Malley to get rid of that short left-field fence.

Big Beth Jacob Halloween Party

I RECEIVE dozens of bulletins from synagogues and organizations, and recently my sense of the ridiculous concentrated on one announcement after another: "Big Beth Jacob Halloween Party," "Big Jewish Halloween Dance."

Halloween is the eve of a highly religious Roman Catholic holiday. It is also part of the worship of the Anglican church—the High Church of the Episcopalians. It is one of the most Catholic of all Catholic observances. November 1 is an important day on the church calendar. It is All Saints' Day. Catholics are required to hear Mass that day and pray for the glorification of the saints. The night before, Halloween (hallowed eve), is when the saints rise out of their graves and together with the martyrs of the Church visit the surroundings of their earthy existence. Tradition says that many strange things happen on this eve of All Saints' Day, and of course the pranks of farm boys putting the cow on top of the church steeple has its basis in these legends. The game of bobbing for apples, which is associated with Halloween, was a game of relaxation in the monasteries of Europe for many centuries, and somewhere along the line it was incorporated into this religious holiday.

The question will be asked, why did the Puritans bring this observance to Massachusetts? The Puritans were certainly not Catholics, and they had fled from England to escape the persecution of the Anglican Church. In fact, the Puritan religion, like Calvinism itself, was a complete return to Biblical Judaism within the framework of Christianity. Yet why did the Puritans celebrate Halloween? This is a story within a story. When you see kids in masquerade costumes on Halloween, this is not a part of the original religious Catholic observance. Its origin was just the reverse, intended as an insult to the Catholics. In the year 1605 the Roman Catholics of England were having a tough time of it under King James. A few of their leaders organized a conspiracy known in history as the Gunpowder Plot. One of their number, a soldier by the name of Guy Fawkes, volunteered to store some gunpowder under the Parliament and blow up the House of Lords on the day the king spoke from the throne. The plot was carefully planned and was to be executed on November 5. But a relative of one of the Lords wrote him a letter, and giving some flimsy excuse, pleaded with him not to attend Parliament that day. Guy Fawkes and many others were arrested and executed, and to this day England celebrates Guy Fawkes Day. An appointed committee goes through the ritual of exploring the cellars of Parliament with lighted candles to see that everything is all right. Part of the observance of Guy Fawkes Day was for the kids to put on grotesque costumes (to call attention to the "foreign" aspect of Catholicism) as a mockery.

And now on the eve of a strict Roman Catholic holiday, thousands of Catholic kids put on masquerade costumes and the Jews hold a "Beth Jacob B'rith Halloween Dance." Amerika goniff.

Brocco's downfall

I REMEMBER the case of Brocco, the greatest of the six-day bicycle racers at a time when this sport filled Madison Square Garden around the clock for six days. It was a tremendous sport, and Brocco was the king. Up in the gallery were always four thousand Italians cheering themselves hoarse for their countryman, and they used to shout in unison, "Brrrroccco!" as the racer would spin around the track. Then one day, at the height of the season, Brocco, the dope, tells a reporter that he is really a Frenchman. The next night instead of four thousand cheering Italians there were two French chefs waving handkerchiefs.

Hindu custom of suttee

THE custom in which the wife dies on the funeral pyre of her husband, which the British finally succeeded in abolishing in India, was not instituted because of any wifely devotion—"I cannot live without you," and all that sort of thing. Centuries ago there had been a great epidemic of wives poisoning their husbands. It became a fad. Hindus married child brides. It was common (and still is) for a grown man to marry a little girl of seven or eight. Then he waited a few years and they consummated the marriage. Fifteen years later this girl was in the prime of life, say about twenty-two, and the husband would be pushing sixty. This led to many poisonings so the young wife could be rid of her weary old husband. To stop this husband killing the Hindus adopted the custom of "suttee," throwing the wife on the funeral pyre of her dead husband. Of course when the husband died a natural death she had to go along, too, but that's what made it a custom rather than a punishment. The poisonings stopped, but suttee became part of the religion, and that's hard to stop.

Sunday radio schedule in Dixie

9:00 A.M.: The Gospel
9:15 A.M.: Unitarian Service
9:30 A.M.: Back to God

A Jewish secret

IF ALL the Jews decided to go back to the Orthodox dietary laws, I am sure that *shrimp*, and not ham, would be the problem.

You will notice that in all discussions about the dietary laws no one ever mentions shrimp. They keep their fingers crossed. Maybe they'll overlook it altogether. Does anybody tell the chairman, "May I please have tomato juice instead of the shrimp cocktail?" Are you kidding? Shrimp is the best kept secret of Jewish communal life in America. Once a week the middle-class Jews of America empty out the ocean.

An architectural dilemma

THE greatest problem in modern architecture is how to build a synagogue large enough to hold everyone who wants to come on the High Holy Days but small enough so that the regulars who come every Sabbath won't feel self-conscious or lonely in some huge cavern. There seem to be only two answers: build only ultra-Orthodox shuls so that only people within walking distance can get there, or get hold of an up-and-coming Frank Lloyd Wright who can figure how to build an accordion-type synagogue which can be collapsed after Rosh Hashanah and Yom Kippur services.

Jews pray for Gentiles

WHEN I tell my Gentile audiences that five million Jews are praying for their continued success and good health, they look a little skeptical. But it is true. The reason for this goes as far back as Nehemiah and has persevered since. In every country the Jews have thrived during the days of peace and prosperity. But during war and depression and social upheaval they suffer. And they suffer more than any of their Gentile neighbors. Jews understand this by instinct. We are a political seismograph. We hear the tremors first.

One has but to read the prayer for the Queen as it appears in the prayer books in London's Jewish sanctuaries: "May the Supreme King of Kings in his mercy put compassion in Her heart and into the hearts of Her counsellors and nobles, that they may deal kindly with us and with all Israel."

Jews face a double jeopardy.

If, for example, the textile mills of the South shut down (God forbid!) it would constitute a major catastrophe for all Southerners. For the Jews it would mean something more—the fear that victims of the calamity would look around to see on whom this wretched burden could be shifted and blamed.

That is why Nehemiah is one of the greatest of Hebrew prophets. He told Jews to pray for the good and the welfare of the country in which they live. That is why I am right when I tell Gentile audiences that five million Jews are praying with all their hearts that their Gentile neighbors stay healthy, physically, economically, and spiritually, and that God will protect them from all harm.

Most rabbis are doctors now

I ATTENDED a luncheon in New York recently and sat among one hundred rabbis. I was as happy as a mouse in a cooky jar listening to "Hello, Doctor. Hi, Doctor. How's everything, Doctor?" Doctor, Doctor, Doctor. I thought, God forbid, that I should suddenly develop a serious case of heartburn. With a roomful of doctors not one person qualified to prescribe the necessary bit of bourbon and water.

PART 9

Still More Complaints
and Free Advice

How to win an argument

During my life, I have made countless friends by arguing—
and I am a Northerner living in the South, a Jew in the most
Gentile community on the continent, an integrationist among
white supremacists. I have a lot to argue about. But I have made
friends over discussing a difference of opinion because I make up
my mind about what I believe but I do not make up my mind
about people.

Back in 1954, when the Supreme Court ruled against racial
segregation in the public schools *The Carolina Israelite* was one
of the few Southern publications that applauded the decision.
Since then thousands of people have come to me by letter and in
person, and said they disagree. And we argue. These people who
disagree are still people. They are millworkers and lawyers, radio
announcers, bankers, and salesmen. I do not believe that you can
win the fight for the civil rights of one individual at the expense
of dehumanizing another. I listen with respect to my "opponents" and I have found this idea to be contagious. They listen to
me.

I remember one important occasion. I was invited to address the
student body of Davidson College, the leading Presbyterian institution of higher education in the United States, and where
Woodrow Wilson had studied for a year. Many of the one thousand students would one day occupy Southern pulpits, and I
urged them to become leaders in striking down the caste system
which is involved in racial segregation.

During the open forum, a student asked a simple question:
"What about the senior-class dances in our Southern high
schools?" It was the more respectful way of asking, "Do you want
your sister to marry a Negro?"

I could have sneered and said something clever about a "sense of guilt" or Mr. Freud. I could have said many things to indicate that the question was not intelligent and that my interrogator was stupid for asking it.

But the question is not stupid and the man who asked it is not unintelligent. You have to see the man who asks it as just that—a man, much like myself, worthy of respect. This man knows that a Southern high school is where boys and girls meet and later get married.

You could have heard a pin drop in that noble Presbyterian institution as the student body and the faculty waited for my answer.

I explained that the South had not had any immigration from the Mediterranean and eastern Europe, and therefore constituted itself into a single homogeneous society of white Anglo-Saxons. And because it was a "club," the Southerners did what all other people have done under similar circumstances; they permitted their social lives to overlap into their public institutions. We did the same thing on the Lower East Side fifty years ago, where we were a single homogeneous society of Jewish immigrants. The teacher spoke Yiddish to your father when he was summoned to school and your mother walked home from the ritual baths with the unwrapped towel under her arm. There was no embarrassment and there were no inhibitions because we were all *one*. Then one day the Italians began to move eastward across the Bowery and suddenly there were "strangers" in the classroom, and it was not convenient and it was not particularly pleasant. The schoolhouse had ceased to be a club. That public school was not ours. We learned to understand that the *public school* and all other tax-supported facilities of our society belong to all of us—equally. In fact, the character of the public school in particular is that it is both free and public. And I may add that we did not marry the Italians. And they did not marry us. We just went to school together.

I tried to explain that it is unfair to suspect that a Negro who wants a share in the industrial age of the twentieth century covets the high school co-eds. For the democratic principle there are some

sacrifices we have to make, and one of those sacrifices the Southerner has to make is *to separate his private life from his public
institutions.*

The Davidson College audience rose to cheer me, even though
I knew that I had not convinced my questioner. But at least he
had listened.

The woes of the intellectuals

IN SEVERAL of the intellectual enclaves along the Eastern
Seaboard, places like Nyack, New York, and Bucks County,
Pennsylvania, the drive for status does not miss a single beat.
The big thing there is *not* to have a television set, and the folks
are having a pretty rough time of it, hiding the set in the broom
closet every time the doorbell rings. The reception is very bad, too,
because they wouldn't think of installing an outside aerial. Now
if some smart hillbilly invented a sort of invisible aerial or one
that could be hidden down the chimney, he'd be doing the
intellectuals of the North a very great service.

Romance is dead

SOME time ago I saw an item in *The New York Times*
that the public library on Rivington Street on the Lower East Side
was being torn down. It was a small news item; but it meant a
very great deal to me. The item also gave the name of the last
librarian. I had spent many hours in that Rivington Street Library
when I was a kid. I remember that on one Saturday I went in
there and the librarian at the time, Miss O'Day, laughed and
laughed when we both realized that I had read nearly all the books
there (except, of course, the technical works—mathematics, engineering, trade, and commerce books). Miss O'Day said that she

was going to write me up in some library journal, but I never followed it up to see whether she did.

Anyway I now sat down and wrote a letter to this librarian in the news item who was in on the obsequies of this wonderful institution. I told her about my years in that library; I told her about Miss O'Day and the books on the shelves; the shelves of Henty, McMasters, Dumas, Bulwer-Lytton, Hugo, Emerson.

But it was like talking to the wall. No imagination. No sense of history. No sense of time and place. Romance is dead. I received a reply from this "liquidating" librarian which said, "Your inquiry concerning the Rivington Street Library has been referred to the such-and-such department, on such-and-such street." Pfui!!

How to tell a rich city

No MATTER what town, village, or city I visit, there are two statements I know I am bound to hear.

The first will be, "This town contributes more money per capita to the annual UJA Drive than any other town in America." This may or may not be true. Anyway the UJA is not eager to correct this mistake. If people are charitable, there is no reason why they shouldn't be indulged in thinking they are the *most* charitable.

The second statement is always, "This is a rich town; there's a lot of money here." But I know the difference between a town that is rich and a town that says it's rich. I have an infallible method for determining this and I do not need census or income-tax reports either.

The primary difference between a town that really has money and a town that merely says it has money is whether or not you can get a shoeshine easily.

I have been in Hartford, Connecticut, a town with sixty-seven major insurance companies. The post office daily delivers more money throughout this city than is delivered in any other in the world. Everyone will tell you, "There's a lot of money in Hartford." This doesn't mean that residents have the money. They don't. There's only one place in Hartford to get a shine. All those insurance presidents either go to work with dusty shoes, shine them themselves, or wear sneakers.

In Louisville you can get a genuine soap shine at any one of six different bootblack stands, and Tucson, New York, and Charlotte are filled with bootblacks.

What to do with drunk drivers

WITH the one millionth casualty carefully recorded, the question remains whether a civilized society can do anything about this mass slaughter by the recklessly and carelessly driven automobile. My friend, editor Vern Dollase of Fort Atkinson, Wisconsin, has a sound solution. He says that we should put the car in jail instead of the driver. He is absolutely right. There is something about getting behind that wheel for many people that turns them into monsters. In a way it is understandable. Most of them lead stupid, dull, insipid, uninteresting little lives. They go from one set of comics to another Gene Autry recording. They eat, sleep, dream a little, and then nothing, nothing at all. Then suddenly they get theirselves behind that there steering wheel and all hell breaks loose. If they were threatened with the loss of the machine, they'd go stark, raving mad, and get some sense. Why not try it? The next case of drunk or reckless driving, let the judge sentence the car to six months and see what happens. It's easy for him to stay in jail while he dreams of that nice shiny car resting comfortably in front of his house, but if he were on the outside and that car was locked up, I think we'd get some results.

Easing a friend's pain

I FOLLOW an age-old principle of appeasement. A fellow comes up to me and says, "Well, I see you're a big shot now," and

I immediately ease his pain by saying, "I'm having terrible trouble with my teeth." People love that. It strikes a "balance." It is not all going my way. Tell the next man you see that you are on the way to the dentist and see how his innermost soul lights up.

But of course my "terrible teeth" gambit performs another great service. The evil eye thrives on such designations as "big shot," and because of my quick thinking in answering, "I'm having terrible trouble with my teeth," I have not only diverted the steady gaze of the evil eye, but I have actually sent my friend away much happier than when he came.

In all seriousness I suspect that people discuss their ailments and their operations for precisely this reason. Like that famous salesman of Arthur Miller's play, we not only want to be *liked*, but we want to be *well-liked*, and some instinct tells us that we can more readily endear ourselves to our friends and companions by telling them that we are in pain or in trouble. When *you* are having trouble, pain, and distress, it somehow makes him feel safer.

"Reverend Fathers and gentlemen"

OVER the years I have prepared a mountain of "research" for politician clients in New York and in the South. I wrote many a speech for an Irishman which started with the salutation, "Reverend Fathers, ladies and gentlemen," and the phrase fascinated me. Over the years I have delivered most of the speeches, in one way or another, that I had written for others, but in the Protestant South there was little chance of ever using that "Reverend Fathers" greeting.

Think, then, of my good fortune three years ago when I was invited to address the graduating Student Government Council of the Roman Catholic monastery, Belmont Abbey College. I was very happy when I saw the four or five priests on the dais, and, savoring every word, I spoke very slowly—"Reverend Fathers and gentlemen." But I had such a big smile on my puss that I had to explain it all to my audience.

"Broken homes"

THE lecturers and many clergymen are having a big time making parents and "broken homes" responsible for "juvenile delinquency." What is "juvenile delinquency"? In 1905 they were called "bad boys," and there were some; and in 1920 they were called "products of the jazz era," and there were some.

The boys of 1905 won World War I and laid the foundation for our huge industrialization. And who are the middle-aged men today who run the banks and the laboratories, who build the bridges and design the automobiles? Are they not the "products of the jazz era"?

There is a restlessness among the youth, and boys get into trouble, but this has very little relationship to parents or "broken homes." In fact Shakespeare wrote something exactly the opposite: "Happy is that child whose father has gone to the dogs."

The following men had mothers who did not care a whoop for them and/or fathers who were habitual drunkards: George Bernard Shaw, H. G. Wells, Lord Byron, Percy Shelley, Charles Dickens, and Leonardo da Vinci. The poet William Morris observed, "Of all the guardians a child could have, its parents are probably the worst." Many a boy has spent the years of his childhood trying to straighten out the old man:

"Mr. Gallagher, is my father in there?"

"Stay away from those swinging doors, son."

Charles Dickens, who knew more about "juvenile delinquency" than any man since the days of the Prophets, pointed out that drink does not cause poverty, but it is poverty that reduces the poor to drink. (Even if it is not poverty in the economic sense, his observation still holds perfectly true. Heavy drinking may be the result of some other deeply felt inadequacy, some rejection equal to that of poverty.)

I would say it is about fifty-fifty. As many juveniles have re-

deemed "delinquent" parents as the lecturers claim to have been
seduced by "broken homes."

> "Father, dear father, come home with me now,
> The clock in the steeple strikes one . . ."

This is not an advertisement for "broken homes" and it does
not mean that if your father is a drunkard you'll wind up another
George Bernard Shaw. But I hope I have made my point that it
is ridiculous to make parents the scapegoats for a problem that
confronts us all in a civilized society.

I am sure the parents would be willing to take the blame if it
would solve anything, but all it does is sweep the problem under
the carpet and earn some fees for the civic-club speakers with that
same old stuck whistle about "parents" and "broken homes."

No more sports

WHEN I sold newspapers as a kid, I used to see men dressed
in Inverness capes escorting their fine-looking ladies, and they
were very considerate people, especially with newsboys, mes-
sengers, and waiters. Things were a bit slower, but there was
some form to it, and class. Enrico Caruso was a sport. He received one thousand guests at the Hotel Knickerbocker cele-
brating his twenty-fifth anniversary as a singer. He was forty-six
years old then, and he announced with pride that he had paid
$153,000 income tax for the preceding year, when the rate was
exceedingly low.

Another great sport was John Ringling, the circus man. When
the circus came to New York Mr. Ringling had an entire floor in
the Hotel McAlpin devoted to entertaining newspapermen and
friends of the circus. All you had to do was step up to Mr. Ringling and say, "Wonderful show this year, Mr. Ringling," and the
place was yours—champagne, beefsteaks, and all the trimmings.
Another sport was Mr. Herrmann, the man who owned the Cincinnati baseball team. He traveled with his team and for him the

whole thing was a picnic. There was a full car of good Cincinnati beer and when his team played in New York, Mr. Herrmann went all out to entertain everyone who could find his way to the Hotel Ansonia on upper Broadway.

Today there are no sports. There are just chronic drunks sitting in an overpublicized café society joint, which is about as exclusive as Grand Central Station.

A public relations feat

STEEL, coal, oil, and automobiles: these industries are the basis of American life and the direct cause of American prosperity. Yet in thinking of them, you cannot forget Memorial Day at Republic Steel when armed troops killed seven strikers and wounded hundreds of others. And you remember Flint, Michigan, where several hundred workers went on a sit-down strike against General Motors. And there were the random murder of wild-catters and the unjust eviction and dispossession notices served on farmers as the big oil companies moved in. And in the coal towns of Harlan County, Kentucky, National Guardsmen sat behind machine guns as the operators tried to break the strike.

One thinks of steel, coal, oil, and autos, and conjures thoughts of labor strife, of the Molly McGuires and Pinkerton agents, the court injunctions.

But the American Telephone and Telegraph Company conjures up nothing more than the image of the telephone serviceman valiantly atop the telephone pole during the torrential downpour while lightning cracks all about.

The Telephone Company has impressed the idea of service upon us and this is without question one of the greatest jobs of public relations ever achieved in the course of the Industrial Revolution. We should salute the geniuses who brought this about. We do not think of the telephone company and strikes, lockouts, or even negotiation, but only of that serviceman dangerously high on the pole in the bad lightning rainstorm.

Wall-to-wall carpeting

I REMEMBER my mother forever scrubbing the floors of the tenement we lived in on Eldridge Street. As soon as she had scrubbed them clean, she carefully put down newspapers over the entire area. She wanted to *keep* those floors clean. Two days later, when the newspaper started to tear and to show footprints, she gathered them all up, scrubbed the floors again, and put down fresh newspapers. I never saw that kitchen linoleum of which she was so proud. Newspapers always covered the entire kitchen floor.

Although it has been argued that a younger generation will try to break from the customs of the older generations, this is not always true. Wall-to-wall carpeting is another way of putting newspapers on the floor. To be sure, it is an adaptation somewhat encouraged by builders, but wall-to-wall carpeting is also a tenacious grasp on the past. Its origin is in the tenements with their constant and neat arrangements of newspapers on the newly scrubbed floor.

A noble institution is gone

How is the cause of temperance served by selling twenty-one drinks at a time in a bottle (package stores), instead of selling one drink at a time in a bar or café? It would be nice to find out how people arrived at that conclusion. When you go into a package store, you can get twenty-one drinks by merely saying, "Please give me a fifth of so-and-so." Now if you wanted to get the same twenty-one drinks at a bar, you'd have to say it twenty-one times. "Give me another drink." Anyway, no decent bartender would sell you twenty-one drinks in an evening. I fail to see where the package stores help the cause of temperance. There were thousands of people who never bought a bottle of whisky in their lives.

They stopped off at a bar for a few drinks and went about their business. Of course you had barflies and drunks, but you have the same proportion of drunks with package stores (I insist there are more), and you had even more drunks when there were no bars or package stores. Contrary to the folklore (no one had the courage to speak up for that noble institution, the corner saloon), vast thousands of men stopped drinking after they had their one, two, or three drinks and went on home or about their business. But when a man must buy a bottle, you know very well that it makes him nervous until he sees the bottom of the bottle. Prohibition made drinkers out of girls and women. The corner saloon was a male institution—and that is what made it so desirable. You discussed philosophy there, and politics, and heard some mighty good poetry too. Then the singing—where do you have that fine singing today?

Once in a great while a woman would come through the side entrance (family entrance) and get a can of beer, but one thing you were sure of—if you ever did see a woman in a saloon you knew it was a disreputable place and gentlemen stayed clear of it. The greatest advantage of the corner saloon, in addition to its value as a temperance factor, is that it provided gentlemen with a convenient restroom on nearly every corner. Today you have to walk blocks, and you can drop dead before you find a likely place to go, and usually it is a restaurant. You have to squeeze through occupied dining tables and maybe ask a waitress where it is, but that's only half the battle. On the way out, you have to stop off at the cashier's desk and in front of a dozen people paying their checks, you practically have to give her an affidavit that you did not come in to eat.

I don't understand hi-fi

THE people with the stereophonic sets and the dials and the gadgets who brag to me that their speaker is bigger than the one in the Charlotte Coliseum are making a big mistake. While it is true that hi-fi reproduces music better than the ordinary victrola, music was never intended solely for the ear any more than food was intended solely for the stomach. There is something homey and heart-warming about a roasted turkey, something delightful and delicate about an éclair, and something substantial about a pastrami sandwich. These qualities enrich the table and inspire the taste buds. Similarly there is something more than the highs and lows the hi-fi bug is listening for in the recording of Tschaikovsky's Piano Concerto performed by Van Cliburn. There is an emotional tone which no set recaptures (but which you can, often by humming the melodic line to yourself). And I remember the advice of a fellow years ago who told me, never take a girl you're fond of to the Met to hear *La Bohème*; you'll marry her if you do.

Music should not be considered as only the mechanical reproduction of sound: music is the loneliness of Beethoven, the joy of Mozart, and the authority of Arturo Toscanini conducting in Carnegie Hall.

Here in Charlotte, I have an old victrola in the bedroom which is played during the working day. It has no highs, no lows, nothing to twist or turn or adjust. One of the secretaries is crazy about Beethoven's Emperor Concerto and the other has conceived a passion for some old Union Songs sung by Pete Seeger, and we all listen to Carl Sandburg.

The decline of murder

MURDERS no longer sustain newspapers. Once upon a time if the police found a murdered blonde, any editor who could make up some kind of mystery about her past, and why she was dead automatically guaranteed his publisher that they would finish the year in the black.

Today's reporters have lost the urge for sheer exaggeration. They are better trained and do better research. People nowadays are fingerprinted, registered, enrolled, and processed by so many institutions of one sort of another that it is impossible to pretend a murdered blonde might well be a Princess of Liechtenstein or an unhappy blackmailed debutante out of the 400. "Waitress found murdered" is a sad and tragic story, but it's good for only three inches of type in one edition.

Bar mitzvah of "Orson" Goldberg

IN THE Orthodox tradition in which I was brought up, the bar mitzvah was strictly a *man's* world. The thirteen-year-old was brought up to read the Torah on the Sabbath morning and his father and grandfather were standing beside him. Occasionally this was a tremendously thrilling event for the boy's father, who was perhaps a factory worker or a peddler, and here he was for the first time standing on the beema (altar). After the ceremony we had lekach (honey cake) and wine—strictly for men—while the women, the mother, the sisters, and the aunts, stood at a distance and watched and beamed. I have seen the time when the young boy and his father led a procession from the synagogue to the home, the men still wearing their prayer shawls, and the father of the boy handing out wrapped-up pieces of the honey cake to the Irish cops along the way.

Today the bar mitzvah is a woman's project, which is of the greatest significance, since it spells out the story of the progression from the immigrant Orthodox status to the entry into the American middle class and its reflection of the habits and the mores of the Christian community. In fact, it is no longer the bar mitzvah of the thirteen-year-old boy upon his entry into the household of Israel. It is now the bar mitzvah of the mother—"Brenda Goldstein's bar mitzvah," or just, "Did you go to Brenda's bar mitzvah?"

Now, it's a matter of twenty-three rooms reserved at the leading hotel for the out-of-town guests. The program includes: Friday night, the bar mitzvah in the temple and the reception; Saturday, lunch for the out-of-town guests; Saturday night, the dance; and

Sunday, brunch. All of which would make a piker out of Petronius Arbiter and his silly little banquets in the days of Nero. Now, the kids march in to the tune of "The Stars and Stripes Forever" —the bar mitzvah and his friends, with a red, white, and blue spotlight playing on the "head table." There is always one, a great big fat kid, who makes the balabatim gasp, "This is a thirteen-year-old boy?" and this kid is immediately followed by a teeny-weeny little kid who looks like he's about eight, if that much. The kids march twice around the head table and finally stand at attention with the Boy Scout salute and Pledge of Allegiance. This is followed by the reading of the telegrams and the opening of the presents. And all through this bar mitzvah I keep hoping that the Prophet Amos does not show up wagging his bony finger prophesying dire consequences.

Summer TV

ALONG with the blistering heat, we are withstanding the ravages of summer TV. This fall we will again pause to think: Why? Why is nature so malignant? Why is summer TV so bad? Nature refuses to answer for herself but some of the executives answer for summer TV. They say, well, sponsors are discouraged from putting their money into programs no one is around to watch.

Where do TV people think everybody is? Not on vacation. Vacation lasts only two weeks and there isn't a hotel below the Mason-Dixon line that doesn't have color TV.

Ah, no, say the executives. People don't watch television, they are on their front porch, But, ah, no, television executives. You have eyes but do not see. Houses do not have porches any more. People are in their air-conditioned living rooms, turning off those re-runs and pilot films you are foisting on them. If the TV people don't watch out, the English teachers will beat their time. They will start handing out required summer reading lists to students and if that happens—watch out for the winter programs.

The ball point pen

I AM surprised that no one has yet written a good magazine piece about the ball point pen, which one expert said was "the greatest invention of the postwar period." They are selling for ten cents and fifteen cents now, the same pen which swept the nation at five dollars and seven dollars each, and in some cases as high as twelve dollars. The "fake" would make an interesting story since it actually took away as much money as the Mississippi Bubble, Ponzi, and the Second Louisiana Purchase. Maybe it really writes under water. We know now that it doesn't write on the land.

Why must we have a speaker?

EVERY organization insists on a speaker either at the beginning of or at the end of the campaign. Nor can it be just any speaker. Preferably it should be somebody from out of town. Now why do they need the speaker? The answer lies in the motive of the people who join the organization. The motive is a compound one. It is not simply to do good, but to do good in some social context. The campaign devoted to raising money or cheering up antiquarians must also become a social event for those involved.

In engaging a speaker, the organization knows it must plan a luncheon or a tea or a cocktail party. And this will emphasize both society and common humanity, since people will partake of food together. Successful campaigns are never launched in the offices of the fund director, but at the country club. And the old folks don't get cheered up when their welfare is plotted in the downstairs lobby of the Old Folks Home. But they have a whale of a time when the plan is proposed by a visiting geriatrist who cheers the effort on while the hostess and the maid arrange the canapés.

Bigness

BIGNESS, I read, is the thing. Bigness in corporations, in government, and in military operations. It's smart to be big. And the first man to vouchsafe this information is the G.M. stockholder. G.M. is big and it pays big profits. It is a little unnerving to think, however, that if G.M. were smaller maybe the profits would be as big, if not bigger. What makes me think this is that most bigness hides. G.M. announces its dividends and how they got them is not for public ears. The government has every sort of bureau, none of which is privileged to give you the straight story. But if you really want to investigate what bigness looks like, visit your State's Bureau of Motor Vehicles. That's bigness. It is true that every car in the State gets licensed—but at what a cost in time and confusion! I am convinced that the reason a chauffeur gets so much money is not because of his talents. He is like a doctor. You've got to help pay for the time he has spent applying for his license.

The public is blasé

YOU have but to go into a movie to see the stepped-up program of violence, with no holds barred. A TV program some time ago had one brother—a cowboy, of course—solve a mental-hygiene problem by taking his crazy brother out to a clump of sagebrush and shooting him through the head. It did not awaken any thundering consciousness from the public. So it must be above par for the course.

How to get rich—by classes

1. Buy low and sell high.
2. It's not what you make but what you save.
3. The third shift is what pays off.

"The hook"

"AMATEUR NIGHT" is another sign that we don't see any more. I believe it was Miner's Theatre on the Bowery that pioneered the Amateur Night idea. The London Theatre, which was in this area, also sponsored an amateur night. I do not know that it was Miner's Theatre that introduced "the hook." Amateurs, even when they know they are particularly terrible, have not the professional sense to get off. Once the crowd began to hoot and boo, the stage manager reached a big hook out from the wings and with it gathered the amateur from the stage.

The three things

THREE things help a man live a long time: if he is lucky to have picked parents and grandparents who lived long lives; if he can keep his weight down; and if he can live and work without tension. I am gambling that two out of three (the first and third) will do it for me and permit me to write lots of books.

BBC television

I'LL have to change my mind about this "no commercials" deal now that I've watched BBC television in London. I watched an hour-long program, A *Picnic at Margate,* and a half-hour program about a collective sheep farm on the Isle of Skye in the Hebrides; another half-hour of A *Trip to Bologne,* and after an hour of madrigals, with a skinny gal doing a here-we-go-gathering-nuts-in-May dance, I began to yearn for those wonderful American fellows who can cure hemorrhoids without an operation.

How to get time off

EMPLOYERS hate like the devil to see employees take time off, especially if they think the employee is enjoying himself or earning extra money.

But if you need time off the best way is to take it when your boss takes it. Failing this, you have one recourse. You tell your boss you have to take a basal metabolism test. For some reason bosses always give you this time. But if you say you have an appointment with the eye doctor, bosses suggest that the optometrist's office won't be as crowded after five, why not wait? Or a dental appointment. The boss is sure to suggest that Saturday is a better time. But a basal metabolism—they buy it every time.

Resolution

I HAVE decided to go the rest of the way down life's path without ever eating anything that's squeezed out of a tube.

The obsolete pocket

PROBABLY no more than one man in a thousand uses the little watch pocket any more.

In the old days the first thing you did to honor a good watch was to buy a black silk watch fob with your initials in gold. In the winter you carried the watch in your vest pocket with maybe a charm or two hanging on the chain across your chest. An Elk's tooth was very popular with the members of that fraternity; there were a few fellows with a Phi Beta Kappa key, and many others with a charm that looked like a Phi Beta Kappa key. The Heinz people put out a little green pickle with a gold loop, and lots of sports wore that little green pickle on their chains.

I use my watch pocket, but there are no watch fobs to be had anywhere. In the winter I carry my watch in the handkerchief pocket of my coat with a chain: and I had to go to a pawnshop up on the Bowery to replace a little button that holds the chain in the lapel. There are no more watch fobs, and I guess the pants makers are sentimental fellows with a nostalgia for a more placid era, and so they continue to insert that obsolete little pocket on the right side of the pants.

Judgment awaits

ON THE Day of Judgment, I'd hate to be in the boots of those fellows who conduct the "Early Morning Rising" programs.

The important story

IN THE hallways of Barnard College, the women's college of Columbia University, there are printed signs warning the girls not to walk along Riverside Drive unescorted. If I were managing editor of *The New York Times* I would reproduce that sign and run it across five columns on page one. What is more important than that?

Do New Yorkers and the New York press have to look elsewhere for problems to solve?

Is it any wonder that Times Square no longer has its cheering crowds on election night?

Teaching classical music

IF YOU want your children to acquire an appreciation for the opera and classical music, I would suggest that you play the records of *The Pearl Fishers*, by Bizet, *La Bohème*, by Puccini, and *Aïda*, by Verdi, and play them over and over again. The child will identify the melodies with many of the details of his imagination and daydreams—mother, father, home, lullaby, marching soldiers, parade, dancing, and pageant—and identity or familiarity will eventually grow into affection and appreciation.

Highlighting my speech

I DELIVERED the address at the tenth anniversary of Carver (Junior) College of Charlotte and here is a portion of the printed program:

Ladies and gentlemen

WHEN I make a speech I always begin, "Ladies and Gentlemen," or just "Gentlemen," if there are no ladies present. In recent years this "Gentlemen" has become a vanishing term. Now we use "men," "women," or the meaningless "friends." The word "gentlemen" once meant a good deal. When a firm advertised "Gentlemen's Luggage" it did not mean "Men's Luggage." Not by a long shot. You knew at once that this luggage was extra good, probably handmade, and it was not necessary to add that it was genuine leather. That would have been an insult. Now we have reduced everything to the level of "men" and "women," even to the changing of the signs on the restrooms, and they certainly look it, too.

Togetherness

WHAT's this "Togetherness" the fancy magazines are talking about? On the old East Side, did we have Togetherness! Three of us slept on the "lunch," four of us slept on the fire escape, and on the roof you literally had to step over bodies in the summertime. That's what I call "Togetherness."

This book was set in
Electra and Baskerville types
by The Haddon Craftsmen.
It was printed and bound at
the press of The World Publishing Company
Design is by Larry Kamp.